THE WORLD THAT CRUMBLED

THE WORLD THAT CRUMBLED

by Malka Moskovits

HOLOCAUST LIBRARY
NEW YORK

Library of Congress Cataloging-in-Publication Data

Moskovits, Malka, 1924-
    The world that crumbled / by Malka Moskovits
        p.   cm.
    ISBN 0-89604-155-7(pbk.) : $13.95
        1. Jews — Ukraine — Berezove (Zakerpatskaia oblast') — Per-
secutions. 2. Holocaust, Jewish (1939-1945) — Uk-
raine — Berezove (Zakerpatskaia oblast') — Personal narratives.
3. Moskovits, Malka, 1924-   . 4. Berezove (Zakerpatskaia
oblast' : Ukraine) — Ethnic relations.
I. Title
DS135.U42B485   1993
940.53'18'09477 — dc20   93-6758
                                                              CIP

Cover Design by The Applebaum Company

Printed in the United States of America

Foreword

I first met Malka Moskovits over ten years ago. She was enrolled in my section of Introductory Psychology which I was teaching in a special evening program for returning adults at Brooklyn College.

I have always found those special sections fascinating because my students inevitably teach me as much as I teach them. The unit on the psychology of prejudice is particularly enlightening, because many Brooklyn College students are recent immigrants or have grown up in hardship and have first-hand accounts of most of the principles of prejudice.

It is always tempting to want to describe discrimination as a phenomenon that is ending or as an abomination we will not allow to happen again. However, Malka Moskovits' story is a riveting reminder that a former victim of prejudice continues to be a victim. Not only do the scars from her days in the concentration camps refuse to go away, but her memories of those days are unrelenting.

Malka Moskovits approached me several years ago with the request that I help edit her story in the hope that committing the memories to writing might finally put some of them to rest. Yet every time we have worked on the book it has been obvious that she constantly relives her experiences as vividly as ever.

Malka has won my deepest respect for persevering in this project. She believes that future generations should have some first-hand accounts of what happened during World War II, despite the fact that it has been so painful for her to write it.

As a psychologist, I find her story to be a very important lesson in how much physical and mental pain a human being is capable of enduring. It is also a horrifying reminder of how insensitive nearly everyone can be to the sufferings of individuals who have been dehumanized.

Marilyn Rall

Job

When suddenly a
Great wind came across
The desert and smote the
Four corners of the house, and
It fell upon the young people
And they are dead; and I alone
Have escaped to tell thee.

I dedicate this story to the memory of my mother, Bila Hendel and my father, Yisrael, my brother Azick and his three lovely children, to my sister Alta and her three-year-old son, my sister Rivka and her two-year-old blond, blue eyed son, and to the memory of two young brothers Shmuel Moshe and Chaim Hersh, who were all murdered in cold blood by the Germans.

We, the six million who were slaughtered beseech you through this memoir never to forget the Holocaust. Otherwise, we will have died in vain.

Acknowledgments

I wish to thank my teacher and friend, Professor Marilyn Rall of Brooklyn College, without whose valuable help this work would not have been published.

My thanks also to Joyce Finks for serving as editorial assistant and James Byrne for insisting that I undertake this project. I am grateful for the encouragement of the staff of the Brooklyn College Corporate Careers Program, and for the technical guidance from its director, Dr. Matt Kahn.

All the details in this narrative are true. However, some names have been changed at their request to protect their privacy.

Prologue

I am about to tell you a sad and depressing story, but I have a problem. I don't have the words at my command to adequately relate it. Many survivors of the Holocaust have written about their experiences during the tragic years between the time Hitler came to power until the collapse of the Third Reich. To summarize, six million Jews died horribly and needlessly. I will tell you about one who did not die, but perhaps she would have been better off if she had not survived. When death seemed imminent, I fought hard to stay alive, at least long enough to cheer the downfall of the "super race," to see their numbers wallow in their feces as we were forced to do.

Many others wanted to live to relate what happened to them and to others in the ghettos and camps, to tell how the highly cultured Germans erected factories in which the chief project was the development of sophisticated technology for more efficient killing. As for

1

me, I never intended to record anything. The whole world knew what was happening in Auschwitz and Bergen-Belsen long before I was brought there, yet no voices were raised in protest, nor were there any concrete steps taken to stop the wholesale slaughter by the Germans. I have nothing to add to their knowledge of the subject. They do not deserve the effort that would be expended to recount the painful episodes. I write this story for myself. Maybe, just maybe, I will finally rid myself of the guilt that has tormented me all these years.

I first talked about these experiences and my feelings of culpability to a psychiatrist in Kings County Hospital in New York City some twenty-five years ago, and then later to a group of psychiatrists at Mount Sinai Hospital. However, it did not make me feel any better or less self reproachful. I am so preoccupied with my thoughts of what occurred and why that when people meet me in the street I seldom see them or hear what they're saying when they greet me. Instead, I see all those relatives and friends who are dead. They live on in my mind and in my heart. I even concoct stories about how I saved them by finding a bunker in the forest in which we all hid and escaped the Nazi slaughter. They are all with me and I with them, and it will always be so. As time passes the pain intensifies with each passing day. During the Holocaust and for many years afterwards, I could not even cry or mourn.

The last time I wept was a few days after I arrived in Auschwitz when my bread was stolen. I mourned the loss of the bread but I did not cry for my mother when they murdered her in the gas chamber. Not only was I unable to cry and find release for my pent-up emotions, but I lost the ability to laugh as well. Much

2

later, maybe ten years after the British tanks rolled into Bergen-Belsen, I began to cry every night, and every time I mentioned those that had perished. I still haven't learned how to laugh again. I keep remembering that for a just a smile, I received a blow on my head in Auschwitz from a Polish guard.

THE WORLD THAT CRUMBLED

Even if you look very closely at a map of central Europe you won't find Berezov. It was such an insignificant, godforsaken town that nobody ever bothered to mark its existence on a map. It did not appear on the map of Czechoslovakia either, although it had belonged to Czechoslovakia since the end of the First World War. The whole region, Carpathian Ruthenia, was taken from the Austro-Hungarian Empire and made part of the newly formed republic of Czechoslovakia. The old generation kept remembering the good old days of the Hungarian regime under the liberal Emperor Franz Joseph.

4

Berezov's lack of identity was due to its shortage of any appreciable natural resources, and the absence of a single factory in the town. Most of the people, the Ruthenians, who were in the majority in Berezov, were small farmers. The entire town consisted of two main dusty streets on which could be seen piles of manure from the passing animals. The region came to life only during war. The main road was situated just a few hundred yards from town over a wooden bridge across the river Rika. It was used by the marching armies on their way to the East. The only feature with which Berezov was blessed was the forest that surrounded the town. Control over this area, however, was shared by the various governments. The Czechs and Hungarians who administered the region reserved the right to cut down trees. Anyone else found doing this was subject to imprisonment. When the cold winter arrived there was always someone who ventured into the woods anyway, felled a tree, and sold the wood in the village. Usually it was a brave Ruthenian or one who was hard pressed and needed money desperately for salt or kerosine for his lamp during the long winter nights, or to purchase tobacco when he couldn't get a smoke from a friend. Life in Berezov was difficult.

The second natural resource in our region was children. Large families were in the majority. The trouble with this valuable asset, unlike the woods which did not inconvenience anyone, was that the children had stomachs that needed food, not to mention clothing. Both of these necessities were hard to come by. It was particularly unfortunate when the father of a household passed away. The family was left without an income. The mother, with the help of the townspeople, managed somehow until the children grew up and could provide for themselves. It was even more tragic, however, when a mother died leaving small children. This happened fairly often, because many women in our area died in childbirth. There was no doctor in town for medical emergencies. The Czech government finally tried to remedy this situation by training a Ruthenian woman to become a midwife. She had to be paid for her services, however, so many called her only in an emergency. When the mother of young children died, the father remarried very soon thereafter. Quite often he would marry a young girl with no dowry, and could not expect to wed anyone except a widower or an old man. She now had an instant family, but was likely to have problems because money and provisions to care for the large family were usually unavailable.

Not only did young women die in childbirth in our region, but the mortality rate of young children was much too high. In my family, my mother bore ten children. Three never reached adulthood. Actually, almost four died. I was the fourth, who became gravely ill. I was about six or seven years old when a severe epidemic struck Berezov called "scharlach fieber" (scarlet fever). In many territories it has since been eradicated. But during that year the disease killed hundreds of children in Berezov alone. I lay on my death bed for weeks, and was not expected to recover, as so very few children ever did. I remember having a severe sore throat, and could not swallow. A rash covered my entire body which ached terribly. It was early spring and the Jewish community of Berezov was making preparations for Passover, epidemic or no epidemic. The traditional pre-Passover chore was the baking of the matzos in which everybody participated. The actual baking was done somewhere in town. Since I was sick with a serious disease, I was left alone in the house. When mother and the other family members came home for lunch, mother opened the door to the room I was in, and said to somebody in the kitchen, "Sie lebt noch." (She is still alive.) After lunch everybody left again.

We had no social service system, no doctor, no post office, no telephone, no electricity, no running water and no library. I, however, managed to find reading material, at least until my parents found out. Every week I took corn over to a mill to be ground. The mill was owned by a wealthy Ruthenian. His son, who studied in the city of Chust, was suddenly brought back home before he matriculated. Instead of continuing with his studies he was forced to work in the mill. The young man was very bitter towards his father. He liked school but was not allowed to complete his studies and amount to something. He brought back many books and magazines and offered me something to read every time I came to the mill with the corn. He also enjoyed talking with me about his problems. He told me that he did not want to marry a Ruthenian peasant girl as his father had insisted. We also discussed the books after I read them. We had something in common, since I too wanted to study, but could not afford it. High school was not free. Only elementary school did not require a fee. The nearest high school was located in Chust. One couldn't commute daily. Transportation was difficult and costly. A residency in Chust was a necessary requisite to attend school. Tuition was also expensive and few in Berezov could afford it.

When my parents learned where I had been getting the books, they changed mills. Someone else took the corn to the other mill. My parents were afraid that something serious might develop. He was a handsome young man.

7

My father not in favor of reading books in the first place. It was his belief and that of the other pious Jews in our region, that books degraded morals, except of course, the Jewish religious writings which were not taught to girls to begin with. All that the girls need to know how to do was housework, sewing, and mending.

Berezov's Jewish population consisted of the ritual slaughterer, Reb Nachman, who was the authority on Jewish affairs. He was the one that officiated at weddings and funerals in Berezov. There was the "blechner" (ironmonger) who fixed all the leaky pots and roofs. That is, only if your roof was covered with tin. On most roofs in Berezov wooden planks were used. The rich could only afford tin covering. He couldn't earn a living in Berezov alone, so he traveled to other towns and villages and wherever he could find work. He would come home for the Sabbath or for every other Sabbath. There were the Yiddish instructors, like my father, who were called "Milamed." They taught the Jewish boys reading, writing Yiddish, and the Hebrew religious works, the Bible and the Talmud. There was the blacksmith, but he wasn't Jewish. The "starosta" (mayor) was first a Ruthenian and never a Jew.

There was the tavern where Jews and Gentiles could obtain a drink. It was frequented mostly by the Ruthenians. The Jews would save their money for emergencies. Berezov Jews lived in relative peace and harmony with their neighbors. These ideals however were only superficial. The Ruthenian would taunt us with, "Zside do Palestina" (Jews go to Palestine). They could also throw stones and snowballs at us in the winter. We never fought back. It was unheard of for a Jewish child to strike a Gentile. We fought among ourselves, but never with the Ruthenians.

I was confused about Palestine. I used to wonder, since I heard from my father, who was a great story teller, that Palestine was such a wonderful place. He described quite vividly all the holy places: the Western Wall, all that was left of the holy temple in Jerusalem; the "Maarat Hamachpela" where the Patriarchs and Matriarchs are buried; and the wonderful soil that yields crops twice yearly. There is no snow there in the winter. The sun shines the whole year round. Firewood or warm clothes are not needed to prevent one from freezing. It sounded too good to be true. All I knew were cruel winters. There was always a problem in obtaining clothing for warmth, never had enough. I always thought how wonderful it would be to visit all those places that my father described.

Of course, he never went there himself. He just learned about them from the books he read, the Bible, the Talmud, and the Commentaries, about which he was a great scholar. I wondered if Palestine was really so wonderful, why the Ruthenian kids teased us about that land. Their intent was surely to degrade and insult us. They implied that we did not belong to the forsaken region. They proved it soon enough at the first opportunity that presented itself. Not one of them showed the slightest compassion or sorrow when we were dragged from our homes by the Germans and their Hungarian allies. They would not help a Jewish friend by hiding him in his home or on his premises.

When a woman's husband died in Berezov, her children would often try to collect whatever anyone would contribute. On many occasions my mother would insist that I take a liter or so of milk to some poor family. She would sometimes wrap herself in her shawl and take a supply of milk to a little house where two hunchbacks, a brother and sister, lived. Mother would stay for a while and talk with them. They were very lonely and appreciated the human contact almost more that any gift that she might bring.

I was particularly fond of Esther Mirl Wolvovitz, who was widowed with five children. One of Esther Mirl's daughters, Lea, was my friend. Once, on Passover eve, when the men had already left for the synagogue, my mother told me to fill a bucket of potatoes. When it was full, she placed some red beets on top. She then told me to carry the bucket to Esther Mirl. I was extremely happy to do so. When I arrived, Esther was so grateful that she began to bless me, started to cry, praising my mother for remembering her. My mother would also provide homemade borscht for Esther Mirl on Passover. Esther would often send one of her children with a pot for some milk. The child never returned empty handed. If an emergency arose, Chust was only twenty kilometers away. It was a ride of two hours in a horse-drawn wagon on a bumpy road. The stricken one had to survive the trip as well as afford the doctor's fee before any help would be forthcoming. The Jews cared for their needy in the best way they could. The Ruthenians were supposed to attend to their own. Every Thursday afternoon, two God-fearing ladies, carrying several homemade clothes bags, made the rounds from one Jewish house to the next to collect whatever each housewife could spare for the poor Jewish families. The Jewish population of Berezov was divided into two classes; the poor and the poorer. There were no rich Jews in Berezov. They earned a living by bartering services among themselves.

Although most of the Berezov Jews were poor, nobody

really relished that condition. In fact, they all tried to hide their poverty from friends and neighbors. All week long it didn't matter what one ate, as long as one could scrape up the few pennies needed to buy a piece of meat, candles, and flour to bake the challah bread for the Sabbath. It was a tradition, but it was practiced as if the order to do so came from above. Everyone tried hard to attain this end, unless, of course, when especially hard times hit, and no one could afford even the most modest of contributions.

One Friday night, our neighbor and friend, Chaim Shevas, who visited us frequently, walked in as usual. We were all seated at the table, which was not covered by a white table cloth. On that Sabbath we also had no candles. We were eating potato soup and corn bread, the same food we ate on any week day. My family had no money that week to purchase those Sabbath necessities for a festive meal. Needless to say, we were all terribly embarrassed, but none more than Chaim himself. He knew that he was witnessing what he was not supposed to, and he never mentioned it to anyone.

Many housewives today might wonder how my mother could sometimes make two meals from only one pound of meat. Many other ingredients that were more readily available were mixed into the soup pot: large lima beans and other vegetables. The soup tasted good every time. No one ever complained.

Each season brought hardships to the Jewish population of Berezov. Winter was the worst because of the severe cold. There was not enough wood for heating and cooking and there was a need for adequate clothes which had to be bought. Money was always a problem. It was quite scarce. The children, however, would sometimes have fun in the winter. When the snow was piled high, we would sneak away from the house, get a sled, and slide down a hill. If no sled was available, a narrow wooden panel would serve to slide down the slippery street as one child would stand on the panel while two other children would each hold on to one of the first child's hands, and run alongside.

In addition to the other handicaps we suffered in the winter, we had to face as best we could the problem of the cursed taxes. Soon after the Christmas holidays a Czech tax collector appeared in Berezov. The deputy with some fan-fare announced that everybody should bring his assessment, or furnishings from the house would be confiscated, if one waited until the collector came to the house. Very few people showed up, since not many of Berezov's inhabitants had money for taxes or for anything else for that matter. The collector waited three days for the people to appear. Then he would make his rounds with two deputies. He was very cruel, confiscating everything of value he could find in the house: such as a quilt or a warm coat, leaving the family without blankets for the children and the head of the family without a coat to weather the bitter cold. People tried to borrow money to redeem the seized possessions. He didn't seem to try to collect from the Ruthenians.

Since we could not raise the money to pay the government, we emptied the house of all valuables, such as candlesticks, bedding, clothing, and linen that mother always gathered for this daughter or that. My mother had a friend who could pay her own taxes. We carried all our valuables to her house for storage until the collector left town. The authorities knew of these ruses and warned those few who had paid not to hide anything, or risk punishment. But a good friend could not refuse. We had to be very careful so as not to endanger her.

It was not very often that one could obtain a new dress, and even more infrequently a new coat. It was exciting to own something new. Ready-made dresses were never bought, material was purchased and then Ruchel, the seamstress, would custom tailor the garment in the style the customer wanted. The dress was worn till it faded or wore out. If it was not torn, it went back to Ruchel, and she would open it at the seams and resew from inside. When I was growing up, the dresses for me were made a few sizes larger so I would fit into them as I grew.

Laundry was washed by hand. The final rinse was done in the 'potick' (brook) which ran behind our house. It usually took all day to clean the clothes. Sometimes a Ruthenian woman would help my mother. It was particularly difficult in the winter. The laundering was done in the house, while the rinsing was still accomplished in the ice-cold brook. The rinser had a little pot of hot water near her. When her hands became very cold she could dip them into the heated water. Every now and then another pot was brought to her. The drying was a difficult and lengthy procedure. It was hung outside on a line. It took three days for the clothes to dry. Each evening, mother would bring the frozen clothes into the house. They couldn't be left on the line over night for fear that they would be stolen. Even the line had to be taken into the house. The clothes were defrosted indoors and mother had to hang them out again the next morning. When I was small, it was a lot of fun to see the frozen, stiff clothes. They resembled people without heads.

13

Summer was especially delightful when I was permitted to go to the Rika river to swim. Usually I stayed home to do the chores. My main job in the spring and summer was to care for the geese, as every other little girl in Berezov did. As long as a few of us were together, we had fun. We drove the geese to the outskirts of the town where they could graze. Then we played. We would sneak into orchards and pick up fruit from the ground under the trees. We also picked fruit from the lower branches. Sometimes, as a last resort, we would throw stones or sticks at the trees so the fruit would fall. Climbing the trees was a bad idea. What if the owner came? You couldn't run; you were trapped and risked a thrashing. I was very good at finding fruit since I knew the orchards well. I enjoyed munching on a juicy apple, pear or plum. My father would say that in the morning I opened my eyes and my mouth at the same time.

I was especially familiar with the orchard of our good Ruthenian neighbor, Miklush. He had several trees in front of his house and many more at the rear behind the corn field. When there was a strong wind or storm many pieces of fruit would fall to the ground. I would take a bucket and pretend that I was going to his well to fetch water. (We used water from his well in the summer because the water in the stream was not clean, as it was in the winter when it was frozen on the surface.) Instead of getting water I would fill my bucket with juicy pears.

The orchard of the widow Esther Mirl Wolvovitz was almost completely dominated by the children of the town. She did not have the means to chase the children away.

When I was about eleven or twelve years old, I realized that I would not be able to roam the through the orchards forever. I did not like to grow up. I started to feel embarrassed to raise my dress and fill it with fruit or walnuts.

I somehow felt at that early age life for me would not be a bed of roses. I had already felt the impact of growing up by the time I finished elementary school. School was my first and only love, and I was a good student. I wanted to continue my studies but my father said, "I have only a parcel of land for your dowry, and if you waste that, there will be nothing left for your marriage." a Czech teacher, who lived in our house for one school year, told my parents that no matter how excellent a student I was, the government would not permit me to pass the final exams because the Czechs invariably failed Jewish students. I did not even get the chance to try.

When my final days of school approached, the political situation became very grim. Hitler was threatening Czechoslovakia. Our teacher, Maria Kandiskalova, took the entire class to the home of the head of the Czech police where the window was opened wide. A large set radio was placed near the open window. We all crowded around to hear a speech by President Benes. He spoke emotionally, describing the grave situation the in which country was. The only solution to the German threats, he claimed, was to defend the country. Some of the students left their place and went into the yard where they cavorted and noisily chased each other around.

Those who remained at the window, listened but did not realize what the President meant later when he acceded to the Germans' demands and relinquished the Sudeten. He was forced to do so by the Allies chiefly by the British Prime Minister, Neville Chaimberlin, whose policy was appeasement towards Nazi Germany. He thought he had achieved, "peace in our time." That was the beginning of the end for the Jews, but it had dawned on us yet. How few of the youngsters who stood in the yard, by the open window, and listened to the President's speech would be alive when it was all over. That was in 1938, and nobody knew then, but I felt very sad and depressed. Just a few weeks later a number of students, including myself, were matriculating. The situation was tense, and the school principal delivered a speech to the graduates about the serious threat our country was facing, and how unclear and bleak our future seemed.

I tried to suppress my emotions and my tears while I was at school so as not to be laughed at. Later, however, when I was alone, I cried a great deal. When I reached home I found my mother in the vegetable garden weeding the beds of vegetables. I told her what the principal had said about the situation. She shook her head sadly. We did not know then that she would be one of Hitler's victims in his mad mission to rid Europe of Jews.

We had no radios or even a regular newspaper delivery in our town, but people commuted to Chust every day and sometimes from further away, where they could read newspapers and listen to the radio. They brought the news back to Berezov. The politicians of the town argued about and discussed the latest events. They all agreed that the situation was grave, but observed that we are all in God's hands and, besides, Hitler "wet nisht derleben," wouldn't live long enough to harm us and achieve his racist goals.

We had heard the anti-Semitic rantings of Hitler. We

also knew of the attacks on Jews in Germany, who were killed, their possessions confiscated, and Jewish houses of worship burned. The Nazis seized all Jewish prayer books, including the holy Torah scrolls, burned them in the streets while German mobs cheered and laughed as the fires consumed the ancient written records of a cultured people. We heard of victims disappearing from their houses in the night or from their homes or from the streets. Our hearts bled for the Jews of Germany.

Then "Kristalnacht", the night of the broken glass. This was the first overt slaughter of Jews by the Germans, and it was supposedly a spontaneous mass reaction after a German had been assassinated in Paris by a desperate young Polish Jew, after he learned of the plight of his family who were expelled from Germany and forced across the border into Poland. The Polish government at first refused to accept these penniless Jews. In reality, the German government had organized the killing and robbing of the Jews that night. It seemed that they were just waiting for an excuse to slaughter Jews with impunity.

The Nazis then stretched out their murderous arms and began reaching beyond their own country towards us. They conquered Czechoslovakia and the republic crumbled. Potkarpatska Rus, as our region was called by the Czechs, was ceded over to Hungary as a prize for cooperating with Hitler. All the Czech teachers, police, and other officials left. They emigrated to Bohemia and Moravia. My eighth grade teacher, Maria Kandiskalova, did not leave. She was married to a Ruthenian teacher. From the time the Czechs left and the Hungarians arrived, anarchy was rampant. Some of our Ruthenian neighbors were said to have compiled a list of Jews they wanted to behead.

There were even rumors of who in Berezov might be on this list.

Before long, the Hungarians arrived. Suddenly everybody became a patriot of Hungary. Flags and banners of welcome appeared on houses and public buildings. A delegation of respectable Ruthenians carried a welcome banner and flags appeared some distance out of town towards Horinch to great the incoming Hungarian army. They were anxious to prove that they had been loyal, all along, to the Hungarians who had controlled the region before World War I. Many noisy children trailed after the grown-ups.

As I crossed the wooden bridge over the Rika river to the main road, I noticed my teacher, Maria. She, too, had come to welcome the Hungarians. Although she was a Czech, she wanted to show her loyalty. When she noticed me, she came over and took my hand and pressed it firmly. We walked together toward Horinch after the welcoming party. We were both very sad, because we were witnessing the passing of an era and the beginning of a new one. What it bode for us did not seem very promising.

My former teacher, Maria Kandiskalova, lost her job. She was no longer needed to the teach Czech language to Jewish children. No one used Czech anymore. Jewish children, who had previously attended a segregated Czech school, were now forced to go to the Ruthenian school. The official language was now Hungarian. In Berezov, of course, Jews still spoke Yiddish among themselves and Ruthenian with their neighbors.

A few months after the Hungarians invasion, new faces appeared in Berezov. A Hungarian family took over the grocery store which was previously owned by the Kahan family. They also owned a school building. After the Czechs left, and classes were canceled, they lost the rent on this building too. An other school structure belonging another Jew was also abandoned.

A new general store called "Hongyo" opened. It was completely staffed and operated by Gentiles. All the Ruthenian customers who previously shopped in Jewish stores now patronized the Hongyo, because it was managed by Ruthenians. Jewish stores went out of business. The Jews, too, were compelled to buy in the new shops because only they carried rationed foods, and only there could one redeem food coupons. As a result, many Jews lost their livelihood.

The Czechs had guarded the woods with their lives, the only natural resource that this region possessed. The Hungarians, however, raided attacked the woods like hungry wolves. They couldn't chop down the tall trees fast enough. Trucks, loaded with lumber cut into ties, cluttered the roads.

Previously, one could get to Chust on the bus which passed Berezov twice daily, in the morning and in the afternoon, or for a smaller fee, one could travel by a horse-drawn cart. The ride in this manner, however, took much longer, two full hours, and it was much far comfortable. You took your pick. Most people rode in the wagons and seldom used the bus. Now, however, a pretty, young girl could hitch a ride to Chust with the Hungarian truck drivers at no cost. Later, others could get a ride to Chust and back for a fraction of the regular bus fare.

Because of the war and the Hungarian occupation,

Jews suffered many hardships. Almost everything was rationed, but that was the least of our problems. As soon as they occupied the town, the Hungarians conscripted all Jewish men from age 18 to 60 for hard labor. My father was among those who were ordered to report for special duty. Later, older people, including my father, were sent home. However every able-bodied young man, including fathers of young children, toiled in the work battalions throughout the war. They would wear a yellow band on their left arm. Many were sent into the woods to chop down trees and, of these, quite a few were killed or maimed by the falling trees. Our neighbor and good friend, Chaim Shevas, died this way. Hunger and disease also took its toll. Many were slain by the Hungarians. Others were sent to the Russian front, when it opened in 1941, to dig ditches for the Germans, to clear mine fields, and, in general, to serve as cannon fodder. My sister Alta's husband was called in and was never heard from again. She remained alone with a small child. I stayed with her for a few months. She lived in Tecso, another town quite a distance from Berezov, and had no any relatives there.

As soon as the Hungarians occupied our region, they began to issue decrees for the Jews. In 1941, it was ordered that all 17,000 foreign or stateless Jews residing in the Carpathians were to be expelled to the East. Our hearts broken as we watched the blechner (iron-monger) bidding farewell to his wife and five children. He was a well-liked member of our community He was forced to leave his home and family because he was a foreigner, who was not born in the desolate Carpathians.

Only one year later, in 1942, our turn came. The Hungarians surrendered to German demands and agreed to "resettle" the Jews to the East, namely to Poland and the Ukraine. (The Germans used the term "resettle" as a euphemism for liquidate.) I was in Tecso with my sister Alta. She wanted me to return home to our parents, to face with them, whatever fate had in store for us. She did not want the responsibility of having a teenager to care for.

The whole region was in turmoil. It became very dangerous to travel by train. People were dragged off them, and disappeared. Nobody knew what happened to them. A relative of Alta's neighbor was in Tecso and had to return to Chust. In order to avoid traveling by train he hired a car. This relative agreed to take me to the station in Chust where I could get transportation to Berezov.

When I arrived, Berezov was in an upheaval. Every face looked sad and haggard. People were apprehensive. We were ordered to be ready for deportation with enough food for three days. Mother transferred all of our possessions to good neighbors for safekeeping. The house was emptied completely except for the furniture. Mother even took our little kitten to Marika, our closest Ruthenian neighbor. She said that she pitied any little creature who had to be left alone in an empty house. "Who will feed it?" she said. "It will die, the poor thing."

The old "shochet" (ritual slaughterer), Reb Nachman, who also served as rabbi in Berezov, designated a day of fasting. Everyone including the very young were not to eat, but pray. Other towns had the same observance. All the men assembled in the town's only synagogue and draped in their prayer shawls, prolonged the morning prayer. After that came hours of chanting the Psalms. People were told to visit the cemetery and take with them innocent sinless babies. They were told to pray on the graves of their ancestors and cry and plead with the souls of the departed to intercede on their behalf before the Almighty, that He in His infinite grace should nullify the deportation edict.

I visited the cemetery for the first time. Before, I had only glimpsed parts of the monuments because they were almost entirely hidden by high bushes. We were always respectful in this place. No youngster ever dared enter the cemetery alone. We never laughed when we passed to avoid offending the dead. Mother showed me where my paternal grandparents were buried. I read from a prayer book. Later, I whispered whatever I felt like. Mother lit candles. She said she wished she could pray on the graves of her own parents, but they were buried in Sinover, her hometown.

Meanwhile, the women engaged in something more practical. They baked bread for the trip. Mother's choice was black corn bread since she could not obtain any other flour. The bread made from this grain was sticky and wasn't very tasty. No one liked it, but we ate it anyway because we were quite hungry. Laundry was washed and bundles were all packed and ready. Mother called on the Herskovits family, who sold kerchiefs. The black silk one decorated with the little gold florets that she wore only on the Sabbath, had been packed away and left with our good neighbors. Her everyday kerchief was quite faded and worn from daily use. Using her credit she bought a black kerchief. She said, "If we live, I'll somehow pay for the kerchief. If not, nobody will lose. I am embarrassed to wear a faded kerchief." My mother always covered her head as did all the married Jewish women in

Berezov. That night, as I lay without sheets with my mother in a bed, she caressed me and said, "Why do you have to die? You are so young. Now your body is covered only with a layer of flesh. You were always so thin. You grew so rapidly."

"It's been halted! It's been halted!" shouted the stranger who was riding through Berezov in a car. He was choking with emotion. Elation swept through the town as the news spread that deportation decree had been negated. Our happiness knew no bounds. It was only later that we learned that the order was merely postponed for two years. "In two years a great deal can happen," said the optimists. "The war can end, and they will lose their opportunity to harm us." My father who looked on the brighter side said that if they did not hurt us now they would not do so in the future. To show his faith in the future he said that he would marry me off if he found a nice young man. My mother retorted angrily, "Leave the child alone. Marriage can wait until after the war."

Mother brought back the things she left with the neighbors and put everything back in place. We were greatly relieved and happy. The house looked habitable again. The last thing mother did was bring back the little kitten from Marika, who told mother that the little thing would not eat. It just sat glumly in a corner and would not respond to a show of affection. When mother put the kitten down, it started to jump and run from one place to another. It was evident that the creature was as happy as we were to be home. Seeing the joy of the little animal, we lost all control of our emotions and tears. For the first time since the decree was promulgated, we all cried.

We heard, however, that other towns weren't as

lucky. The young and the old in the entire region along the Mala Rika river, from Chust all the way to Sinover at the Polish border, were loaded on trucks, and driven away. Among those unlucky souls were my brother Azick, his wife and two of their three children. The third child was in Bilki with my sister-in-law's parents. We grieved a long time for Azick. He was my parents' oldest son, and they were extremely proud of him. He was handsome and talented. Pictures of him regaled in red britches and black polished boots as a proud Hussar in the Czech army adorned the walls of our house. Azick could accomplish things that others found impossible to even try. While he still in the army he once told us the story of a wild horse that his brigade wanted to transfer. No one was able to get the horse to the train. It would rear up and kick her front legs in the air so no one could approach her. After many attempts had failed they called for Azick. He promptly delivered the horse to its destination. People lined the street to watch him maneuver the wild mare which had posed such a problem for all the others.

As for me, I owed him my life. It was a story repeated to me many times. When I was three years old, Azick was home on leave and had brought a friend home with him who came from the neighboring town of Horinch. Mother, lost in their conversation, forgot about me for a moment. When she looked around for me, I was nowhere to be found. No more than five minutes had elapsed, she claimed, and I was gone. She ran out to the yard and not seeing me focused her eyes on the creek that ran at the back of our house. It had rained on the previous day and the present one as well so the creek overflowed its banks. She suddenly saw my red dress as I was being carried away by the powerful rushing water. She screamed hysterically, and the two young men came running from the house. Azick's friend started to unlace his shoes. Azick didn't hesitate. He jumped into the deep water and started after me. After a few hundred feet, he caught up with me. When he brought me out of the water, I was blue and had swallowed a great deal of water. He immediately turned me upside down to shake the water out of me, then they massaged me vigorously to revive me.

In another second, without mother searching for and spotting me, I would have been carried away by the rushing water. Were if not for Azick's immediate and heroic action I would have been lost. After that incident Mother had nightmares, she would wake up screaming, and would reach out her hand to touch me, to make sure that I was still there next to her in bed.

I was fifteen and a half the first time I visited to stay with my sister Alta, in Tecso. I was a child when I left. While in Tecso, I emerged a woman. I developed physically, my body filled out and became well rounded with all the proper curves. I had blossomed into a beauty. Alta bought me a very becoming new dress and a pair of very pretty shoes.

When returned home that Passover, Azick happened to be visiting our parents. He was married and lived in the town of Drahive. He was very proud of me, kept asking the other family members whether they saw what he saw; how pretty I was. Azick also became the leader of a Zionist organization in Drahive. As a reward for his devotion and leadership, he was granted a certificate that would enable him to legally enter Palestine. As all other pious Jews would do when confronted with a crucial problem such as marriage or investing a large sum of money in a business or embarking on a long trip, the rabbi was always consulted. My parents called on a prominent one for advice. He advised them not to let him go, it was not the right time. The Messiah hadn't come yet. We had to wait for him in the diaspora, and when he arrived we would all meet in "Eretz Yisrael". Azick was a good son. He listened to my parents. In his place somebody else went to Palestine and to salvation. Azick went by truck to Kamenits Podolskiy to die an untimely and cruel death. He and all the rest of the Jews of his town were taken across the border to the Ukraine which the Germans had already occupied. He was shot in a ditch by the "Einsatzgruppen", the death squad commando groups. As soon as the Germans invaded Poland, vast areas of Russia, and the Ukraine, these death commandos were ordered to execute the Jews in those areas. They accomplished mostly their grim task by shooting the victims at the side of their heads. Before my brother was killed he was forced to dig his own grave.

That summer, when we were almost deported to the East and to certain death, another misfortune befell us. It rained all summer long. The crops, upon which our livelihood in great part depended, rotted in the fields. Fewer crops were harvested in the fall than had been planted in the spring. It was quite evident that the people of the entire region were going to starve, and they did. Rationing was enforced, and the allotment of flour or bread was very difficult to get because money was also in short supply. Even in normal times the area of the Carpathians was one of the neediest in Europe, but as long as the fields yielded a good crop enough food was available. Other necessities, however not dependent on bountiful crops were the acute problem.

Life in Berezov continued to be dismal. The recent events, the hunger and the continual inclement weather contributed to our low morale. One day I passed an apple orchard, and noticed a few mounds of apples nicely piled and grouped by their varieties. In a good season the orchards yielded abundant fruit, but this was a bad year and the harvest was poor. The small quantity of fruit produced was guarded very closely. As I passed and noticed the assortment of apples, I stopped and stared hungrily at them. My friend, Ilonka, came out of the house. She did not live there, but the orchard belonged to her family. She noticed me admiring the fruit, so she brought me an apple. I thanked her, and because I was hungry, I ate the apple immediately, wondering why she gave me only one. I told my mother what Ilonka had done and she mildly reprimanded me for not bringing the apple home to share with the rest of the family.

After a day of steady rain, and imminent prospect of starving that year, in addition to the recent deportation order, contributed greatly to our depressed mood. Late at night, we heard a knock on the door. Nobody moved. The atmosphere was fraught with tension. We all realized what could possibly happen to us without much warning, and we were very frightened. The knock was repeated, this time, somewhat louder. It was parent that whoever it was wouldn't leave. My mother went to the door and asked who was there. After learning who it was, Chaim Hersh from Sinover, the oldest son of her younger brother, Moshe, walked in. We were all aware that he and, his family, and all the Jews of his town had been taken by trucks to Poland. We all crowded around Chaim. He looked tired and weak. His clothes were ragged and he was very hungry.

Mother served him some food and we asked him about the families and people on the transport. He stated briefly, that everyone on the transport was dead. They were all shot in a ditch. He witnessed the slaughter. He was near the forrest and saw men with machine guns, in German uniforms shooting at everybody. As those in front fell dead or wounded, others were forced to come forward only to be shot in the head. He managed to escape, unobserved, among the trees. As he was running, he continued to hear the shooting. They echoed in his ears. He started to run faster from the site of the slaughter. He continued all night. In the morning a Gentile woman gave him a piece of bread. He was afraid to walk in daylight, and waited for nightfall. He kept off the main roads and hid in the forest. We had heard enough, really, more than we could hear. Mother prepared a place for him to sleep. In the morning he started to talk again. He said that while they were still in the trucks in Hungarian territory, they heard that the deportations had been halted, and that no more Jews would be expelled from the Carpathians. For them, however, it was too late. They would not turn the trucks back. Escape was impossible because they were scrupulously guarded. They kept rolling towards the border. After they crossed it the Germans took charge of the trucks. The Jews were forced to walk to a huge clearing in the forest and to dig a large ditch. When it was completed they were lined up and the shooting started. The SS threw babies into the air and used them for target practice. He still had more grisly stories to tell, but we refused to hear them. It was just too much.

Word of his returning from the dead spread among the Jews. Everyone found his recitals unbelievable. He was thought of as a lunatic who concocted incredible stories. Mother told him to stop talking. We, nevertheless, got a good idea of what the Germans had in store for those Jews who were unfortunate enough to fall into their hands. We were surrounded by the Germans, and Hungary was Hitler's ally. What awaited us was on everybody's mind.

The dead, of course, do not need to eat. The living, however, must. There was no food in Berezov or in any of the small towns in the region. We had none for ourselves, and now Chaim Hersh was an additional mouth. When the rain stopped for awhile my younger brother, Chaim Hersh, who was named for the same grandfather as Chaim Hersh, my cousin, and I went to the garden where corn, beans, and cabbages were planted and had rotted from too much rain. We dug up the cabbage roots and ate them. We could not find enough of them.

Our Ruthenian friends became suspicious and started to ask questions. Mother was afraid that the police would also have some. He was not "legal" any longer. He was supposed to be dead, shot in a ditch. He just had no right to be alive. My parents discussed solutions for him. We had a cousin in a town much larger than Berezov. They decided that he might be safer there and would be able to move about unnoticed. He would not be as conspicuous as he would be in Berezov. My parents scraped together the money for his transportation. Reluctantly, he left. He would have preferred to stay with us but my parents could not feed themselves and their own children that year, let alone take care of one more. There was no work available in Berezov for him or anyone else for that matter. After he was gone, the legacy he left weighed heavily upon us and on those who had heard his tale.

The villages and small towns of the Carpathians all looked alike. Drahive was no exception. It was about the same size as Berezov, with a larger population. It was about twenty kilometers from Berezov across a wide range of mountains and forests. There were two ways to reach Drahive: an expensive means by bus around the mountains and a less costly way, on foot over the mountains. For hikers, there was no road or pathway. One could easily get lost in the dense forest. When my brother Azick settled in Drahive, we would frequently cross these mountains.

As my brother, Chiam Hersh, and I descended into the valley, I saw them from a distance. The feathers in their helmets were fluttering in the light breeze. I thought; what I should do? turn around and go back up the mountain?, they would see me anyway. Hiding among the bushes would be useless too. The gendarmes would easily spot me in my red dress, because the bushes, having shed their leaves, offered very little protection. I decided to continue to walk. I had not committed any crime. I took my brother's hand and we headed toward the two gendarmes on patrol who stopped and waited for us.

As we approached them, they asked who we were and our destination. Our answers did not satisfy them. They ordered us to accompany them. Much to my dismay, we were leaving town, in the direction of the Polish border. After walking for quite a while the Ruthenian "Starosta" (mayor) of Drahive stopped by. He asked the gendarmes with whom he was very obviously very friendly, who we were, and where they were taking us. Then he asked me who we were. I explained that our mother was in Drahive at the house of my brother, Azick. He further inquired whether my father was the man who taught the Jewish children. (My father had worked there previously for a number of years. The pay was a little better than what he received in Berezov.) I nodded. He told the policeman, whom he called Tokach Ur, that he knew us and entered into a long conversation with him. He told them that he would guard us until the policemen returned. We were glad to be walking in the direction of the town rather than away from it. I was also happy to be in the company of the "Starosta" rather than with the other two. When we reached the town, I noticed how deserted it was. It resembled a ghost town. In place of the Jewish houses and yards where children once played and laundry hung on a line to dry, geese and chickens were the present occupants together with stray cats and dogs, sniffing the garbage. The "Starosta" chided us for coming to Drahive. It was no longer a safe place for Jews. He led us into his house and locked us in a dark room. I was very frightened as I had been from the moment I spotted the gendarmes.

When we first met the Starosta I had hoped that he would release us since he knew our father. Instead, he informed us that he would have to hold us until the gendarmes returned. We were locked up like criminals. What had we done but cross the mountains from Berezov to Drahive, as we often did many times previously? After a number of seemingly endless hours, a Jewish man came to the window. He was very angry, "What the hell are you doing here?" he yelled. "Don't you know what has happened?" Drahive was almost "Judenrein" (Jew free) except for himself. He paid an enormous "fee" for the privilege of polluting the pure Aryan air. I tried to tell him who we were. He informed us impatiently that he already knew. The Starosta had told him. He said that he had been a pupil of father's but that wouldn't save us.

31

We were in serious trouble, he said. Tokach, known far and wide for his sadistic treatment of Jews, was determined to shoot us for his own amusement. Jews had no rights and anyone could do whatever he pleased with them. The Starosta succeeded in getting Tokach to postpone the shooting until the evening. "What on earth are you doing here anyway? Your brother is gone," he said. I explained to this man that we had a mother in Drahive, quite probably in Azick's apartment. He left, and we were upset and frightened in the dark, locked room. He came back much later with the Starosta. He unlocked the door and told us to leave. We breathed a sigh of relief. We were warned, however, to travel through back alleys and gardens. "Do not use the main road. Get your mother and leave immediately. Never return to this town again."

My younger brother, Chaim Hersh, and I had been sent to Drahive where our brother Azick and his family lived. We went via the short, inexpensive route on foot across the mountains, a trip that would take two to three hours, depending on how fast the pace. Azick and all the Jews of Drahive were among those who were deported to Poland. Why?, there was no logical reason. Mother had arrived in Drahive a few days earlier to see what was left of Azick's home, his store and his household possessions. In the previous year, my parents had convinced Azick to lease a parcel of land for planting potatoes. Since business for Jews was bad, his family would at least have an abundance of food. Now he was gone and probably dead, although no one wanted to admit it.

Mother hired some help and together they harvested the potatoes. Azick had planted his crop on a hill (this was the poorer land) where the water drained off.

His crops had not rotted like the ones the neighboring farmers planted in the valley. Father had sent us to help mother with the potatoes. She wanted to bring them home because we were starving.

When Chaim Hersh and I arrived at Azick's apartment, mother had already sorted the potatoes and was putting them into sacks. When she heard what had happened to us, she ceased working and, leaving the potatoes, we set out through the back streets, running until we reached the mountains outside which were beyond the jurisdiction of Drahive. Here, we felt a little safer.

Our need for food became acute. Only a few days after our narrow escape from Drahive, my parents talked again about getting the potatoes. If they were not removed from the cold, empty apartment they would freeze or probably be stolen. In the meantime, we would starve. We knew it wasn't safe to go: The town was restricted; no Jews. We were also aware that the potatoes were Azick's. He was probably dead, shot in a ditch somewhere, yet all that concerned us were his potatoes. Hunger, however, triumphed. Mother returned to Drahive determined to be especially careful not to be visible, and to avoid public places. My parents managed to get a horse and wagon to bring the potatoes over. The potatoes arrived safely via Chust. Each time we ate those potatoes, we thought, sadly and bitterly, of Azick, his misfortunes, and how close we all came to sharing his fate. We hungrily devoured the potatoes, nevertheless, each one of us feeling silently guilty. Only mother verbalized her thoughts.

Later that same year, mother talked continually of going to Bilki where one of Azick's young daughters lived with her grandparents, and thus escaped the fate

33

of the rest of her family. That year was an economic disaster for us. She could not raise enough money for her fare. She kept talked of making the trip, but she was never able to visit her granddaughter, who lost her parents, sister, and brother in the German attempt to implement their plan to make Carpathia "Judenrein".

About a week after that episode in Drahive, on a late, dreary afternoon, aa unexpected visitor arrived at our house. He almost scared the wits out of everyone. The situation for us was extremely tense. Each day could bring, and often did, another decree, another restriction. But on this particular afternoon we were shocked and surprised when Mikula, the Starosta of Berezov, walked into our house unannounced. What frightened us so about his appearance was that he never came personally to serve a summons. His deputy would run errands for him. When he called in person, we thought the worst. Mikula was among the richest Ruthenians in Berezov and was respected and feared by Jews as well as Ruthenians. He was the political power in the town. That afternoon when he entered our house my father offered him a chair and they started to converse. They made small talk about the weather, when suddenly Mikula asked my father about the whereabouts of his daughter. My father pointed to me and said, "that's her." "Not her," Mikula said, "the other one." "She lives across the street. She is married." "And you don't have another daughter?" Mikula persisted. "Yes," my father said, "but her home is in Tecso." "I don't understand," said the Starosta. "Which of your daughters was in Drahive last week? The one that Tokach almost killed? He is a very mean man." My father again pointed to me. Mikula went on. "Yesterday, I met Tokach in Chust, and we began to talk. He said that he knows you. Your girl, the one that he saw, is very pretty.

34

Tokach wondered how it is possible that an ugly Jew like you would have such a beautiful daughter."

My father did not answer. The room we were in was very quiet. I was leaning against the wall near the stove and did not move. Mikula glanced in my direction once more and shook his head. "I've got to go," he said. "I have a lot of work." My father walked out with him. When he returned, he faced the eastern wall and recited the evening prayer swaying slightly backwards and forwards.

Just a few weeks later when I journeyed to Chust, I met the Starosta of Drahive. Thanks to him and to my former father's pupil, my brother and I were saved from the notorious Tokach. When the Starosta saw me, he greeted me warmly and shook my hand. We talked for a few minutes and then said goodbye. When I told my mother that the Starosta of Drahive recognized me and talked with me, she reprimanded me for not offering to buy him a drink at the bar.

The Hungarians were continually promulgating new decrees among us. It was bad enough that all the young men were drafted for work battalions, they also ordered that those who couldn't prove that they and their predecessors were born in the region, would be deported to Poland. On the other hand, those with citizenship papers would be spared that expulsion. A frantic search began for papers to establish one's right to live in the region. These poor people who already had a difficult time making ends meet, used up their last pennies or, in many cases, borrowed money for birth certificates of long dead and forgotten ancestors. The prices for these documents soared as more and more people tried to obtain them. First, I tried on behalf of my sister Alta's husband, to search for papers.

The husband was one of those who had to prove his citizenship, not that of his wife. They were exempt from having to produce documents, but wives shared their husbands' fate.

I traveled to distant towns in the dead of the winter in search of certificates. The officials intentionally made my task difficult and did not offer much cooperation. Some townships made it virtually impossible to obtain these papers. Officials often had to be bribed before they would even open the old books to look for the names of people who had once lived there. First I had to learn whom to bribe. Then, after paying off the first official I went to the township to pick up get the papers and was told that I had to pay another fee. These papers had to be certified once more, even, by a higher official in Chust.

I traveled to these towns in a horse-drawn wagon from Chust. To return, however, there was no transportation available, and I had very little money left for fare. So, on a blustery cold day I walked all the way back to Chust. I was very cold and hungry too. On the previous evening I had eaten two small baked potatoes with a bit of sauerkraut at the Starosta's place in one of these villages. I had to see him because he too had to sign those papers. I met another man in his home who was there for the same purpose. We were invited to stay the night because it was very late. I slept on a wooden bench.

As I wearily trod the long distance to Chust on a slippery road, icicles formed on my eyelashes and eyebrows. When I arrived in Chust I went to a designated office to have the papers signed once more. The official I had to see was not at work that day. I was told that he would be in on Monday. Since it was

Thursday I decided to go home for the weekend instead of returning to my sister in Tesco.

Some of the towns that I visited were already "Judenrein". In one of those desolate villages I found only one Jewish family who had managed to return from Poland. They too, like my cousin Chaim Hersh, had miraculously escaped the slaughter. Their children had been killed in Kamenits Podolskiy. They saved themselves, but not their children. They had run through forests and over mountains to return to their hometown. They allowed me to spend the night in their home which was now empty except for some items of furniture. They had a few blankets which some kind Ruthenians returned. They were changed people. For one thing, they refused to talk about what happened. They scrupulously avoided the subject. They kept it within themselves, unlike my cousin who was eager to relate everything in full detail. Gloom and a sadness was evident in their faces. They moved about like wraiths.

When I arrived home, my father was teaching a group of students in our house. He could not conduct his classes in a different location because of the severe cold during that winter, and his lack of adequate clothing. He decided that it would be better if his students would come to our house, though the rest of the family didn't like having thirty kids ranging in age from three to thirteen occupying the kitchen, the warmest place in the house. When I reached home that Thursday, father asked me whether I had any money. Flour was available for those with ration coupons, but he had no money to redeem the flour. I had none left from the supply my brother-in-law had originally given me. All our funds had been expended on certificates.

When I came back from my sister's I had to start all over again to obtain documents for ourselves. It was difficult for a Jew like my father who wore a beard, to travel even if he had the time. He was devoting all of his efforts to teaching Jewish boys the Bible and other Jewish religious writings. Unlike the public schools these studies were not government subsidized. Each child's parents paid for his tuition, but as money became scarce people could not pay this obligation.

I had to travel as far away as the city of Sighate to locate the papers. It was extremely difficult to find the birth certificate of my father's mother. She was not listed anywhere, as if she never existed. At that time my father's favorite witticism expressed to his friends was that he shared a parental anomaly with Jesus Christ who had no father just like himself who "did not have" a mother.

After much scurrying around and expending money which we could hardly afford, all the papers were finally gathered. Then, suddenly, the Hungarian authorities decreed that all these documents were worthless unless they were signed by some high ranking military official. It had to be done immediately or we would be deported. On that Sabbath, every Jewish girl and boy of Berezov was on the road waiting for a ride to Chust. Although the Jews of Berezov were strictly orthodox, and did not travel on the Sabbath, this situation was declared an emergency, and as such, an exception was allowed. On the way I noticed other Jews also waiting for rides. In Chust I asked for directions to army headquarters.

As I approached the place, I saw that the whole area was jammed with people from all the towns surrounding Chust. The pushing and shoving was dreadful.

Everybody was trying to get to the door which was guarded by a soldier. The entrance was occasionally opened to admit a few distinguished looking men. I heard cries of despair from the crowd. After a few hours it became apparent that none of us would have our papers signed. In desperation we left.

I soon thought of my parents who were depending on me. How could I go home without the last precious signature? I had to go back for it. When I returned to the army headquarters there were very few people left at the door, and the guard was gone. I walked right in, thinking whatever happens, happens. I walked up two flights of stairs and asked where I could find the official for whom I was looking. His office was pointed out to me and I entered. Much to my pleasant surprise, the man signed my papers immediately. I could not believe that I finally had all my bloody documents properly validated.

I returned home and word spread that I was the only one of all the people who went to Chust that Saturday whose papers were signed. I was queen for the day, and the talk of the town. Everybody envied my parents. I was very happy and proud. The documents proved worthless. It was just a ruse to empty the pockets of us Jews before their annihilation. Although most them in the region were poor, they were suspected of having money secreted away. Often, in times of crisis, the Jews of our area were forced to pay to save themselves. They could not afford nice homes, good clothes, or nutritious food. They seldom, if ever, were able to give their children a higher education. They rarely went on vacations, nor could they send their children to camp. They never bought gifts or toys for their children. They just couldn't afford these normal necessities and niceties. However,

Jews always managed small sums in emergencies. As one official of Berezov once said of the Jews, "Chortovi tay rabinovi musath biti" (For the devil and the rabbi they always have). The Jews saved a little for a rainy day.

During that winter we had little food. Our major staple was potatoes; Azick's potatoes. Occasionally we were able to obtain some flour with ration cards. Mother either baked matzos in the stove or made a porridge from the flour alone, since there was nothing else to add. We also had no firewood, despite our close proximity to a dense forest. The wood had to be purchased, and there just wasn't enough money available, even though father worked as usual. He kept teaching as he had done previously. However, his students' parents lacked the means to pay for their children's Jewish education. My father had a choice. He could send his students home or continue to teach them and hope that their families would pay him when money became available to them.

Food and wood became the two important items around which our lives revolved. New clothing was out of the question. It was impossible to survive without food and wood during the bitter cold winter. When the fire stopped burning in the brick stove, it became unbearably cold. On many occasions we would sit on the oven because that was the warmest place in the house, after the fire went out, and we had no wood left. One time Chaim Hersh and I went to our parcel of land, the Walentroses, from which we obtained hay for our cow, and there we chopped down some thick bushes. We brought the wood home on a borrowed sleigh to warm the house for awhile.

As all things good and bad eventually come to an end,

this winter was finally over. Passover, which was always a happy time for us, was celebrated. In the fall, when the potatoes from Drahive arrived, my parents dug a hole in the ground in front of a window so that they could watch it. They stored away some potatoes and a few beets. My parents took extra precautions to prevent the potatoes from freezing and to protect them from thieves. We were afraid that somebody's life-threatening hunger might drive him to open the hole and steal the potatoes. Now, with the arrival of spring the potatoes were taken out of storage. We barely had enough for the Passover holidays. We planted the rest in the best parcel of land we owned. We saved some beans and corn, too, for planting. It was very difficult for us to "deposit" the good stuff into the ground while we were hungry. But it had to be done.

After the Passover holidays we depended almost entirely on rations, which were quite unsubstantial. My brother Baruch Bendit, who lived in Ungwar and worked in a bakery, would send us two loaves of bread almost every week. The mail was slow and the bread would be stale when it arrived, but we ate it anyway. Then Baruch Bendit was conscripted into a work battalion.

That spring and early summer weren't any better than the previous winter as far as food was concerned. We had none. On the seventeenth day of the month of Tamus, which is a date in the early summer, all pious Jews fast, in observance of the day the siege of Jerusalem by the ancient Romans began, some two thousand years ago. Mother went to visit my sister Alta. My father, Chaim Hersh and I remained home. We all fasted. We had nothing to eat anyway, and no food for supper. Late at night when the fast period had passed, my father returned and brought a piece of mushy pie made from some unrecognizable grain substitute. He had obtained it from one of his students' mothers who lived on our street. She had served this ersatz pie to her family for supper. Her name was Esther and her husband was Mortche Leib Neuman.

When the Czechs were in power, this family operated a flourishing grocery business which both Jews and Gentiles patronized. They also had an extra room which rented to a Czech teacher. After the Hungarians arrived their business failed. The owner, Mortche Leib, who was only about forty years old, was drafted into a work battalion and later died at the Russian front when the Germans poured gasoline and fired the barrack in which he was quartered. Esther and her children were sent to Auschwitz. Only Molly, the youngest of a family of three daughters and two sons miraculously survived the war. The rest of the family perished. She was about twelve years old when she was condemned to the gas chamber in Auschwitz from where she somehow escaped and mingled with other girls in the camp.

Later that summer we looked forward to harvesting the new crop. The weather was good. The fields and orchards promised bumper results. News from the war was promising too. The allies had made progress. The Germans were badly beaten at Stalingrad in the previous winter. The prognosis was that they would surely lose the war.

Jews who escaped from Slovakia and from Poland to Hungary told dreadful stories of what the Germans were doing to the Jews in the places they occupied. Escapees were hiding in Jewish homes. My brother Baruch Bendit gave refuge in his house to such a man.

He came from nearby Slovakia. The gendarmes, on a tip from an informer, conducted a search in his house. By sheer luck they didn't look in the one place where the fugitive was hiding. Baruch Bendit was in grave danger. Had the man been discovered, both would have been turned over to the German butchers across the border, or just shot on the spot by the Hungarians.

The Hungarians were always on the lookout for escapees, many of whom were young men who lived and worked in Budapest. I had seen some of them on my visit to Budapest. They spoke Hungarian fluently, better than we did. Their survival depended on how well they could integrate with the Hungarians' population.

A number of Jews from Hungary were sent to Berezov to work in the forests as slave laborers, instead of serving in the work battalions on the Russian front as ditch diggers for the Germans. Every able-bodied Jew was forced to work for the "Motherland" Some stayed with relatives. Others rented rooms. One recently married man rented a room in our house and brought his new wife with him. They remained for a few months until he was transferee to a different area. There were no young men left in Berezov. Only the very young, the old, and the women. And, yes, the Hungarian gendarmes with the cock feathers in their hats, and the Hungarian drivers who drove the trucks loaded with railroad ties, and flirted with the Jewish girls.

The streets of Berezov were usually safe, not that it was a good idea for anybody to walk alone at night. Once during this period late time of day I was returning from Chust, I walked home alone through the dark streets. I was a distance from our house when suddenly Tokach, one of the Hungarian gendarmes who was stationed in town, appeared. He immediately began to hug me, and I could tell from his alcoholic breath that he was drunk. In fact he was seldom, if ever, sober.

Tokach started dragging me into a dark backyard. I couldn't very well fight him, so I tried to talk him out of whatever he intended to do, to save myself from being raped. I took his arm and we walked towards my house. I had hoped to meet someone in the street who might come to my rescue, but not a soul was there. The streets were deserted.

As we passed the Catholic church with its spacious grounds the front and in the rear, Tokach started pulling me towards the churchyard, saying that it was a good place in which to make love. I tried strenuously to remain in the street to prevent him from taking me into the churchyard. We were standing in front of the church. We struggled for a while and I finally succeeded in leading him away from the church.

After this, I felt a little better. But I was not safe yet. I still had a long way to go before I would reach home. I counted the houses. How many more to my house I wondered? I was getting nearer. There was no one in the streets, as if the whole damned town had suddenly died. A few more houses to go. Another minute or so and I would be home.

Even as I entered our yard, I didn't feel safe. Tokach still held on to me, and I was scared. I started to talk loudly, hoping that somebody in our house would hear me and come to my rescue, but nobody came. I was on my own. As I stepped on the front porch, only the door separated me from the safety of my home, but no one came.

I finally persuaded Mr. Tokach to go his way, promising him that next time we met I might be in a better mood. He said good night and left. I was saved. I entered the house hoping that my parents had not heard me and so could not help me. I learned that in fact they did hear the commotion but wouldn't respond. My mother admitted later that she was quite confident that I could handle the besotted policeman by myself. She felt she could not have stopped Tokack anyway. In fact, it might have infuriated him.

Since no one was in the street during my confrontation with the drunken gendarme who wanted to rape me, I thought that nobody in town would know about it. I was mistaken.

On the next day the whole town was talking about the episode. As I arrived the next morning at the Kahan's where I studied sewing with their daughter, I was asked whether I had a good time with Tokach last night. I tried to look innocent and thus imply that I didn't know what they were talking about. But in vain. Apparently, many people had watched from behind drawn curtains. No one, however, was courageous enough to help prevent a rape. They all knew what he had in mind and still did nothing. They all minded their own businesses. I was left alone with the menacing drunken cop in the deserted streets of Berezov.

The Jews of Berezov had lost their rights in 1939 when the Hungarians moved in. They were the masters and we were less than their slaves. Had Tokach actually raped me there would have been no place where I could go for assistance or sympathy. Not even from my parents. I would have been blamed, and the incident would have been considered my fault, even though I was the victim.

I wasn't the only person in Berezov that Tokach preyed upon. Just a few days after his attempt on me, he tried to rape another girl named Sosy, in whose house Tokach lived. Tokach had tried persuasion with me. He used force with the girl. Nevertheless, she managed to escape with her mother, but not before Tokach viciously beat both of them. They hid from his fury in a barn. He made yet another attempt on a girl named Sarah.

It had become dangerous for Jews to walk out in the evening, to say the least. Aaron, who was my father's partner in the baking of Passover matzos, once left a house at a late hour, and when he stepped out into the street and headed for home, Tokach greeted him with the Hungarian curses for the Jews, "Budos Zsido" and "Zsido budos kurvo" (dirty Jew and dirty Jewish whore). Tokach then started striking Aaron on the head and face with his fists.

Aaron realized that his life was in danger, and ran to the nearest Jewish house. He screamed that Tokach was killing him. The occupants wouldn't open the door for him. He went back to the street where Tokach accosted him again, hitting him with full force. He ran to the next house which belonged to his uncle. He pounded on the door and screamed, "Uncle Moshe, Uncle Moshe, open the door, Tokach is trying to kill me." This door to did not open for him. All the Jews of Berezov were terrified of Tokach and feared reprisals from the brutal policeman. When he tried the third house with the same negative results, Tokach pulled a weapon from his pocket. With nothing to lose, Aaron tried to defend himself. He was able break from Tokach's grip and then ran all the way home. He hid in the house, because he knew that Tokach would come after him. When he appeared, Aaron's mother told him that her son had already left. Tokach cursed and walked away. He also beat the old shochet (ritual slaughterer), again without provocation.

Tokach was only one of many who persecuted the Jews of Berezov. We had ceased to have any civil rights and had become virtually defenseless against legalized theft, abuse, and terror. All possessions from Jewish homes were confiscated. Jews were arrested for no reason at all. Yosel Froimovits, a Jew from Berezov, was arrested for selling barley to other Jews. The authorities seized the belongings of Zise Nojovits.

The Nojovits family in Berezov had guarded the possessions of their relatives from the town of Toron. Two years earlier Toron was evacuated because it had become a war zone. The Nojovits' relatives who also lived in Toron brought all their best things to them. Our relatives from that town also entrusted their possessions to us in Berezov, but they repossessed them as soon as it became safe to do so. The Nojovits family, however, left them there.

Actually all the Jews of Toron were on the transport to Kamenits Podolskiy in 1942. Now, in 1943, the Hungarians were confiscating the silver, clothing, foodstuffs and other valuables of the Nojovits household. Everything that belonged to that family in addition to what they were safeguarding for the relatives of Toron, was seized by the Hungarians.

The authorities took an entire trousseau from a girl named Yehudith which she accumulated over the years. They confiscated a horse and wagon from another family. Aaron, who was dealing in apples and nuts, lost everything to the authorities.

The Catholic priest, who waged a vendetta with Tokach, called Aaron the day after he was beaten and told him that the Jews deserved what they were getting. It was true that Jews had no recourse, but Tokach had no right to beat anybody at will, except, of course, the shochet, who deserved a beating. He, the priest, could get rid of Tokach because he tried to engage in sex with Jewish girls. Everybody knows that all Jewish girls are spies. Aryans are not allowed to have intercourse with Jews. It was then that the chief of the police called me to testify against Tokach. In an effort to get rid of him, who was almost always drunk, the priest reported all the crimes that he believed Tokach had committed. They wanted to use me as a material witness to prove that he betrayed the motherland by going to bed with a Jewess.

One late Friday afternoon a deputy came to our house. I was summoned to attend the hearing immediately. I did not know why I was being called. When I learned why, I refused. I was advised to tell the truth, not to be afraid. I decided not to admit that he raped me, because in fact, he didn't. I said that he just escorted me home, kissed me, and that was all he did. They were very disappointed and thought that I was not telling the truth, and that I was ashamed to admit that he raped me.

Despite all the evidence against him, Tokach's punishment was only a transfer to a different town. We didn't have time to rejoice, however. After he left we were confronted with problems much worse than Tokach ever caused.

The year was 1944. The war was surely going to end this year, all the experts agreed. The Germans couldn't win. They were virtually defeated already. The two-year extension on our deportation might be prolonged, or invalidated. Why would we be deported in the first place? I think everyone had forgotten that we lived on borrowed time. The experts said that the Germans had more important matters to worry about than the Jews of Hungary, especially now that the war was going badly for them. Then in March it happened, the event we dreaded and feared most: The headlines reported that said the Germans had invaded Hungary. They were actually placed in Budapest.

It hit us like a bolt of lightning out of the blue. As soon as the Germans entered Hungary, their first priority was the Jewish question. They invaded Hungary with the express purpose of liquidating the Jews. We learned to live with the Hungarian decrees promulgated by Germany's ally. They proved to be extremely devastating and humiliating. Immediately upon entering Hungary on March the 19th, the Nazis forcibly removed all Jews who were riding the trains. They were arrested and sent away. No one knew where. They just disappeared. Other Jews were seized as they walked in the streets. The Hungarians were most eager and happy to collaborate with the Germans in rounding up the Jews. People were afraid to leave their homes. Nobody travelled to Chust anymore. Identification papers were being scrupulously checked everywhere. Jews were virtually under house arrest. It took some two weeks before we actually saw a German in the region. In nearby Horinch, German officers were housed in the nicest

Jewish homes. A German officer stayed in my cousin's house. He behaved very gentlemanly.

This was the beginning of the end for the Jews of Hungary, and the end wasn't long in coming. We hoped and prayed for a miracle. Since the Germans were already here, only a miracle could save us. In 1941, Hungary had approved the deportation of stateless Jews living in the new territories. In 1942, the Hungarians had delivered a few thousand Jews from our region to the so-called new territories that Hitler had "given" to Hungary for becoming a German ally. They were delivered to the Germans in Poland to be massacred. My brother Azick was among those who were forced across the border into the Ukraine and slaughtered there. We were next in line. However, the new prime minister, Miclos Kallay, opposed the deportation and the Jews of Hungary gained a two year reprieve.

As long as it suited the Nazis, they did not bother the Hungarian Jews. But the war was going badly for them and their defeat was imminent. The Nazis wanted victory on their more important "front," the total annihilation of all European Jews, before it was too late for them to achieve their goal. With the Third Reich crumbling, they had to act very quickly to murder the remnants of European Jewry who still lived in Hungary. The Jews in Hungary and the new "territories" were in sort of oasis. They totaled almost one million.

As soon as the Germans occupied Hungary, the notorious Adolf Eichmann and his murderous henchmen arrived in Budapest. They began to issue decrees just as they had in the other countries that they occupied. There was one difference, however;

with us they proceeded swiftly. They had no time to lose. By this tome they had become quite proficient in the art of killing, garnered by a great deal of experience. After all, they had already annihilated most of Europe's Jews. As soon as they entered, dire events ensued. It seemed as if God and all of mankind were concerned only with the fate of Jews in the godforsaken Berezov, a town that nobody ever remembered except at tax time. Now we were recalled in order to humiliate us. We were forbidden to go outdoors between five P.M. and eight o'clock in the morning. We were not allowed to commute to other villages or towns.

The most debasing act for me was the Star of David decree which was announced on March 31 and would be effective as of April 5. The village crier reached the house next to ours, as was his custom. He beat his drum long enough to allow everyone to assemble. When he finally stopped he shouted, "Attention everyone." He then intoned in a lilting voice, emphasizing every word loudly and clearly. "From this day on," he said, "The Jews of Berezov ages six and over must wear a six-pointed, yellow star on the left side of their chests, visible from a distance to all. The star must be made of bright, yellow fabric. Its size should be eight centimeters in diameter. Any Jew seen in the street not wearing this yellow star will be immediately arrested."

The Jews responded quickly in order to comply with the order by the stipulated date. Yellow material was brought in from Chust. No one in Berezov had such fabric. It was a very sad time for us when we had to sew the yellow star onto our clothing. Jewish girls were distinguished from the Ruthenians by their clothing. Most Ruthenians wore their national attire:

dresses made of embroidered, white home-woven fabric with colorful aprons tied at the waist. Jewish girls, on the other hand, wore more stylish clothes. Only those Ruthenian girls who had studied in large cites wore chic clothes. We often dressed in fancy Ruthenian clothes for Purim and in school plays. The Yellow Star Decree, however, humiliated us, but then that was its real intention. When the Hungarian gendarme started flirting with me, I told him, "See, I wear a star."

"There are many stars in the sky" he said, and pointed towards a clear sky covered with millions of stars. Our future, however, was certainly not as bright as those stars to which he pointed. We were branded. We avoided looking at one another so as not to notice their embarrassment. We hoped that, maybe, if we ignored it, it would go away.

Of course, it did not. We went about our business as usual, out of habit, I suppose. Our hearts, however, were not in it. We prepared for the approaching Passover holidays; the traditional cleaning of the entire house, and mother painting the interior of our house as she did every year. The windows were removed and washed. Everything else was brought to the stream behind our house, scrubbed and polished as tradition dictated. Mother, as was her custom, force-fed two birds for Passover, a goose and a rooster. Actually, preparation for Passover started in our household much earlier. The melting of goose fat was accomplished in the middle of winter. The goose and the rooster were set aside for Passover. Money was saved to buy new clothes for the holidays.

Before each Passover, there was much hustle and bustle in the house, with the cleaning and with the baking of the matzos, and everybody participated. Father and his partner, Aaron, were the sole bakers of the matzos in Berezov. Often, they were baked in our home, and sometimes in Aaron's. As a child, I was the one who poured water for the kneader and my older brother, Shmual Moshe, poured the flour. When I was a little older I took care of the flour and my younger brother, Chaim Hersh, added the water. We were paid for our work, and allowed to buy whatever we wanted, provided we didn't spend our money foolishly.

When I grew older, I was promoted to rolling out the matzo leaves. All the girls and women of the town participated, and we competed to see who could roll out a better, thinner matzo in the least time. It was not so boring when we competed.

This year we baked matzos as usual, but it was a solemn occasion. My father's partner who was a young man had been called up to serve the work battalions. It seemed the authorities had previously forgotten about him, so my father baked the matzos with another Jew of Berezov. Because Jewish law forbade eating leavened bread on Passover, we ate matzos as a substitute for bread.

The Germans tried desperately to stop the advancing Red Army. They rushed masses of soldiers and equipment to the Russian front. On their way there, they passed Berezov where they stopped for a few days to rest and conduct maneuvers before continuing on their journey to the East. While in town they were housed in, the best Jewish homes. They requisitioned only two Ruthenian houses. We were ordered to empty the largest and best room in our house of all furniture except for one bed which we were to leave with its bedding. The floor was covered with straw which was collected from Ruthenian barns. Right after, a platoon of soldiers led by a sergeant, moved in. The privates occupied the floor, while the sergeant placed his personal belongings on the bed.

Soon after they moved in, the officer tried to befriend me and my family. He was a "Volksdeutscher" (a German living outside of Germany) or what they were called in our place, a "Shwab". He was from a town in Hungary. He befriended my mother too. He liked her cooking. At least, he preferred it over the food he received at the army kitchen, which was set up as soon as the army moved into town. He would sometimes skip going to the army kitchen for lunch or supper and would eat at our table. He became a regular house guest. He observed everything that was going on in our house. He soon learned about the forthcoming Passover holidays. He knew who our friends were. After a few days in Berezov he familiarized himself with everything. Once, in town, he was asked where he was housed, He answered matter of factly, "at pretty Moncika's." Some did not know who Moncika was, because I was known by my Jewish name, not the Hungarian.

He had a packet of photographs of the German-held Russian and Polish territories. He had been fighting on the Russian front previously, where he was wounded and sent to the rear to recuperate. Now he was ordered for a second time, to the same fighting area. He showed these pictures to only a few carefully selected people, and I was not among them. He said that I was too young. I, nonetheless, learned that some of the photos were scenes of gallows from which bodies dangled. He explained that those people were hanged by the Germans. They were partisans who attempted to survive underground in a German dominated world. However, he did not reveal whether these victims were Jews or Gentiles.

He also told of Germans shipping trainloads of Jewish goods from Russia and Poland to Germany. Everything that could be loaded on wheels was sent. Furniture, clothing, silver, art, foodstuffs, anything that could be moved was packed and shipped. They "employ" Jews to clean and pack the "stolen" items. To his Ruthenian listeners, he related terrible stories describing what the Germans were doing to the Jews in the East. He also told them that we would not be eating the two birds that mother was fattening for the holidays; we wouldn't have the time. Our work was in vain.

Once he casually asked me to show him pictures of myself. Not realizing what the consequences might be, I let him see my collection which consisted of photos of my family, friends, and me. He looked through all of them and picked out my most recent one. It had been taken in Chust by a professional photographer. I was standing with my friend, Monci Kahan, with whom I had studied sewing. He asked me to cut off Monci, and give him the half of myself. On the back of the photograph, he wanted me to write a dedicatory inscription dedicated to him, and sign my full name. I declined to give him my photo. He kept asking why I refused. I told him that I had deep seated reluctance to giving my picture to passing soldiers. A girl did not offer a picture of herself to a casual acquaintance.

He also liked to amuse his listeners with jokes. Once he told us an amusing story about three people who wagered among themselves as to who was going to win the war. One said the British and Americans. The second picked the Russians, and the third chose the Germans. To determine who would win without having to wait until the war ended, they decided to toss a coin. Heads, the British and Americans would be victorious. Tails, the Russians would be victorious. And if the coin remained suspended in midair, the Germans would conquer. "Ha ha ha," he laughed. Nobody else dared to join him.

Although the Germans were being beaten on all fronts, as far as we were concerned, they were very strong. They were doing to us what they damn well pleased and nobody was stopping them. His favorite quip was that if the British and Americans won the war, he would marry Moncika. If the Russians prevailed, he would wed my Ruthenian friend and neighbor, pretty Chrestina. Should the Germans be victorious, he would return to his home.

He always associated us with the British and Americans. I wondered: Why don't these great powers, if they are our allies, do something in our behalf? Our very lives are hanging by a thin thread and at any moment the town crier with his drum might appear once again to announce a new harsher decree and we are helpless.

The soldiers spent about two weeks in our house. When the officer received his orders to march on to the front, he asked me for one last time to give him my photograph. I still refused. He bade good-bye to everyone including me, and then he and his platoon departed. We were told to leave the room as it was, ready for the next arrivals. He left on a Friday.

On Saturday I was sent to the town hall which was on

the Kuzi across the Rika, to sign some papers. When I reached the main road it was crowded with soldiers and equipment. Some people were walking, others were riding on horseback. As I returned from the town hall, I saw the sergeant a few hundred feet down the road, riding his horse among the horde of soldiers. When he saw me, he prodded his horse and emerged from the long line to the shoulder of the road where I stood. He dismounted and approached me. "Moncika," he asked, "did you bring me the picture?" I was very embarrassed. At this point, if I had the photo on me I would surely have given it to him. If he could still think of my picture in this miserable weather, on his way to the front, I would let him have it. He looked so humble and vulnerable. The potholes on the road were filled with water, and it was teeming. Puddles and mud were everywhere. Although spring had officially arrived, it was bitter cold. His clothes were wet and seemed to weigh him down. I suddenly forgot my principles about not having my picture circulating among the German-Hungarian soldiers, who might later claim, as they all would, "See, I had a Jewish friend." I said, "I don't have the photo with me, but I will run home and bring it to you in a few minutes." "No, Moncika," he said, "it is too late for you to do that. I have to go now. I am delaying the entire column. Go home and stay there. It is not good for you to be here on the road with so many soldiers, and in such bad weather too." He stretched out his hand, and I put mine in it. He shook it hard and long. "Moncika, I will return," he said. "I promise, I shall. Good-bye." He mounted his horse, nudged it slightly with his riding boots and rode off. When I turned around, all I saw was his back and the tail of his white horse. I walked home as fast as I could. He kept his word. He did come back, but we were not there to see him.

Marika, our good Ruthenian neighbor told me after the war that she saw him. It was about Christmas time when the Germans and the Hungarians were retreating. The soldiers ran as fast as if the devil himself was chasing them. And maybe he was. As they ran they wreaked havoc on the region. They looted, burned property and left dead animals in their wake. The Ruthenian population stayed out of their way. No one was safe. "We locked ourselves in the house," she said. "We were afraid to go out. Suddenly, I saw an officer on a white horse approaching. He stopped in front of your house and stared at it for a long time."

Then he rode over to Marika's house. He alit and passed her gate. At that point she recognized him. She opened the door and noticed that he had risen in rank.

He inquired of Marika: "Where are the people who live in that house?", pointing to our place. She shook her head and told him that she didn't know.

"What nice people they were. Oh, such nice people," he mumbled. He stood there for a few more minutes and then started to leave. She asked him if he wanted some food, but he shook his head and walked out, leaving no message for us. He mounted his horse and rode off in the same direction from which he came.

After this first group of soldiers left, others followed. We got used to their presence. Father was worried about how he would be able to conduct the seder rituals with the soldiers in the vicinity. But the cleaning and scrubbing proceeded as if nothing out of the ordinary. Mother asked me to paint the outside of our house. In normal times she wouldn't have trusted me with that job. When somebody asked her why she worked so hard fixing up and cleaning the house, considering the terrible times in which we were living ("Isn't it useless?" they would ask), she would shrug her shoulders and answer sadly: "I can't help myself. I just can't. It is Passover."

A few days before the holidays, Chaim Hersh, my younger brother who worked in Budapest, returned. Normally he would have come home to observe the holidays just as my other brothers always did for Passover, until they were married. And even then, they would sometimes arrive with their wives. This year, however, the holiday spirit was missing. Chaim Hersh had been advised by the good lady in whose house he lived in Budapest to return to his family to face with them whatever lay ahead. Had he stayed in Budapest he might have been alive today. Many Jews of Budapest were spared our fate.

In spite of the circumstances, he brought me a jar of Nivea cream, the first gift that I had received in a very long time. I cherished that good cream, although I never had an opportunity to use it. Just before Passover, he asked me to give some of the cream to our mother so that she could apply it to her painful hands, which were severely chapped from all her scrubbing and cleaning.

On the eve of Passover, as we did every year, we rose early to for a breakfast of non-Passover food. After that, we were not allowed to eat "chumetz" (leavened food) until the holiday was over. After the dishes were washed and put away in a corner of the attic, another set was brought down. These were used only during Passover. Among them were a few antiques that had been handed down from one generation to the next. Some of these dishes belonged to my grandmother. My mother pointed out to me a few bowls that were hand-painted, ones she had received from her mother. Chaim Hersh and I, as small children, had our favorite special bowls from which we ate.

In normal times, when the Passover dishes were brought down, we were thrilled that we would once again eat from these favorite plates of ours. We all liked Passover. In fact, our lives revolved around the Jewish holidays, the Sabbath, and the occasional wedding in the family or of our friends. We really had no other entertainment.

I often heard the story about my oldest sister, Alta, when she was a child. One year, she started to cry when she saw mother clear away the Passover dishes to take to the attic when the holiday was over. When asked why she was crying she said, between sobs, that she didn't want dearest Passover to go away.

This year we did everything as we had done in the past but without enthusiasm, without life. We behaved like robots, going through the motions. We even made the traditional wine without which Passover couldn't be properly celebrated. About two weeks before the holidays, somebody from Berezov, at great risk to himself, went to Chust and brought raisins which we used in making wine for Passover. Mother had a special earthenware pot in which the raisins were placed and to which water was added, and put in a warm spot. After a number of days they would begin to ferment. After two weeks, they were squeezed out through a cloth. The remaining liquid was wine. Maybe it wasn't the best wine ever, but it was certainly the best anyone in Berezov could afford.

This is how we celebrated Passover for the last time as a family. For my parents it would be the last Passover they would ever celebrate, and it wasn't a very happy one. It was a very sad and gloomy ritual. No one could disguise his or her fear and apprehension over what lay in store.

We observed Passover among the soldiers. Nevertheless, we did eat the two birds for which the friendly German-Hungarian sergeant predicted we would not have time. I never did wear the slightly used rain coat and the new shoes that I bought in Budapest before the Germans invaded, even though I had kept them especially for the holidays.

It was chilly during Passover. After the holiday everything was in an upheaval. It seemed that the whole world was crumbling and coming to an end. It did. But only our world, the world of the last remaining Jews of Europe.

On the last Sabbath in our home, mother and father recited the Psalms after the services at the shul. I went for a walk with my friend Frida. We left town and reached the place where as children, not too long ago, we played hopscotch, where we once played marbles using stones instead of real marbles, and where we use to jump rope while watching the geese to make certain that they didn't enter any of the fields where corn and beans were growing. This time no Jewish girls were gaily playing. The place was deserted. There were no sounds of laughter. We only heard the rat-a-tat of machine guns coming from a short distance away.

We walked slowly and solemnly as if we were part of a funeral procession. At times we remained silent and then we would talk strangely about survival, a theme we had never discussed before. At one point Frida said that she was sure that I would survive. I asked what made her think so. She replied that she just knew. As for herself, she didn't have much hope. As she predicted, she would later die in a bed next to mine in a British makeshift hospital near Bergen-Belsen, Germany, a few days after liberation.

The town crier came again and again with new, more restrictive edicts. He announced that Jews were forbidden to mingle with aryans. No business transactions were allowed between Jews and Gentiles. Jews were further forbidden to speak to or greet non-Jews. They were forbidden to deliver any household articles, clothing or money to Gentiles. The Gentiles in turn were not allowed to receive anything from Jews. Punishment for any violation would be severe. We became isolated and alienated.

The worst, however, came to pass a few days later. At that time, about the beginning of May, the town crier appeared again to announce our imminent departure from the town. Any Jew found hiding would be suffer greatly. Also, any Gentile in whose house or on whose property a Jew is found would also pay the price. It seemed that all else had ceased to exist. Everyone apparently was concerned with the Jews. We were given three days to vacate the town and move to a ghetto, Izo, about fifteen kilometers from Berezov. I heard the word "ghetto" for the first time.

Despite these restrictions, interactions between Jews and Gentiles not only continued but were intensified. As a result of these clandestine transactions, money, horses, cows, clothing and jewelry changed hands. They were secretly transferred from one owner to the next. Ruthenians acquired Jewish real estate, mills, houses and other valuables. We were apprehensive, confused, and terribly frightened about our future. On the one hand, we were convinced that this was the end, yet, at the same time we were worried about our possessions. We wanted them hidden in a safe place when we returned.

Our friend, Marika, refused to take any goods from her Jewish friends and neighbors. She only accepted a few pieces of jewelry from us and from my sister Rivka. She took the threat of the authorities, seriously. She said that she was afraid. In 1942 when we were about to be expelled to Poland, the Ruthenians were not forbidden to safeguard Jewish possessions. However, at this time they were barred by the authorities from engaging in this practice. We just had to find a way to safeguard our meager possessions.

One of our Jewish neighbors, Mallie, had an uncompleted room in her house, only walls and a roof. There was no floor, just earth. To insure the safety of our valuables, during the night so that no one would see what we were doing, our two families dug a large hole in the ground of the unfinished room. While we were frantically transferring our valuables to the hole we discovered a Ruthenian watching us from a hiding place behind the unfinished window.

Consequentially, everything had to be removed from the hole, and we now had to look for a safer location. We found a "good" place at the Balabans, a highly respected Ruthenian family that lived a few houses from us. It seemed that they just couldn't resist the temptation of accepting Jewish goods in spite of the threats from the authorities not to interact with Jews.

We carried our possessions to the Balabans at night, as did my sister Rivka and her two sisters-in-law. Everybody in our family was told where our belongings had been hidden so that when any one of us returned, he or she would know where to find them.

The "shochet", who acted as the rabbi for Berezov, declared a day of fasting. Other towns in the vicinity did likewise. Every able-bodied person was obliged to fast. Men were to spend the day in shul, praying and reciting the Psalms. We all went to the cemetery to plead with our dead ancestors to intervene in the heavenly court in our behalf for redemption and deliverance from the bloody hands of the Germans. It had worked two years earlier and it might work again at this time.

Old men, women and children visited the cemetery. The young were taken there for the first time, so that their pure, innocent prayers would reach God. Only He in His infinite mercy and goodness could reverse the decree that announced our imminent deportation and doom. Nobody knew what else to do. We were just inundated by the tide of current events. We Jews were too stunned by the sudden invasion of Hungary by the Germans, to make plans to protect our lives. Some, however, did talk with their Ruthenian friends about hiding in their homes. Several agreed to help us for money, of course, or for a parcel of land.

Udel, our neighbor and friend, who was quite a bit older than I, had an arrangement with a good comrade of hers who lived a long distance away in the woods. This person said that no one would ever come to his house looking for Jews. We would be safe with him. My parents decided that I should save myself by hiding there. They wanted at least one person from our rather large family to survive. We decided that Udel and I would hide together, either at Udel's friend's house in the forest, or at one of several other pre-arranged places.

The town was in great turmoil. Jews were ordered by the authorities to prepare to abandon homes their families had lived in for generations. It had been a very difficult life for we Jews. Under normal circumstances we lived in deprivation and want. In times of war it became even more burdensome, especially during this conflagration which dragged on and on. But it was still our home, and now we were being forced to leave it.

When it became evident that we would be consigned to the ghetto, I packed a knapsack with clothing, some food, and said good-bye to my family. Then I went to sleep in Udel's house. The bed had no sheets, because Udel's family's bedding and other valuabies, together with ours, were all "safely" stowed away at Antza and Shtefan Balaban's.

Long before dawn we left Udel's and made our way to the outskirts of town. We reached the house of a good friend of both our families. Udel suggested that we stay with him for a while.

We approached his place but we couldn't get close to it because a ferocious dog was tethered to a long chain so that he blocked the entrance to the house. The dog was barking very loudly, and he was trying desperately to free himself to attack us. The snarling canine opposed our intrusion, and obviously so did its master. The wild barking continued in an effort to scare us away. We, however, refused to leave. After a long time elapsed, our good friend finally came out. He had obviously looked out of the window to learn why the dog was barking so insistently. He knew what we wanted. By ignoring us he hoped we would go away. But since we remained outside for so long he had to come out. He was angry that we had disturbed his sleep. He said that it was a dangerous business to harbor Jews. He was old, scared and didn't want any trouble with the authorities, and so he told us to go away and leave him alone.

Silently, we walked into the night and climbed the mountain. When we reached the top, we turned off the path and sat down to rest. I was very tired since I had not slept at all that night as well as on the previous few nights also. I was quite upset about having to leave my family, and that kept me awake. As we sat down to rest I fell asleep for a few minutes. I woke to find that I was a fugitive on the same mountain where I once roamed free as a bird.

As the new day dawned, we hid in the woods. We spent the whole day there. At nightfall we arrived at another of our prearranged hiding places, the house of a man who once worked with my parents. We owned a large parcel of land called the Walentroses on which we grew grass. This was the land that was designated for my dowry, and this Ruthenian took care of it. He trimmed the bushes, and watched to see that no one trespassed or brought animals to graze. When the grass was good and tall, he would cut and dry it until it became hay, which we shared with him. We fed our cow with the hay, and she provided us with milk. Once a year she gave birth to a calf which we sold. The hay from our land provided him with the same benefits. Now this same man told us that he would let us sleep in his barn overnight, but that we would have to leave early in the morning.

He didn't offer us supper. He wouldn't even let us into the house. I expected a little "tokan" (a porridge of corn meal), but he didn't give us any. So we climbed into the barn and lay down on the hay without undressing. The only thing we removed, were our coats which we used as covers. We were cold during the night and we shivered. He came to wake us up before dawn, and brought us each a little milk, which we drank thirstily. We were parched, having walked all day in the woods without food or drink. When we were finished, he went out and looked around in all directions to make sure that nobody was watching. Then he told us to leave and asked us not to return. We had become pariahs, and no decent person would allow us into his home.

We went back into the woods. At nightfall we called on yet another good friend. This one also didn't allow us into his house. He, too, took us in for only one night. He told us to stay in the stable with the cows and oxen. The floor was covered with manure and reeked. The only available space was in the manger. So we settled in there for the night. There wasn't even room to stretch. Again, we didn't remove our clothes. The bulls might have been embarrassed. So once more we covered ourselves with our coats to keep warm.

This friend warned us not to go out during the night, even to relieve ourselves, and cautioned us not to talk with each other, especially in Yiddish. That language had become outlawed. He had one other condition under which he would allow us to spend the night in his stable: if some one caught us he would claim that we entered his stable without his knowledge. We had to promise to corroborate this story. We agreed; we had no choice. He went back into his house and returned

67

with two bowls containing a little corn meal and porridge. It was fresh, warm and good. We ate it hungrily in the manger with the cows looking on. He too observed us eating. When we finished, he took the bowls and the lantern and left.

That night was awful. Without the lantern it was pitch dark and the manger was narrow. The heads of the animals were on top of us and they were sniffing us constantly. They made noises while scavenging for food. It was impossible to sleep. The straw irritated our skin. But it was at least beneficial in one way. We were not cold in that stable. The cows kept us warm.

Early in the morning when it was still dark, he entered the stable and told us to go. We left and again spent the day in the woods. We had two more stops to make, and the people who would care for us in both places had received advance partial payments on the total amount they would receive for hiding us.

In the evening we made our way to the first of these refuges. We arrived after dark. A woman was living there alone. She put us up in the attic of the stable which contained hay for her cow. Since the attic was clean, we were able to undress for the first time since we left home. We lay down on the hay. Udel and I had some food in our bags. He ate some of it that evening and again the next morning. I couldn't eat. I missed my mother so very much that I spent the entire night crying. Udel urged me to stop it. I wanted to join my mother, but I didn't know what was happening in town, or where my family was. Late Friday afternoon, the woman went to town to shop. She told us she would find out what was happening.

Since her place was quite remote, she allowed us to leave the attic and spend a few hours outside while we waited for her to return. I was pacing back and forth in front of the house and Udel was just standing around when we both heard a sound from behind the bushes. We were terribly frightened, not only for ourselves but for the woman as well. As we dashed for cover we saw Itzik Leib from Berezov. We were very glad to see some one who was Jewish and were relieved that it was not a gendarme.

Itzik Leib with his wife, three children and an old mother lived near us. He said that his family had agreed that he should hide to try to save himself. They realized that with three small children it was not feasible. We asked him what was happening in town. He said that Berezov had become Judenrein. All Jews had been taken to the Izo ghetto. He wouldn't tell us where he planned to hide. "You can't reveal what you don't know," he said. He bid us good-bye and wished us good luck as he lifted his heavy rucksack and left.

We watched as he disappeared into the woods and was swallowed up by the rapidly approaching night. After he left I realized that it was Friday evening. I hoped that I would wake and find myself at home, that this would turn out to have been only a nightmare. Father would come home from shul as he did every Friday night. Mother would light her nine candles, one for each member of the family. The table would be set on a white table cloth, and we would all sit down as mother served the Sabbath meal. What was I doing on a Friday night in this far-off place? I cried bitterly.

The woman returned from town. I had hoped that she would bring some good news, that the deportation order had been suspended and that everything would be well again. Instead, she brought bad tidings. The town crier, as he had in the past few weeks, still occupied himself exclusively with the Jews. This time he announced that any Ruthenian who harbored a Jew in his house or on his premises would be severely punished. On the other hand, those who turned in escaped Jews, would be rewarded.

Our hearts sank. So this was really the end. She now had second thoughts about hiding us in her house. She had difficulty in finding gentle words to tell us that she wanted us to leave. She knew that she was reneging on her agreement. She said that she was terribly frightened, but that she hoped that we would understand. Every one, in town reminded her that harboring Jews was very risky. "They mean what they say about punishing those who are found hiding Jews." She would allow us to stay one more night in her barn attic and then we would have to leave early in the morning. She did not offer us food even once.

After leaving, we wandered through the woods. In the late afternoon, we sat down by a spring. We hadn't eaten all day. We drank lots of cool fresh water from the spring. Udel ate some of the food she saved in her knapsack. I took a small piece of bread, but I couldn't swallow anything. I was too upset, too miserable, too sick at heart to eat. I certainly missed my mother. I couldn't stop crying. Udel said that she was disappointed in me. She thought that I was more mature, more adult. I told her that when I heard of the persecutions of other Jews, I felt sorry for them and could deal with their misfortunes, but it was impossible for me to bear my own travail. How much more difficult it was to suffer ourselves then hearing about the misfortunes of others.

I yearned to be with my mother, no matter what the consequences. I couldn't bear being separated from her. Although I had been away from home many times before, this time I missed her more than I ever had previously. Maybe I felt that I would never see her again. If I don't get to the ghetto, I will miss my last chance to be with her, I thought. I tried to convince Udel to surrender ourselves so that we would be taken to the ghetto. She remained adamant about going to our last, and supposedly best hiding place. "You cannot do a thing for your mother," she said, "and she can do very little for you. Now stop crying and behave yourself."

Udel might have been overly optimistic because this last refuge we were heading towards belonged to a Ruthenian who was a lifelong friend and business associate of Udel's family. Of course, he had already received an advance payment for hiding us. When I told Udel that he too might have second thoughts after he heard about the threats to anyone giving aid and comfort to Jews, she still had faith in this man. When he accepted the fee, he had sworn on his mother and children that he would treat us as he would his own children until the war ended, no matter how long it took.

After we had our drink of water we rested near the spring. We then continued our roaming in the woods. As we walked in the dense forest, feeling protected by the many trees, we hadn't realized that this area came to an abrupt end. We suddenly found ourselves in a clearing. A Ruthenian family: father, mother and two daughters, were cultivating the land. We instinctively wanted to turn and go back to the woods, but they had already seen us. If they told the authorities, the gendarmes would soon be searching for us. We decided to approach the family and say hello. Neither Udel nor I knew them. They seemed to be friendly. The man acted very fatherly. He soon pointed out how useless it was for us to wander in the woods. "Why don't you join your families? It will be impossible to escape the fate that awaits you," he told us. After the advice, we left them and returned to the forest. I was persuaded to give myself up and go to my mother. Udel still refused to go with me. We realized that we should be more careful in the woods. Ruthenians could be working almost anywhere.

For the Ruthenians life went on as before. The fact that the Germans had invaded Hungary changed nothing for them. They and their children were safe at home. They continued to work in the fields as they normally did.

Isn't it spring? I reflected. Everything is returning to life. The meadows are covered with wild flowers, the trees are alive with new leaves. The animals are grazing in the pasture for the first time after a long, cold winter. Boys and girls are walking hand in hand. After all, they are the superior race, the favored people of God and men, because they are Aryans and Christians. God wreaks his wrath only on the Jews. The Gentiles live happily. For us there was no spring, no flowers, no sun. We were the doomed. Our death sentence had already been pronounced. Our executioners had already arrived.

My thoughts proved to be truer than I knew. Adolf Eichmann was already settled in the Hotel Majestic in Budapest. From there he loudly proclaimed that we, the Carpathian Jews, would be the first in the country to go to our death in Auschwitz.

We had not yet heard or known about the gas chambers that awaited us. We were deluded. We thought that some miraculous forces would save us. But nothing happened. No deliverer appeared. I was very miserable and I cried that I was not with my family.

The longer I was separated from my mother the more I missed her. Udel, however, said that I would get over it. We had to get nearer to where our last, and hopefully our best, benefactor lived. Then, at night, we would approach his house.

We got close to where he lived, but stayed in the woods until it was dark. Then, we carefully walked through a meadow, avoiding the main path leading to his house. We arrived at dinner time. Our Our "benefactor" did not welcome us but answered our greeting between his clenched teeth, reluctantly. We sat down on a long wooden bench against the wall. His wife was at the stove finishing the preparation of corn meal porridge. The family sat down at the table for dinner. We were not served any food. I knew, then and there, that we were trapped.

If you are in a peasant's home and he doesn't offer you food while he is eating, it means that he is contemplating hurting you. A thought passed through my mind. Maybe he thinks that we have a great deal of money on us. If he kills us he will get it all without having to hide us on his premises. I didn't tell Udel in Yiddish what I thought. Maybe these people would be offended if we talked in Yiddish, which they didn't understand. We looked at one another instead. Udel had her own thoughts. I saw fear in her eyes.

The family finished dinner and prepared for bed. We

were not offered a place to sleep. No one even talked with us. We remained seated on the bench like beggars. The man put on a short, white home-woven coat called a "voyosh" and walked out of the house. He bolted the door from the outside. We were trapped inside.

Udel and I whispered to one another about what we ought to do. But there was no way for us to escape through the bolted door, and there was only a small window in the kitchen where we sat. His wife went to bed in the next room. We sat there for a long time. Finally, we decided that perhaps everything was not lost. Maybe he had to conduct some business and did not want to bother his wife to open the door for him when he returned. That could conceivably be the reason he locked the door from the outside. We were very weary so we stretched out on the bench and tried to sleep.

Early in the morning we heard voices outside. The door was opened and our host entered, along with two other men who were armed with thick, long clubs. We no longer had any doubts about what he had been up to. He had gone to get reinforcements. He wanted to share the big reward from the authorities with his friends.

If we had previously thought about escaping the situation had now deteriorated. There were three armed men with clubs against two girls. Our chances of escape had become quite hopeless.

We were ordered to leave the house. It did not take us long since we hadn't undressed the night before. We took our few belongings, which we had never unpacked, put on our coats and walked out. One of the men stepped in front of us while the two others formed a rear guard. We were warned not to try anything foolish.

We marched through meadows, farm land and forests for a very long time. We crossed streams, valleys and ascended mountains until we arrived on the main road near a village named Bistra. It was located about six or seven kilometers from Berezov. As we entered the village many houses, Jewish ones, seemed deserted. There were no Jewish children playing outside or Jewish women standing by the doors talking with each other. The whole town was "Judenrein". As we came to the center of town, wonder of wonders, there appeared a single Jewish woman who came out of her house to look at us. I knew who she was; a member of the most prominent family of Bistra. One of her daughters was romantically involved with the magistrate of both towns, Berezov and Bistra. This daughter used her influence on the magistrate to allow her mother to stay home for the time being.

We proceeded to the police station. As we reached it, a policeman came out. He immediately realized what was happening and told the three men with the large clubs, to wait outside. He led us in and brought us before the officer in charge who cross-examined us. When he learned who we were, he wanted to know where my parents had hidden their money. "What money?" I asked. "We don't have any." He had seen our house, he said, and was sure there must be money in there. "I don't know about any money," I answered. He mentioned photographs he had seen in our house.

In the meantime, a policeman was sent to dismiss the three club bearing "heroes". Our captors did not receive the reward they had counted on; the money that was promised to anyone who exposed fugitive Jews. These three men learned that the Germans and their collaborators delivered on threats but never paid rewards. The promised money was only a ruse to entice the Ruthenians to cooperate. We watched them leave after they threw their clubs away. They walked with bowed heads, not as proud as when they brought us in, the Jews who tried to escape from "justice."

We were told by the gendarmes that later in the day they would take care of us. In the meantime we were confined in a room. At noon they offered us a lunch of noodles sprinkled with sugar and walnuts. We politely refused. They said that we could eat our own food if we didn't want theirs. I couldn't eat anything, I was too upset.

One of the officers, a young fellow, asked me to accompany him to the garden. He wanted to show me something. I followed him. The garden which was in front of the police station featured beds of freshly planted vegetables. Just outside of the garden was a shack, probably containing tools. He suggested that I accompany him inside this shed. He wanted to have sex with me. When I refused, he was surprised, and said that I had nothing to lose. Where I was going, it wouldn't make any difference one way or the other. I still shook my head in refusal. When I returned to my friend Udel, she immediately asked me whether I had been propositioned. It was that obvious. I was lucky that he only made a suggestion and did not attempt to rape me. I had no rights as a citizen. I was a nonentity.

Later in the day we were taken to Berezov. This town had also become "Judenrein". Berezov never looked so forlornly deserted. People still lived there as they did previously, but only in the Ruthenian houses. The Jewish ones' looked like tombs. They were abandoned. Their former, rightful occupants had been forced out and sent away.

Although it was daytime, few Ruthenians were in the street. They remained safe in their homes. If any of my previous friends saw me through the windows, they ignored me. No one would to say hello to me.

I entered the house of Marika, our close neighbor. She told me that when they were rounding up the Jews for the ghetto, my mother had been ill; no wonder. She was forced out of the house she had lived in for more than forty years, where she came to as a bride from her hometown, Sinover, to join her husband.

During all of this time I was escorted by an armed gendarme wearing flying cock feathers. As I approached my house, self the guard stationed himself downstairs while I went up to the attic to take foodstuffs. There were many things in the attic. The dry beans, for example, were in their shells, just as we had brought them in from the fields. We peeled as many as we needed. We left the rest in their shells. Corn for tokan and corn bread was still on the cob, and I did not have the time to remove the kernels and go to a mill for grinding them into flour. So I asked our Ruthenian good neighbor, Antza, who had come to the fence to see me, to let me some dry beans. She gave me two "itzes" worth. (An itze was a wooden container, used by the peasants in our region for measuring dry food items.) I gathered up some more items, not very much, and stuffed everything into a sack. The officer told me to hire somebody to carry the load for me. I told him that I could manage it

77

myself.

He took me to the Kuzi which was across the Rika river at the main road. I saw a few other Jews there who, like me, had been attempting to survive by hiding with Ruthenians. They had either been informed on or had left their refuge of their ov n free will, because they decided to join their families for better or for worse.

I saw Itzik Leib, whom we had seen going into hiding that Friday. He said that he felt very guilty for having left his wife, his three children and his old mother to fend for themselves in this time of life-threatening danger. No, he had not been betrayed like Udel and me. He had a good hiding place. But his conscience really bothered him.

I also saw Mendel Kahan, with whom I had gone to school and with whom I competed in mathematics. He always said that girls didn't know math, only other subjects. I wanted to prove him wrong so I studied it very intently. I asked Mendel why he came out of hiding, whether he was betrayed like Udel and I. He answered that he had not been turned in, but had come back because he was the oldest child in the family and just couldn't abandon his parents and younger siblings. He was sure that they needed him, and he was going to join his family come what may.

There were a few others with whom I spoke with who had also been betrayed to the police. There was a group of ten young people, eight men and two women, who had been hidden by a Ruthenian friend. After they stayed in his house for only a short while, he demanded more money and they gave it to him. They knew only too well that he would continue to ask for more. He would never have enough. When they refused his third request, he brought reinforcements, three men with axes. They forced them to march to the police station. Only two men of all the ten, survived. I knew them all. One of them was Sarah Herskovits, another girl Tokach had tried to sexually abuse, and Rivka, the daughter of Zise Nojovits whose entire possessions were confiscated by the authorities. Ruthenians wanted to show how well they obeyed the law by turning in hiding Jews. They were actually more interested in the monetary rewards that were promised than by any belief that they were doing the right thing.

That night, we were placed in a Ruthenian school building that was guarded by gendarmes both inside and out. I had previously attended classes for a entire year in this structure. Now I was locked up in it. We all sat on the floor. I walked over to the window and looked out into the night. I saw lights flickering across the Rika river. How I envied the people behind those windows. Maybe, at that time they were all eating dinner, talking, or getting ready for bed. Whatever they were doing, their families were together. Their minds were not preoccupied as ours were, with fears of what awaited us.

Everyone regarded us as if we were corpses or imminent ones. A guard came over to the window where I was standing. He asked me what I was looking at. I pointed to the blinking lights on the dark mountain. He asked whether I would like to go outside. Was he hinting that he would let me go? I would have tried to find out, but I had no place to go, in mind. The world was so big yet there was not one safe haven for me. It seemed that the entire universe was full of Germans and their collaborators. There was no room for me and the Germans in the same world. They didn't want me and my kind around. Unfortunately, they had the power to execute their will. There was however, one place for me, in the Izo ghetto where I still had a family. The gendarmes took us there on the following day.

That night we "slept" in our clothes on the floor among our bundles of provisions. Before I briefly dozed off, I spent some time talking with Mendel Kahan. In the morning we were allowed to leave the school and go outside. We were constantly escorted by guards and were not allowed to go to our homes again as we did on the previous day. I really wanted to go back home and take more food since I had heard that they needed it in the ghetto. Everybody I talked with told me that there was a severe shortage of food there. Some of the fugitives had already received messages from their families to bring a lot of food with them when they returned.

We went to the only grocery on the Kuzi, which previously had belonged to a Jew named Adler, and now was owned by a Gentile Ruthenian called Baleban. Fresh bread had been delivered from the bakery in Horinch. We bought almost the whole supply. I stuffed a sack, which somebody had given me, with loaves of rye bread. Later in the morning we loaded the bundles of food on a truck. We were ordered to climb on top of the cargo. Two armed guards joined us during the trip. Another one sat inside the truck as we rode the fifteen kilometers to the Izo ghetto.

When we arrived at Izo we could not mistake the location of the ghetto. We saw it from the main road. The residents also noticed us and the word was that some stragglers who wanted to escape the fate of the rest of the Jews, were arriving on the truck. Many people came to the ghetto gate. Everybody who had left someone in Berezov, presumably in hiding, came to the gate where the truck had stopped. The gate was nothing but a wooden barrier that had to be raised by hand. It resembled the barriers that were used to block roads. It wasn't heavily guarded either, just a single gendarme. Those inside were not allowed to come out to greet or embrace us.

My mother had heard that I was on the truck. She had come to the gate with my brother Chaim Hersh, but I could not cross the barrier yet. The people inside were not permitted to do so to help with the unloading. Since we were still waiting outside, we unloaded the sacks of food. We were then ordered to pass the sacks across the barrier. After the sacks were handed over, we officially crossed into the ghetto. Although I missed my mother very much, we did not embrace. We did not want to publicly display affection in public. However, my mother did tell me how much she missed me and worried about my welfare.

Chaim Hersh took one of our sacks, and I carried the other one on my shoulders. I did not want my mother to be burdened with the heavy one alone, as she wanted. I tried to spare her the difficult task. But my mother's feelings were hurt because I wouldn't let her carry the bundle. She felt left out.

I was led to a peasant's hut which would now be home. We dumped our sacks in a corner. My mother looked at me and said that I didn't look well, that I had lost a lot of weight. No wonder. I had eaten very little, almost nothing, and had slept even less, but had done a lot of walking in the woods. I had lived in fear, with

81

mental anguish and pain trying to endure the separation from my family and friends while being subjected to the terrible ordeal of being a fugitive.

Mother unpacked the rucksack which I carried with me during my travels through the woods. She found the round loaf of bread which she had placed in the rucksack before I left. There was only one small slice missing. She asked why I hadn't eaten any more of the loaf. I had no answer for her. I told her that the police in Bistra had offered me lunch but I had refused. She wasn't very pleased with my conduct, and said that I should have eaten their lunch.

Mother also wanted to know whether I had received the note she sent to me with one of her Ruthenian friends, the same person in whose manger Udel and I had slept, in the company of the cows and oxen. This man had promised my mother that he would definitely find me and deliver the note. Well, he hadn't. I asked my mother what was in the memo, and she told me that she wrote that we should come to the ghetto and bring lots of food. If I had received it, I would have brought much more and better food, especially since she mentioned what I should take from the attic.

Mother was not pleased that I borrowed the dry beans instead of taking our own. I could easily have threshed them with my feet or with a stick. She also asked why I hadn't taken the dried fruits and walnuts which were stored in the attic. I didn't tell her that I hadn't spent much time there because the guard who accompanied me had, after a while, followed me upstairs, and I was worried that he might have wanted to get romantic. I felt very uncomfortable with a young gendarme alone in the attic of an abandoned house. But perhaps I could have managed better, even with the man in the attic, and brought more of the food my family had needed so desperately.

Nevertheless, my parents were the envy of all the occupants of the hut because they saw me as a good daughter who had stayed behind and came back with food at the right time. I promised myself that I would return to Berezov, somehow, and get the rest of the food for my family. But I never got the opportunity to go. The Germans were in a great hurry to liquidate us so they didn't let us spend much time in the ghetto. Their time was running out and so was ours. As for me, the newest member of the Izo ghetto, I felt far better there than I had hiding in the Ruthenian barns or wandering through the woods.

My new home was a very rundown one-and-a-half room hut which was stripped of all its furniture. The half room was actually a dark windowless foyer. There were no kitchen or cooking facilities, and it didn't even have an outhouse. The floor was nothing more than tamped soil. This hovel was inadequate for one family. Now ten families were occupying it. We were all from Berezov. I knew everyone.

As I deposited the sack of bread and beans inside the hut, many envied my mother who had a daughter who brought food, especially Chana, who was middle-aged with a husband who was an old man. Chana had married him because she was poor and had no dowry. She had not borne any children because of her husband's age. Chana suggested that I could have picked up a large container of oil at her house. She had left it right at the door. She didn't think that she would be needing it, but she did. If I had at least brought the oil, all of us could have used it.

83

I was now introduced to the ghetto, which consisted of two side streets of the small town. People were set up according to which village they came from. All of us who were from Berezov lived in a few of these huts along with several adjoining small houses and a tent or two. The Nojovits family were housed in a tent.

I found the ghetto a better place than the Ruthenian barns, in spite of the overcrowding. Thank God the weather was clement most of the time. We tried to do as much as possible in the yard. At least there was air outside. In the hut, particularly when all of the "new" inhabitants were crouched on the floor at night, it was stifling. The two small hole-like windows didn't allow in much air to enter.

Now I was visiting relatives who, under normal conditions, I rarely saw. For example, I never called on my cousin Sima who lived in Maydan. I saw her only when she came to visit us. Now when I wished to see her I just walked down the street to where her townspeople lived. My aunt from Horinch was housed across from us on the next street. All I had to do to get there was to cross a field.

The hut was terribly overcrowded. During the day everyone was in the yard. The cooking was also done outside, and each family cooked for its own members. Those who hadn't brought cooking utensils, used stones or bricks they found outside, and prepared their food on those. The poor and not so poor lived together.

In the past what was happening to the others was known to all, but no one could witness the events at first hand. We all observed each other's routines. Now, for the first time, no one could pretend. Every-

84

thing was in the open for all to see. Even the use of the makeshift toilet was not easy to hide from other people. This latrine was nothing more than a hole dug among a few trees to supposedly hide those using it. But it was visible to everyone, never-the-less. We had to wait in line to use it.

Washing was the worst part of ghetto life. When one went to the toilet, the others looked away, pretending that they didn't see. Washing was more difficult. One couldn't chase everybody out of the hut in order to wash, even if a person owned a bowl to fill with water which in fact, nobody had. Cleanliness wasn't as urgent as using the lavatory, so it was neglected. We didn't lack water, only privacy. We drew water from the wells which were in the ghetto's jurisdiction.

Mothers suckled their infants in public. Other "private activities" were also exposed. Parents would scold their children, and husbands and wives would argue publicly. The old and the young were crowded into one small room. Every night when we went to bed, every family spread out blankets on the dirt floor, and each person tried to squeeze in and lie down somehow.

Even at night we witnessed the most private interactions between man and woman. It occurred with my father when he tried to engage in sex with my mother. She was embarrassed, being in a crowd, and reproached him with a single word, "Srul," (my father's Jewish name) which implied "What are you doing?"

He didn't heed her protest, and performed the sexual act in full view of those present: the young, the old and everyone else. These people pretended that they

85

were not aware of what was taking place in their midst.

The following night all the young girls moved out of the hut. Without saying a word to explain why we were leaving, we went to sleep in the yard, where a partially built barn was standing. There was still some straw left behind in the barn. We lay down on it without blankets or sheets. The place was much roomier. There was more air in there than in the one room hut, where all those bodies were lying one next to the other.

After a few nights, however, we were awakened by a strong light that was focused straight into our eyes. When we finally could see, we realized that two gendarmes were there. They had been patrolling the ghetto. We were ordered back into the hut and were told that it was forbidden to sleep outside. It was convenient for us to sleep outside, but not for them. They preferred our being cramped like canned sardines, where we were forced to witness people's weaknesses in the face of imminent doom. We were given no choice, and forced to sleep inside. But after a few nights we moved out again. This time we found a place where they could not see us. My mother came along. We spread our blankets and sheets and slept there, except when it rained. One night while we were sleeping it suddenly started to teem. We had to run back into the hut in the middle of the night and tried to squeeze in somehow among the sleeping bodies on the floor.

Jewish police were organized in the ghetto. Their function was very limited. Mostly they made sure that children didn't disrupt the order. They would also run errands for the Hungarian gendarmes, summoning a young woman with whom the gendarmes wanted to have sex. On occasion, they would also call a doctor for a person who was stricken.

There also a group called "Judenrat" which meant a Jewish council. It was a comprised of three or four Jews. The chief of it was a man from Maydan. He was the one who implemented the German orders in the ghetto. He would decide who should be on the first transport to Auschwitz and who would stay for another three days.

Food supplies were running low. My cousin Sarah, who lived with her parents in the same hut with us, outsmarted the Hungarian police when her family ran out of food. She told them that she would show them where her parents had buried the family's money. My uncle Berl, her father, was thought to be a rich man. He was actually rich only by poor Berezov's standards. He lived in a dilapidated three-room house, which was really only two rooms. The center room was just a windowless hall. He might very well have had some money because he had another daughter to marry off. He was taken to Berezov to show the authorities where he hid his cache. He showed them an empty hole in the ground. As a result, they beat him.

Now the gendarmes, with the black cock feathers that decorated their helmets, were eager to obtain Jewish money. They gave my cousin, Sarah, a free ride to Berezov, since they were sure that she would lead them to the spot where the money was buried. She returned to the ghetto later that day loaded with food. She told us that their yard and garden were full of freshly dug holes and heaps of fresh soil near them. The Ruthenians wasted no time. They searched for gold and money left behind by the deported Jews, even though we were still only a mere fifteen kilometers away.

My uncle Berl actually got his money and jewelry delivered to him in the ghetto. His partner's son, Yankel Markovits, who had been a ghetto policeman, walked to Berezov during the night and brought his own family's money as well as uncle Berel's. Yankel was told where he could find it. It was not buried as the Hungarians and Ruthenians thought. My uncle placed it under a rock in the yard, and that's where Yankel found it. He brought back money and jewelry for another family as well. My uncle most probably took the money and jewelry to Auschwitz. He couldn't possibly have used it all in the ghetto. The time was too short for that.

The ghetto's two streets and a pathway or two with a number of small dwellings contained all the Jews from the vicinity: all the towns and villages along the Polish border, including Izo. The shul at Izo, however didn't fall under the jurisdiction of the ghetto because it was on the main road. So, pious Jews prayed three times a day for their deliverance from the Germans in a make-shift shul. Each village or town prayed separately. There was only one Torah scroll in the ghetto that some one had brought along. The rest of the Torahs were left behind like useless objects in the abandoned synagogues in every town and village. So most Jews had to pray for the first time without a Torah. All the prayers and tears that were shed since the German invasion had not helped us. We were still dragged from our homes and forced to leave our meager possessions with our "good" neighbors.

The ghetto, however, was not as bad as it could have been. Had we been incarcerated during the winter, it would have been much worse. The winters in our region were terrible. No one was forced to work. At this time we still had a little food and hope. Yes, we still hoped that God would help us. I was thinking: We are only fifteen kilometers from our home and there are no limits to the wonders that God can perform for his faithful followers. Even in this cramped space we have something for which to be thankful. It is spring. We don't have to stay indoors. We are in the yard all of the time.

In spite of the good weather our horizon was dimmed by the events in the ghetto. A woman from Horinch, a mother of two young children, died. There were no medical facilities or medicines in the ghetto. There were other deaths too. A man from Berezov died. But we took it all in stride. The only doctor in the ghetto committed suicide. His practice was extremely limited in the ghetto. He could do very little for those who fell ill, although he was occasionally called upon to help. The authorities didn't provide him with medicine. He hanged himself from a tree. We were all saddened by this tragic incident. Taking one's life is forbidden by Jewish law. Perhaps he knew something that we refused to admit to ourselves. As for him, he did not want to face the present situation or experience what he feared, lay ahead. He found a simple way out of the misery called Izo Ghetto.

German officers occasionally came to the ghetto. They took with them a man who was from Volove. He was taken to Chust for interrogation about his alleged money. He never returned to the ghetto. The story was that he had been taken to the Jewish cemetery in Chust and shot there.

There were rumors that the young people would be

taken to work in the forests to plant trees there, to replace those the Hungarians had cut down since they invaded our region. They were busy day and night denuding the woods, shipping the cut trees to the "Motherland." They ravaged the huge forests like swarms of hungry locusts.

Jews were not allowed to leave the ghetto, and Gentiles were not permitted to enter, with the exception of a few German officers. I saw them twice during that period and there were the Hungarian guards, of course. The Hungarians were running the show, although the orders probably came from the Nazis. Only one person was allowed to leave the ghetto daily, but only if accompanied by a guard. She was Ruchel, the dressmaker. In the past, her customers came to her and she would make them clothes. Now she called on her previous customers, mostly the intelligentsia. Her fee was food for her family. Her customers were now only Gentiles, since they alone would think of new clothes. Her Jewish customers didn't consider such an extravagance. They even left behind what clothing they had.

We had no way of learning what was happening in other places. Communication with the outside world had ceased. No mail came in or out of the ghetto. Actually, no one even had an address any longer. We weren't enclosed by a high wall that couldn't be breached. We were only encircled by a single strand of barbed wire that even a child could get over.

We were, however, surrounded by an invisible high wall that kept us within our boundaries. We were segregated from the rest of the world like criminals, and were not permitted to mingle with "decent" people. Our ghetto was narrow and long. I could see beyond the two streets to the main road where people, wagons and trucks passed. I wondered: Why can't I walk there, too, as I did in the past. What terrible crime have I committed to be driven out of my home, out of society and interned in a prison?

The only difference between a prison and the ghetto was that entire families were left together in the ghetto. We had no other privileges. At night it was much worse than any prison. We had to find our place on the bare floor in the dark, because there were no lights in the ghetto or in the hut where we lived. No one brought along a lamp much less kerosene to light it. We weren't given any food by the authorities who had incarcerated us. Those who brought food, ate, and those who didn't were starving. We were even supposed to bring our own firewood. Since we didn't have enough, we took wood from the fences or anywhere we could find it.

The ghetto was situated in the most run-down section of Izo. The peasants who lived there were told to vacate their homes and to take everything with them. I'm sure they were promised that they would be able to return to their homes soon, after the Jews had departed forever.

As a result of rumors that we would be taken to work in the woods, we started to sew work pants. We were worried that there would be a lot of bending and that our limbs might be exposed, triggering amorous thoughts among the non-Jewish guards. Pants were not usually worn by women in our region. However, because of this probable danger, it was permitted.

When I sewed a pair of pants from a piece of white home-woven cloth that I had found, my mother became angry. She didn't share my hope that she might save herself by working. Some married women let their hair grow longer on their otherwise shorn heads. They thought they might look younger with their hair showing on their heads instead of wearing a kerchief, which was the usual custom. They believed that this might help them escape some future, unknown selection. Mrs. Nojovits, the wife of Zise Nojovits was one of these women. She lived with her family in a tent near us. One day when I was visiting, she showed me that she was letting her hair grow to look younger. My father, too, had started trimming his beard ever since the Germans invaded Hungary. I saw him cutting his beard a number of times. Maybe he hoped that a shorter beard would make him look less Jewish and thus make him less vulnerable.

There were rumors that we would soon have to leave the ghetto. But where would they take us? Why did they have to change our workplace? There was plenty to do in the forests in our region that could be of some help to their war effort. We heard a rumor that came from the Chust ghetto that some rich Jews had hired Gentiles to follow a transport of evacuees. They returned and reported that they were able to follow the train as far as Katowice, a town in Poland. There, the transport disappeared. They didn't know what happened to it after it reached Katowice. There was a great deal of apprehension. The word "Poland" had a dreadful meaning to us all. We were all willing to remain in the ghetto instead of any other place. Although the ghetto was not very convenient, we still would gladly have stayed there and waited until the war ended. We suddenly developed a fondness for the ghetto.

The young men were all gone by now. They were

conscripted into work battalions and assigned to dig ditches for the Germans, clear mine fields or serve as "cannon fodder" on the Russian front. Even Avi, my beau, was not in the ghetto. He was on a trip to Budapest when the Germans invaded and he never came back. All the Jews traveling on the trains were removed and arrested. They were taken away. No one knew where. Two young men selected for the work battalions and stationed not far away, arrived on a visit to their families in the ghetto. One of them was David, the son of Esther Mirl Wolvovitz, the widow. The mothers and sisters were delighted to see their sons and brothers, perhaps for the last time.

We were ordered to surrender any money we still had. But hardly anyone admitted to having anything left. Money was useful even in the ghetto. The peasants brought their milk, eggs, chickens and other products to the gate of the ghetto and sold them to the Jews. They had always sold their surplus products to them.

The ghetto gave us a claustrophobic feeling, even though we were not surrounded by an unsurmountable wall. The ghetto border was only symbolic. We could easily escape if we had a destination, a place where we could hide. The Ruthenians had suddenly become law-abiding citizens. Not one of them would even admit that he hid, and thereby saved, a single Jew. They were eager to get rid of them and appropriate their possessions. Not one Ruthenian was willing to risk his life for a Jew, even when a great deal of money was offered.

Our days in the ghetto were numbered. We had to pack our belongings again and get ready. When the order came several days later, a few hundred people from the other street were told to start marching to an

93

unknown destination. I watched them go. There was a long line of women carrying bundles on their shoulders. Their hands held still more items. One hand would sometimes clutch a baby or a child. Older men, older women and even young children carried bundles of all colors. They simply took a sheet, blanket, or a bed spread and stuffed it with the remains of their belongings, then tied all four corners together. It was not fancy. Then they started to walk; an endless line of stricken, ashen-faced people bent under the heavy weight of their bundles. I was quite upset when I saw this procession of doomed people. "There is no God," I cried out, my tears choking me. "How can He let this happen?" I wept hysterically. My uncle Berel, my mother's younger brother, slapped my face lovingly. He, too, was a pious man like my father. He said, "You are not allowed to say that."

His faith in God was not yet shaken, while mine was wearing thin. I cried bitterly. I couldn't control my emotions or my panic. What was happening in front of my eyes moved me deeply. The sight of a seemingly endless line of people walking to their doom was heartbreaking. Babies cried. They wanted to be picked up by their mothers who were carrying bundles. It was a very sad and depressing procession.

I was never so upset in all of my life. I had not witnessed the earlier departure from Berezov, because I had been in hiding, although it was probably similar to this. Now I watched as these same people were once again being marched out of the ghetto and into a burned-out church, whose entire roof was missing. Among the evacuees were women with children and infants as well as old people and pregnant women. They were herded into that church to spend the night.

94

The sky suddenly clouded up and a heavy rain poured down on them mercilessly. A strong wind started to blow. Were these God's wonders for which we had been praying?

The storm raged though the entire night accompanied by lightning and thunder which shook the hut. We, who were spared temporarily, were scheduled to leave on the next transport in three days. We lay on the earthen floor. No one could sleep. We thought of the people caught in the storm and of what was in store for us. It was a very dark night. Thick clouds blanketed the sky. There was no moon and no stars. They too were probably in hiding, ashamed to look down on us and witness this terrible misery. Did God expect us to be grateful that we were indoors while others shivered in the rain in the tightly packed, roofless church? Those who did not manage to squeeze into the church were forced to stand outside in the yard, in the midst of the storm, under close surveillance.

At daylight, we received our orders to be ready to leave immediately. There was room for us on the first transport, after all. About half of the ghetto was being evacuated. We, too, tied our bundles. We really didn't know what to take along. We would have to walk about seven or eight kilometers. What could we take with us? We were told to take enough food for three days. We took as much as we could carry, lined up and marched out of the ghetto. We were not sorry to leave the place, but we would much rather have stayed there, near our homes, on familiar ground, than go to an unknown destination.

We carried our bundles on our backs and we marched. We were together, my mother, father,

95

Chaim Hersh and I; all in one row. We walked to the gate of the ghetto. The barrier was lifted and we walked out. We reached the main road. People were ahead of us and behind us. From where I was marching I couldn't see the beginning or the end of the column. An endless column of miserable, forsaken human beings. We carried the remnants of our belongings on our backs. I had a large bundle on my back and in my hands I carried additional things, as did Chaim Hersh.

Young women either carried bundles on their backs and dragged along toddlers by hand or clutched infants in their arms. My sister Rivka with her two-year-old son was nearby. She had to carry him too. He could walk only for short periods to give her some relief. Old people also shuffled along. We headed in the direction of Chust. In the past, Chust was our district city. All our shopping for clothing and other necessities was done in that town. When had I last shopped in Chust? It seemed like a century ago.

Now we were going to Chust again, but for a very different reason. We would not be there on a buying spree. We left behind even those meager belongings we had in the ghetto. We could only manage to carry just a few of our things. The town of Berezov provided wagons for the doomed Jews when they were ordered into the ghetto. Now there were none available. We walked in a seemingly endless procession past familiar sights.

The Gentiles came out from their houses and lined the sidewalks, or they looked through open windows and doors. They stared at us in amazement and disbelief, as if asking, "Are we really getting rid of the Jews once and for all?" Those few people who worked along the road or happened to pass by, stopped whatever they were doing to look at us, at the peculiar procession. Not one of them exhibited any sympathy or compassion. I looked back at them with envy. What had they done to deserve the right to remain in their homes, safe and content, while we were being dragged away from our homes, when our very lives were hanging by a thread? We were in the hands of the Germans who made no secret of the fact that they hated us and wanted to destroy us for no other reason than that we were Jews. Some of the people on the march tearfully sensed that they were seeing all the old familiar sights for the last time.

Soldiers and gendarmes with black cock feathers guarded us vigilantly making escape virtually impossible. Escape? Where to? The weather improved. The sun shone from a sky of blue. All traces of last night's storm were gone. The sun, however, didn't contribute to our welfare. We became very thirsty. Children cried and asked their mothers for water. None of the spectators offered a drink to a Jewish child. My father and mother dragged themselves along in this miserable parade. They, too, carried bundles, although Chaim Hersh and I bore the heaviest ones. We were trying to protect our parents, to spare them the hardship.

We proceeded to the railroad station, but not to the one we used to board trains in the past. We passed the city through side streets. Our destination was the brick factory. They told us that much. The distance was seven or eight kilometers. This entire group was thirsty, tired and worn out from the heat and long walk with heavy loads. Besides being depressed about our fate, we were terribly tired and our throats were parched. We had very little sleep the night before, and nothing to eat or drink in the morning, no juice, coffee, tea or milk. In order to eat something in the ghetto, we had to cook it first on a fire fueled with wood from the yard outside. We had no time for cooking. The order insisted that we evacuate immediately. We ate nothing on the evening before either, we were too upset, too panic-stricken to even think of food when we saw the long line of unfortunates marching toward their destruction.

When we reached the brick factory we were not given a drink of water. Instead, we were ordered into tents that were hastily set up in order to search us thoroughly. Many times before we had been asked to surrender all our money and jewelry. "You won't be needing it where you are going," they told us. They didn't believe us when we said that we had already surrendered all of our valuables. They arranged to search us anyway.

We were ordered into a single line before a large tent, the men separate from the women. The females were to be examined by a "gynecologist." They searched us externally and internally. When our turn came we were examined by a woman "gynecologist". I wondered whether she really was a doctor. She wore rubber gloves but did not dispose of, or change them, when she was finished with a person. She inserted her finger into the inner areas of the private places. When she finished with one person, she motioned for the next one to come forward. Hygienic methods were was not worth employing the on doomed. After she examined me externally she omitted the internal probing. She must have forgotten, or she may have wanted to spare me the shameful and humiliating act and the possibility of my contracting a disease from her dirty, unsterile gloves.

When they finished with me, I remained at the other end of the tent to wait for my mother. She was being "examined" inside and out.

After the search we were allowed to leave the tent on the opposite side. Others were urged to enter for the check up. A man in civilian clothes who passed by noticed that I had walked away with my earrings dangling from my ear lobes. I was ordered back, and I was searched again completely this time by the same woman. Boxes of jewelry lay about near the gynecologist. I was ordered to surrender my earrings. I took them off and deposited them into one of the boxes among the other jewelry, including many wedding bands, earrings and watches. People did not hide their wedding bands and watches because it was rumored that people were allowed to keep one wedding band and one watch each. I had my little revenge, however. My earrings were not made of gold. They were costume jewelry. I got them as a present from the young bride who lived in our house for a few months with her husband, who worked in the woods as a slave laborer for the Hungarian motherland.

When everyone was searched and many valuables confiscated, we were "ready" for the transport. By this time we were extremely thirsty from the long walk in the hot sun as well as from standing in line waiting to be examined. While arrangements were made for searching us and for the confiscation of our property, no arrangements had been made to provide us with drinking water. We apparently were not worth even a little sip of water to them.

After the searches were completed we were ordered to proceed to the railroad tracks where a long, ominous cattle train was waiting for us. What would it be? No one knew where we were going, but everyone was terribly frightened.

There were many armed police, including German officers, at the station. They all barked orders, "Hurry, hurry into the wagons." We went forward. They counted eighty people and then ordered the group into a cattle car. They wanted us to board the train quietly, without hesitation and without any disturbance, just to fill up the box cars as quickly as possible. They were obviously in a great hurry to get rid of us. Every one obeyed as if dumbfounded by the events of the last few weeks. What could we say or do? It was too late now. We were thirsty and tired, and yet they still herded us into the cars. People from the platform kept disappearing into the box cars. My parents, Chaim Hersh and I boarded the train along with all the rest. We stayed close together to avoid separation.

We were now inside the train. The car was dark and dingy. Each family huddled on the dirty floor. There was no air and no light. There was only one small window which did not furnish much of either. Besides, the window was criss-crossed with barbed wire which decreased the light even more. We crouched in the corner at the far left end of the car. We either sat down on our bundles or next to them. There was very little room left and more people kept coming into the wagon. They were literally on top of each other. I sat with my feet folded under, on top of a bundle. When all eighty of us were crammed in, they brought us two buckets, one empty and one containing water. Then the doors were slammed shut from the outside.

We were trapped inside a dark, cavernous box. When my eyes adjusted to the darkness, I could distinguish huddled shapes. If I hadn't already known, it would have been difficult to determine that these shapes were people. A small amount of light filtered through the rectangular, hole-like window. A little more shone through the cracks in the walls of the railroad car. The window was very high. Even an extremely tall person could not have reached it. Some of the blue sky above was visible. The sky was blue, but not for us who were packed inside like sardines.

We were worried, uncertain, and fearful. We heard the locks turn on the outside. We were caged in like wild animals.

When the anti-Jewish decrees began, I tried to compare the situation with previous historical events that affected Jews. In Spain, the Jews had an alternative. They could convert or they could leave. This time we had no choice. In any case, I know that my father would never have converted, even if his life depended on it. He was a very pious man, somewhat of a symbol to the others. I wondered how his many students would have reacted if he had converted.

I looked at my parents. They weren't young any more. My father was pale. I could read the state of shock in his big brown eyes, similar to the ones all of his seven children had inherited. My mother was also frightened.

As the train started to move we became even more aware of our terrible thirst. There was one pail of water for eighty very thirsty people. There was the empty pail, too. Everyone knew what that was for. My God, I thought. They don't expect us to take care of our human needs right here in front of every one? Do they expect me to relieve myself in front of seventy-nine people captive watchers? I would rather die than suffer such an indignity.

Our thirst was unrelieved. We had walked almost eight kilometers carrying heavy bundles. How long was this one bucket of water supposed to last? We had only questions and received no answers. I envied the small children, at least they didn't seem to know what was happening. Or did they? They, too, were uprooted from their familiar surroundings and jammed into a cattle car. Were they just as fearful as their young mothers?

All the horror stories we had heard about how the Germans mistreated the Jews, came to mind. The shocking tales told by my cousin and others about how the Germans would throw Jewish babies into the air as they practiced target shooting. About how two soldiers would grab a baby, each holding a foot, and rip the infant in half while the mother was forced to watch. There were other accounts of Germans banging a child's head against a rock, until his brains spilled and splashed all around, staining their uniforms. I heard of Germans tying pious men to young girls, then pushing them off a bridge into the water. It was said that some orthodox Jews were ordered to climb a tree and sing Jewish songs from a prayer book. After the Germans had their fun, they shot the Jews. It was also said that the waters of the river Dnester were red with the Jewish blood of those who had been thrown in after they were shot.

At the time we heard these stories people refused to listen. It was just too horrible. It was easier to walk away, to avoid listening and thinking about these atrocities. Maybe if no one listened they would vanish. Now, stuffed in the railroad car under these inhuman conditions, we couldn't walk away from the Germans. It was happening to us, too. We were under their control and they made it quite clear that they hated us, an unbridled animosity that knew no bounds.

A cup containing a little water was passed around. I had only just wet my lips before it was taken away. It was decided that the water should be saved for the children.

The train moved slowly as in a funeral, as we continued our journey to nowhere. The air in the car became foul and reeked of sweat, feces and urine. People started to use the other bucket. We all looked the other way. I wondered who was more embarrassed, the person who used the bucket or those who were forced to witness the shame and humiliation.

The train stopped a few times and each time we thought that we might be leaving. We hoped that we would get off somewhere in Hungary and go to work on a farm as rumored. We were willing to work but we hoped to do so on familiar ground. Anything was preferable to Poland and Germany. But nothing happened. We continued on our journey. Only once during the entire trip was the door opened a little. A German called for some one to go down with the foul smelling bucket that was full by then. It was actually overflowing. Another was ordered to come down with the empty bucket and then brought it back with water.

There was plenty of water along the road we traveled as well as in Chust where we boarded the train. The Germans deliberately delayed giving it to us. Did they want us to be preoccupied with our miseries so that we wouldn't dwell on what they were doing? Or was this merely part of the ever-present wicked and merciless treatment they had reserved for the Jews?

There was moaning in the car. People were sick. The foul smell of urine, excrement, sweat and vomit contributed to the terrible feeling. An overpowering stench emanated from the toilet bucket. As the train lurched, the filthy contents spilled to the floor everywhere. There was no room to move away, so we remained near the dirty bucket. Some one contributed a piece of cloth to cover the horrible bucket. No one wanted the smelly thing near him. It was decided that whoever needed it had to place it near him or her until the next person asked for it. Children were crying for water and food; neither was available. The water from the second bucket was used mostly for the children, just as before. But it was still far from enough. The grown-ups hardly had any water at all.

Some people dozed off. They were exhausted from the previous day's events, particularly from the long walk to the train with their heavy bundles. I couldn't fall asleep. I was too nervous, too afraid of what lay ahead. Whatever it was, it was going to take lots of strength, willpower and especially luck if I was going to survive. My mother kept urging me to sleep, but there was no room to stretch my feet. I sat on one of our bundles, keeping my feet folded under me all the time. I gave the better place to my parents. Finally exhaustion conquered, and I feel asleep, but only for a few moments. I awoke to the cruel reality. My mother kept telling me to sleep but I couldn't, I was afraid. It was terrible to wake up.

It became very hot in the car. People tried to fan themselves with whatever they could find. The train sometimes picked up speed. It was traveling quite rapidly now. I shuddered. Where were we rushing to? What would become of us? I had a feeling that somehow I would survive, but that my mother and father would not. They would perish. Why? Because they were old. Through the chinks in the wall I saw a fine house on a steep hill. How do the inhabitants climb up to that place? I wanted to remember this house when I returned. If, in fact, I did.

The unfortunates in the box car were silent now. All speculations about their destination had ceased. No one knew exactly where we were. One who looked through the openings in the walls said that we were close to the Hungarian border. When we arrived there, a Hungarian guard opened the door slightly and told us to surrender all the hidden money and jewelry that we still had. We were only given a few minutes to comply. After that they would make a thorough search of every one. Those found to have money or jewelry in their possession would be shot on the spot. People in our car became very frightened. They started to produce bills. Hundred pengo ones, and fifties. Bills, bills, bills! They didn't know what to do with their money.

They were afraid to give the money to the gendarmes now because that would mean that a previous order to give up their valuables, one that was announced before we boarded the cattle train, had been disobeyed. People were confused and very frightened. They were at a loss as to decide what to do. They didn't want to die because of their hoarded money.

After a while some one had an idea; throw the money out of the little window. That would be safer than handing it over to them. The bills could be folded and pushed through the barbed wire. Since the window was rather high, somebody suggested lifting a light weight youngster on a tall person's shoulders to push the money through to the outside. Another one said that it would be bad idea. The gendarmes would notice the money coming out of the box car and they would keep their promise and shoot us. Then somebody proposed a better idea. Burning the money would be safer than surrendering it or throwing it out. This plan was accepted by all. Everybody was ready to get rid of the money in this way. But matches; Who has matches? No one; another crisis. Finally my cousin Yankel produced a box of matches. He received the privilege of burning his own hundred pengo bill first. Others handed him their paper money. He lit a match and burned a bill. I watched as people turned over bills of various denominations, mostly large ones, and he reduced them to ashes.

I watched these poor souls who had put aside some money and hid it for the purpose of saving themselves from the executioner. Or perhaps they had hoped use these funds to buy food in a time of a crisis. Now they were burning their life savings in order to save themselves from death. The proud figure of the Hungarian monarch, Miklos Horty, was printed on one of the large bills. Horty, in his grace, had surrendered the Hungarian Jews to the Germans for liquidation. The little flame of the match touched the paper bill with Horty's picture on it and it started to burn. It curled and twisted and finally was consumed by the flame. All that was left of a once valuable note was a little mound of black residue. The match struck again and again, and what was left of these poor people's savings burned until there was nothing left.

Not quite. My cousin Yankel asked again if anyone

106

else had any money. There was no reply. I hesitated for a moment. I, too, had hidden some bills. I sewed it in the lining of my coat, pockets of which had little flaps with buttons. I sewed the money in one of those flaps before going into hiding. But I couldn't burn it. I still remember how difficult it had been to accumulate my very small "fortune" and the necessary things I could have bought with my hoard, like shoes and a dress. But most important, perhaps, it would serve me in good stead the bleak future that lay ahead. I didn't tell anyone that I had money, not even my mother. The burners insistently asked if anyone else had money. I kept quiet. Had my mother known that I had funds and hadn't offered those for burning, and thus endangered myself, she would have been very worried and frightened for me.

We continued our journey of despair. At the border all the Hungarian guards left the train, and the Germans took over. They assumed sole control over us. After we crossed the Hungarian border we didn't know exactly where we were; in Poland or in Germany already? Both of these countries filled us with fear. Then some people sitting by the walls of the car looked through the cracks. They saw signs of Slovakian towns and cities such as Kosice, and later on, completely unfamiliar towns.

As soon as we were locked in the train, the problem of elimination became an acute one for me. I was parched, but this situation was even worse. I knew that sooner or later I would have to relieve myself just as everybody else. How could I use the bucket in front of so many people? There was no choice. Other people had done it. Once again the bucket was full. It had been emptied only once, on the second day of our journey, when a strident German voice called to us inside ordering us to bring it down. Maybe they would ask us again to take down the foul smelling receptacle. What I feared most was starting to happen. I had an unbearable need to relieve myself. I had been holding back for quite some time, hoping we might leave the train. No longer certain of myself, I developed terrible cramps, but I still would not use the bucket. I just couldn't. In my desperation I told my mother. She urged me to use the pail. I just wouldn't. The thought of lifting my dress, pulling down my panties and sitting on the bucket in front of all those people, young and old, men and women, scared me. I suffered. My agony was acute. Once I did try to sit on the bucket, but I couldn't relieve myself. Mother saw my tortured state and tried to help me, she thought of something. She took a blanket and surrounded me with it. In this way, finally, after a long struggle, I was relieved.

We had other problems too. As time passed, we were becoming thirstier. All we could think about was water. No one ate. All we had was some stale bread that I had brought with me into the ghetto. It was three weeks old. We had all lost our appetites, preoccupied as we were, with our thirst and fear.

There was a death in our car. A woman died on the second day of our journey, outwitting the Germans. She didn't give them the satisfaction of killing her. She died on her own. Or maybe the Germans did kill her after all. The strain of ghetto life and the journey in a locked box car without air, food or water where we were tightly jammed caused her death. No one was greatly upset by this event. Perhaps she was better off than the rest of us. Now no one could make her suffer. We were, however, forced to crouch, sit or lean near the dead woman. There was no room to move away from the corpse. The dead and the living lay side by side. It was frightening. We decided to report her passing to the Germans the next time they showed up. They should remove the body. When a haughty German opened the door a bit, someone told him what happened. His answer was to leave the corpse where it was, it would soon be attended to, and the door was slammed shut again.

We were traveling for three days. There was no air in the car. Combined odors from the bucket, the corpse, and the many hungry, thirsty and woefully depressed people in the box car was oppressive. The train's whistle wailed sorrowfully and then the train came to a screaming halt. It was Saturday morning. We didn't know whether we would be let out or continue our trip.

My mother had a feeling that we had reached our "destination," wherever it might be. She told my father to bestow a blessing upon me. Apparently she still believed in the power of the ancient Jewish tradition of the father blessing his children. It is usually performed on the eve of "Yom Kippur," The Day of Atonement, and before the "chuppa" (canopy) on the wedding day of ones children. My father had not observed this custom on "Yom Kippur" or on the weddings of my two sisters and two brothers. My father was not satisfying my mother's wishes. Had he lost faith in the might of the ancient words? My mother kept urging him to bless me. I don't know why she chose me and not my brother Chaim Hersh who was in the car with the both of us. Perhaps because I was a girl and, therefore, more vulnerable than he. Mother was insistent. I never saw her so determined. She was usually submissive to her husband's wishes. Finally, my father yielded. He placed his hands upon my head and silently chanted the age-old prayer imploring the Almighty to bestow upon me the blessing to emulate the Jewish matriarchs, Sarah, Rivka, Rachel and Leah.

We were sitting in the locked car and the train was not moving. When it grew a little lighter outside, some people looked through the gaps in the walls and reported seeing very odd looking people walking about in the station, like creatures from another world. They were clad in striped pajamas, and their heads were shaved. Some one else noticed a large sign reading "Auschwitz." It did not mean anything to us. We had never heard the name Auschwitz before. We weren't even certain that we were still in Poland.

We sat in the locked car, and heard someone tampering with the lock. Suddenly the door of the car was flew open. Two men, a German and someone in a striped uniform, posted themselves at the doorway. In a gruff voice one of them shouted: "Heraus!! Alle heraus! (Out!! Everyone Out!) Schnell! Schnell!" The key word was "schnell," fast. My father grabbed a jar of the watery raspberry preserves that my mother had wanted to leave behind in the hut. At the last minute I had grabbed it and carried it in my hands all the way from the ghetto to the train in Chust. I don't know why we didn't eat it during the trip. We probably wanted to save it for when we arrived. My father took a sip from the jam. Chaim Hersh, my younger brother, also reached for the jar. I said, "I brought it." He put it down and started to cry. I had intended to use it sometime later when we might be huddled together somewhere, as we were in the ghetto. After this journey, even the ghetto looked good.

We were all horrified. SS men with guns appeared,

110

shoving and clubbing people. We started to take our bundles, when a gruff voice yelled, "Leave everything inside." People were trying to descend from the train but just couldn't do it quickly enough. They were hit over their heads and backs with truncheons as they tried to get down from the car that didn't have a ramp. Those who tried to take their belongings were ordered to leave them. Those who couldn't step down fast enough were clubbed.

My father and Chaim Hersh left the car. My father was slow getting off and was hit over the head with a truncheon. I put on my coat. My mother and I were the last to leave the car. I saw that my father was beaten because he couldn't move fast enough. I tried to prevent my mother from suffering so I stepped down first and helped her down from the train. We descended after my father and brother, but we could not find them. They were gone forever. I never saw either of them again.

They were ordered to walk to the left side of the train, where all the men were directed. We did not even have time to say goodbye to them. We were directed to walk in the opposite direction from the men.

The place swarmed with SS men and ferocious dogs. My mother took my right arm. We walked in the direction indicated. My mother clung to my arm and said, "They took your father and your brother away from me. If they take you, too, I would not want to live." I know that my mother and father knew that they were going to die. We walked. We saw high fences of barbed wire and armed guards in watch towers. Machine guns were aimed at us from every direction.

We arrived in front of an elegant, handsome officer, with highly polished boots and white gloved hands. He held a leather riding crop. As we approached him he raised his crop to separate us. My mother's pressure on my arm increased. She held on for dear life. The officer insisted on separating us. I realized that I had to go where he ordered. I knew they were sending my mother to her death. I had to comply with the officers's orders but my mother's grip on my arm grew tighter. I tried to withdraw my arm. The officer saw the wrangle and a smile appeared on his handsome face. Suddenly my mother let go of my arm. She removed her hand, and no longer held on to me. I sensed that she was saying "You want to forsake me too? Go ahead and leave me." I went to the left. My mother, to the right. I had gone only a few short steps when the thought hit me like lightning, perhaps I would never see my mother again. I turned around abruptly to look at her for the last time. I never saw my mother again.

"Mama!" I cry out, but my voice choked in my throat. At the spot where my mother stood just a minute before, only the officer remained. I detested that man. I hate myself for obeying his orders. Why did I let go of my mother? I felt terrible.

I was standing alone in a field, and I was very frightened, depressed and remorseful. I didn't know where I was. The place itself was frightening, foreboding. Suddenly I felt so lonely, and I have been lonely ever since. A deep void formed inside me which has not been filled to this day.

My mother moved off alone to her death, abandoned by God and man. She was robbed of the seven children she had reared, and was left to die a horrible death.

She tried to hold on to her last and youngest daughter who abandoned her too. Why didn't I remain with her as she wanted? Although he tried to separate us, Dr. Mengele (Later I learned that it was he) wouldn't have minded if I had chosen to go with my mother. One more Jew in the gas chamber would not have made much difference. We were all destined to die anyway. They only saved some of us temporarily in order to serve as slave laborers. I constantly live with this terrible guilt of having disengaged myself from my mother who clung to me for dear life, and whom I abandoned.

Those condemned to die were sent to the right and entered a building with the words "Bath and Disinfectant" written on the door. They were handed a "cake of soap" which in reality was a piece of stone and were ordered to strip off their clothes before they were herded into the gas chamber.

I stood motionless staring at the spot where my mother had stood just a few seconds ago, as if by staring at that spot I could bring her back. Perhaps I was waiting for some one to come from the direction of the train, or perhaps my mother would return. But of course, no one came. It was terribly frightening to be alone in this horrible place.

I started walking again. I found myself before a huge grey building. A long line of young girls, all unmarried, in their late teens and early twenties were grouped in front of a large door. Above it there was a sign that read "Bath." I noticed that there were no older women in the crowd, only young unmarried girls. I also realized that the others had been separated from their mothers just as I was. But that didn't make me feel better or less guilty.

The door opened and the column moved forward. We entered a large room that was long and narrow with a low ceiling. The place was bare and chilly. A woman's voice commanded us, "Sich auskleiden! Alles herunter. Los, los." We understood the order and started to undress. At first slowly, hesitantly, and soon faster as we were urged. Clothes began to accumulate on the chilly cement floor. The piles grew with each article we removed. We were told to hold on to our shoes. I was nude in front of others for the first time. I had never undressed in front of anyone except my mother and that was when I was quite young. There were a few young women in their mid and late twenties in the large room who were dressed in ordinary street clothes, along with armed SS men. They stood against the walls staring at us, as they aimed their machine guns in our direction.

We were ordered to hurry. The Germans were in a great hurry to destroy us. No one hesitated more than a few seconds before starting to undress. The atmosphere was tense. We felt it and something else too. This place was frightening. It reeked death. It made me shudder.

As soon as we were all undressed we were ordered to another room, even more frightening than the first one. We were a large group of nude, humiliated women as we entered into the second room. Several women who were dressed in regular clothes were there. In their hands they held tools such as shears, shavers, scissors, clippers and the like. As the first girls were ordered forward, these women started to shave their heads. We looked on in horror at the strange scene unfolding before our eyes.

After someone's head was shorn, they removed the

hair from under arms and pubic area as well. I was petrified. Then my turn came. The woman that worked on me used scissors. Some girls cried as their hair fell to the chilly cement floor. I froze. I was too stunned even to cry. The woman that worked on me was very fast. When she finished with my head, which didn't take her more than a few minutes, she ordered me to raise my arms high and cut off my underarm hair. Then she went for the pubic hair. I was humiliated to such a degree that I was sure that I would have died if I had been the only victim. I took some small comfort in the fact that others were subjected to the same degradation.

After they shaved a few girls, mounds of hair covered the cement floor. It reminded me of the shearing of sheep in the summer in the region where I had lived. They did this to relieve the sheep of the extra warmth and for the valuable wool. Why were they doing this to us? I could think of only one answer, to debase and humiliate us. To remove all semblance of humanity from us. Had we looked human they might have had difficulty, they might have cringed a bit when they destroyed human beings. But if we didn't even look human, they would feel no remorse.

Later, I learned that the reason for shearing us, was to prevent a lice epidemic. A very poor excuse to say the least. It didn't matter. The lice infested us anyway.

At first it was difficult to recognize any of the girls who were with me. Their appearance was so drastically destroyed and altered, turning them into robot-like forms. The sameness was shocking. We were directed to gather in front of yet another door. Armed SS men were still present, observing the scene. Each of us was handed a piece of very odd looking soap. It was etched with the initials, "R J F." I later learned that these letters indicated that the soap was made from human fat, that is, from Jewish fat. The letters stood for "Rein Juden Fett." I didn't pay much attention to the soap. I followed the other girls into a large shower area. Cold water came out from bare holes in the ceiling. There were no shower heads. Some girls tried to quench their thirst by scooping up a bit of water with their hands. I hurried to complete my shower.

As each of us walked out of the shower at the opposite end of the room, we were ordered to dip our shoes into a disinfectant. I did as I was told. The dust, that had accumulated on them when I walked from the ghetto to the train in Chust and from the train along a dusty walkway to this building, came off. My shoes shined. Actually, the shoes were not mine. They belonged to my mother. We bought the same shoes some time ago in Chust. When mine had worn out, I took my mother's who had saved hers. I was embarrassed to walk barefoot. I had only one pair of shoes that I had bought in Budapest. My new pair together with my mother's Sabbath shoes were hidden away by our Ruthenian neighbors. My mother wasn't happy that I appropriated her shoes; she had complained about my taking them. She walked barefoot to her death.

I next came to a woman who was working in the bath house. Her job was to distribute "new clothes" to the recent arrivals. She spotted my mother's nice, brown shoes and took them away from me. A man with a shaved head in a striped uniform crossed the room on the other end. He carried a full bucket of water. Suddenly, I was aware of how terribly thirsty I was. I ignored everything including my nudity and my shoes and ran up to him to beg for a drink of water. He tipped the bucket and let me drink. I drank a lot of the cool, fresh liquid. I couldn't get my fill, I was that thirsty. He was aware that his partner had taken my shoes. He asked her to return them. She answered that I had it too good up till now. I had lived in freedom and abundance, while she had been in Auschwitz during all that time. Now it was my turn to suffer. I, too, would soon find out how it feels to be in Auschwitz without shoes.

The young man again tried once more to persuade her to give back my shoes but she didn't yield. They spoke between themselves in fluent German. I wondered who they were. The man gave up and walked away. She threw me a panty and a brown dress and she handed me a pair of shoes that were mismatched and had high heels. I had never worn high heels. I walked out of the room. I had nothing left from my previous existence. I was truly a caricature. Although I didn't have a mirror to see myself, I could see how the others looked. I put the panty and the brown dress on my wet body. The dress was several sizes too large. It had probably belonged to a grandmother. I tried to put on my "new" shoes. I couldn't walk in them. My feet twisted to the right and to the left. I took them off. I wanted to throw them away. No one can walk in mismatched shoes. Some one advised me not to throw them away. They might have to be accounted for.

I decided to hold the shoes in my hand. Barefoot, I joined the long line of girls who had also been transformed. Every one looked awful. If we had been in a comedy show, we would have been very funny to look at. Avi's sister, my "future" sister in law, laughed when she recognized me. I felt quite bad. For one

117

thing, because I was such a "schlemiel." Every girl had retained her own shoes except me. Mine had to be taken away from me. We waited until everybody was out of the shower and furnished with "new clothes." We were ordered to line up five abreast. "Remember," we were told, "from now on you don't walk, you march in fives." That was the rule. It was probably easier to count that way. German efficiency. To emphasize his point the SS man whiplashed a few of us who had not lined up fast enough. We were ordered to march forward without making a sound. We had already become interned to camp life.

We were a mass of misshapen bodies. When they took away our clothes and cut off our hair, we lost our individuality as well. We looked awfully alike. From a group of more or less fashionable girls, we had become a mass of bodies, easier to despise and destroy. All individual differences had disappeared. We now resembled robots.

I looked around at the girls, trying to find someone who came with me. But I saw no one who was familiar. When I looked more intently I realized that these were all girls that I knew. They were just difficult to recognize. The others didn't recognize me either. My large head was bold and white. My face was tan from spending a great deal of time outdoors in the ghetto.

We were ordered to march. There were camps all along the road on which we were marching. All of them were surrounded with high double fences of barbed wire. Inmates peered out at us and we looked at them. Everywhere were armed guards in watch towers and others accompanied by hounds that exposed their fangs at us, waiting for an order to attack. The armed guards with the vicious dogs surrounded us as we walked along a road that was paved with gravel and dirt.

After marching for a while, we came to a low building with a gate nearby. An armed guard was standing by the gate. Through an open window we saw more guards inside. One of the guards who was in front of us said something to them through the open window and the gate opened. We marched in. We had been officially admitted to the "exclusive" C-Lager.

This camp, like the others we had seen on our way, was surrounded by two five-meter high electrified barbed wire fences. It was guarded by many SS with machine guns and dogs. Additional SS guards were in the watch towers. As I looked around me all I could see was a marshy landscape, a bleak and desolate piece of land. We were ordered to line up for "zahlappell," or roll call. We stood for a very long time.

It was now noon on Saturday. Our deliverance had finally come. Briskly walking, a smartly dressed German in an SS uniform appeared before us. He looked us over much as a general inspecting his troops. He started counting every row of five. The first girl in each row was tapped by the SS's leather riding crop. By the time the count was completed our row from the Izo Ghetto had been separated. We had been divided into various groups and assigned to different barracks.

When I entered the barrack which was number ten and called a "block", I saw a strange scene. It was a long structure without any windows. If there were any, they couldn't be seen; they were very high and hidden by the berths. On each side of the barrack was a row of three tiered bunks. In the center, there was a long structure that reached from one end of the barrack to the other and resembled an oven, which could be used for sitting. To the right of the entrance was a room that was occupied by the "blockalteste", the head of the barrack, who had supreme authority over us. On the left was a storage room. The top layer of the bunks almost reached the roof.

A thousand girls occupied that one block. Other barracks housed the same number of girls. All of them were packed on the berths and they all looked alike. Their heads were shaved and they wore baggy, ill-fitting dresses. The berths stretched from the entrance of the barrack to its very end on both sides. Each unit was linked to the next one. Between each two units of the berths was a narrow passage, where the girls who slept in the rear could climb in. There were twelve of us on each level, six on one side and six on the other, legs meeting in the center. Thirty-six girls were crowded on each triple berth. At night when one girl wanted to turn around, all six had to turn with her, so tightly were they packed. By the time I was brought into this barrack, there was no room for me on any of the berths.

When evening came, everybody was ordered to take her place before the light was turned off. I lay down in my brown dress, at the far end of the barrack on the bare, dirty floor without anything under me and no cover.

After we dehumanized creatures entered the crowded C-Lager we learned an important chapter of the grim reality of Auschwitz. Without being aware of it, we had survived the first selection of the feared god of Auschwitz, Dr. Mengele. He was the tall, handsome devil with the mocking smile, who held life and death over us in his gloved hands.

Earlier, while we were being marched into the showers and stripped of our clothes, hair, and dignity, our mothers, fathers and our sisters and brothers who were under the age of sixteen were being herded into the gas chamber. But first they too, suffered a dehumanizing process. They were also stripped of their clothes and their last bit of dignity in life. In order to delude them completely and keep them from learning what awaited them, they were given a piece of "soap" and were told that they were to take a shower. When the gas chamber was packed to capacity with 2,000 to 3,000 people, Zyklon B gas was dropped on them from the roof of the building through a hollow pipe. While I was washing my body with soap made from the corpses of slain Jews, my mother and father and all those who were sent to the "other" side, were suffocating.

After they all died in agony, their contorted bodies were hauled out of the gas chamber, and checked for gold teeth and other valuables. Every conceivable place was examined for hidden treasures. The hair from the dead women was shorn. After the thorough examination they were ready for the fires. They were packed like logs into the crematoriums to be converted to ashes. To get rid of the enormous amount of ashes, they were dumped into the murky waters of the ponds in and around Auschwitz and into the Sola River. Thus, for some of those who entered Auschwitz on that early Saturday morning an era ended in their brutal deaths. For those of us who survived the first of what would be many selections and who were sent to the camp, a new era was beginning. What it held in store for us didn't seem very promising or encouraging.

Only in camp did I learn what had happened to those
that were sent to the right. I walked out of the barrack and on the left side of the C-Lager I saw a huge,
red chimney rising imposingly to the sky. Thick,
black smoke billowed out from its belly. It curled and
rose higher and higher towards the horizon and formed
a large black cloud which hovered over the camp. The
heavy smoke and the awful smell of burning flesh
dominated the entire region. From now on the low
red building with its tall chimney and rising smoke
was part of our daily lives.

I passed that strange flat-roofed building many times
after that first day. To an unsuspecting person from
the outside, this structure could have resemble a cozy
home where people sat inside by the fireplace, telling
fairy tales to their children. Instead, behind its door
there was hell on earth. Nothing could compare with
it. No purgatory could match it.

Although we now knew that we no longer had
families, that we were orphans, very few of us cried.
For most of us, the rivers of tears would come later,
in my case, over a decade later, as a delayed reaction.
At that time all we were thinking of was how hungry
we were. We didn't eat much on the day the first
group was ordered to march out of the ghetto. We
were too upset. The scene was too heartbreaking to
even think of food. We didn't eat anything in the
ghetto on the following morning when we left. The
order to evacuate came suddenly and we were un-
prepared. We ate very little, if anything, during the
entire trip. We were too thirsty to eat the stale bread.
On Saturday, our first day in Auschwitz, we received
absolutely nothing the entire day, since we were

shoved into the barrack after the midday soup was distributed. I kept thinking of the stale bread in the train that I could not bring myself to eat, although my mother had kept begging me to do so. How glad I would have been to eat it now. I also thought of the bean dish that mother would have prepared for the Sabbath, had we still been in the ghetto. I didn't think of home any longer. It was already too remote, too distant. Although the ghetto wasn't exactly the Garden of Eden and Berezov wasn't exactly Paradise, in comparison to this new hell called Auschwitz, anything and everything was just great.

As I looked around, I saw camps as far as my eyes could see. Adjacent to the C-Lager, I saw a very different kind of place from the one I was in. In that camp, the people wore civilian clothes that fit, not prison garb. I saw middle aged women wearing long pants. I had never seen a woman wear them before. I also saw men and children there. They had all been allowed to stay together while we were separated from our families and segregated from other men and children. After awhile, all these people disappeared. Everyone knew where they were sent.

Not only had I not eaten for a long time, I didn't get any sleep either. During that last night in the ghetto no one could sleep. We thought of the people in the burned out church in the raging storm. No one slept much in the crowded box car either, except for a few cat naps. When I arrived in the barrack there was no room for me in the berths. I lay down on the bare, dirty floor and slept. I really did. As I woke, someone was saying: "How can she sleep so soundly on that dirty floor?" Under strange circumstances, people are able to do many things they never imagined they could. I was terribly exhausted from carrying all the bundles and from the trip in the cramped box car, so I fell into a deep sleep.

Sleeping on the filthy floor wasn't so bad. What was much worse was waking to find myself in the hell known as Auschwitz. It was Sunday morning. Now, after having refreshed myself with a few hours of sleep, I became aware of how hungry I was. I thought about what had happened since we left the ghetto. My God, was it only just four or five days ago? It seemed like ages. So many terrible events had already happened since we left the ghetto. My parents were already dead and so were my sisters Rivka and Alta. What was going to happen to us here? I looked around me and saw many familiar faces. We exchanged a few words. We asked each other about relatives and mutual friends. We avoided talking about those who were no longer alive.

A whistle sounded and the whole multitude started pushing towards the door. When I asked where everyone was rushing to, I was told to line up for roll call. Someone said I should leave the barrack quickly to avoid being hit on the head. Outside, we all lined up in fives in the alley between the two barracks. We stood for a very long time. The blockalteste kept the column in perfect order. Talking was not permitted. Finally, an SS man came along to count us. When he found the count to be correct, he left and we remained standing.

But now the blockalteste and her hand-picked assistants called "stubendiensts", brought out bread. It looked like little dark bricks. There was one loaf for every four of us. Some girls ate their ration while still in line. I saved mine. It was an awfully small portion. If I had eaten it all, it wouldn't have satisfied me anyway and I would have remained hungry. I therefore decided to keep the bread for a little while longer. We also received a small piece of margarine. I thought maybe, just maybe, it won't be that bad after all. How little I knew. Nothing, absolutely nothing, had prepared me for Auschwitz, not the miseries of the ghetto, or the hard life in Berezov. I couldn't have foreseen the miseries of Auschwitz, not even in a nightmare.

I noticed that there was a very fat woman in our block. She also arrived the day before, but on a different transport. After having been in the camp for only a day, I heard that the Germans were performing experiments on a variety of people, including fat people and twins. This woman knew why she had been sent to the camp. She traded her first ration of Auschwitz bread for a cigarette. Was she hoping to reduce her excess weight so that she could blend into the crowd unnoticed by the Germans? She said that she would have been better off had she died yesterday with the rest when she arrived. Then, of course, she didn't known what lay in store for her. She was quite afraid. She sat on the low structure that resembled an oven. As I watched her smoking the cigarette, her hands trembled. Later that Sunday afternoon they came for her. They had not forgotten her and took her away. The SS never rested, not even on Sunday. And they didn't give us any respite either.

We hadn't been assigned any work yet. After the zahlappell we were able to mingle and talk with other people in the same barrack. I met two sisters from Berezov, the daughters of Esther Mirl, the widow. The older one, Leah, was once a good friend of mine before she left for Ungwar to seek employment. She married a gentile and gave birth to a boy. Her hus-

125

band and son remained at home. Only she was sent to Auschwitz. As we talked, they didn't ask about their mother, who had been in the Izo ghetto. They knew only too well that she was already dead.

At midday, we were lined up and given a colorless mush, something the Germans called "suppe". This soup was very bad. In fact it was so awful that no matter how hungry I was, I couldn't bring myself to eat it. It was impossible to swallow. I was very hungry but I still could not eat this so-called soup. I made a resolution that the next time I was given the soup, I would force myself to swallow some of it just to get something into my empty stomach so it wouldn't throb so violently. But when noon came again, it was just impossible to eat more than a spoonful. The "soup" was cooked from grass cut in a field by a commando of girls outside the camp. The trouble was that the sand hadn't been washed off the grass. It screeched under my teeth.

We all existed on the small ration of bread we received after the morning zahlappell. If it rained, we were permitted to return to the barrack afterwards. Then we were given the bread while we were in our berths. No one was permitted to walk around when the it was distributed. In that way, no one could get a second ration in a different place. Occasionally, we were given a dab of margarine.

We were awakened at dawn when it was still dark and cold outside. We stood for hours waiting to be counted, shivering in our thin dresses. I felt as if I was naked with the wind cutting into my flesh. We learned, on that first zahlappell, the meaning of authority. We were directly supervised by a blockalteste who was a Jewess from Slovakia and who also spoke Hungarian. She and the other barrack heads had already been here for more than three years. They let us know that they would avenge themselves on us for having led the "good" life, while they had been struggling to survive against all odds. They kept reminding us that when they came to Birkenau, some three to four years ago, it was just a marshy landscape. They were forced to build the barracks in which we housed, while they had lived in shacks. At that time they froze in the cruel, cold winter and broiled in the summer heat. Of those who were forced to build the camps in Birkenau, most died from the harsh treatment and inhuman conditions. Only a hardy few survived.

They had built up a great deal of anger and frustration which they not able to take out on their oppressors for obvious reasons. Instead, they made us, the newcomers, suffer for it and that met with German approval. On one occasion, the blockalteste counted the long line of girls as she always did, before the SS arrived. She looked me straight in the eye and said, "Wie alt bist du?" (How old are you?) I answered immediately, and then, for no apparent reason, she slapped my face as hard as she could.

These people who were among the first to arrive at Auschwitz had become hardened, cruel and vengeful. They enjoyed the authority given to them by the SS and did not mingle with the new arrivals. They slept in a separate room near the entrance to the barrack.

The blockalteste was the one who woke us very early in the morning, at that hated time of day when the whistle blew outside. We heard the echo of the shrill sound reverberate all over the camp. Immediately afterwards we heard the blockalteste shouting,

"Aufstehen, alle aufstehen." (Getup, everyone get up.) We learned to rise fast, because anyone who lingered was beaten about her head. Our blockalteste told us repeatedly that we were not in a rest home. Auschwitz was a "vernichtungs lager." Here everyone had to look out for herself. The word vernichtung was not new to me. It meant annihilation or erasing.

On the third day after my arrival in Auschwitz I returned from roll call clutching my ration of bread. By this time I had been squeezed into one of the lower levels of berths on the left side. It was about the fourth one from the door. I placed my precious "possession"; my bread, near my head, to make sure that I didn't lose sight of it. I had heard that there were bread thieves in the camp. It was hard to believe that someone could be so cruel as to take away some one else's ration. This wasn't just bread. Indeed it was life itself. We had nothing else until late summer when the "soup" improved a little and at least it became edible. I lay down on the boards (the bunks had no straw or mattresses) to rest after having stood for a long time at roll call. A split second later, when I turned over, my bread was gone. I had not eaten it during the roll call as many others did, because it made me feel a little better to know that I possessed a piece of bread and that I could satisfy a bit of my great hunger, later. When I discovered that it was gone I became hysterical. I sobbed so loudly that I could be heard throughout the barrack. A few girls came over to ask why I was crying. I had many reasons to do so. On the day they gassed my mother I did not shed any tears, but now I was bitterly mourning the loss of one small piece of German bread.

Inmates were plagued by thefts, which were considered almost as serious a crime as killing. Our hunger was so acute that it drove some of us out of our minds. It forced some to steal from others in order to save our own lives.

Why had I held on to my piece of bread? Just the thought that I possessed it and could use to it satisfy some of my insatiable hunger helped me survive for another day.

Whenever a thief was caught, she was beaten severely. In extreme cases they would kill her. It may seem like a harsh sentence but by taking someone else's bread, the thief condemned the victim to starvation.

There was a great deal of another type of "stealing" that went on in all the camps. Even the Germans knew about it. It was called "klepsy-klepsy" or "organizing," which really meant breaking some of the rules of the system in order to obtain something additional. This involved stealing from the Germans and was certainly all right with the other inmates. Anyone who stole from the Germans was greatly admired and envied by the other prisoners. However, one who stole from another prisoner was abhorred and detested.

As a result of the unbearable hunger that tormented everyone, some girls resorted to a sort of stealing, something that resembled "hit and run" piracy. Girls were selected to go to the kitchen and bring the midday soup. They were often attacked by others who lay in wait for the them. They came charging at them and swiftly dipped their bowls into the soup vat. They ran away with full bowls. The soup carriers sometimes returned to the barrack with half the contents of the vats missing. Of course, the rest of us suffered the consequences.

The assembly place for zahlappell was located in an alley between two barracks. Zahlappell could be and usually was a horror. We were driven out of the barracks very early in the morning and were forced to stand still for hours in one place and forbidden to move about. We were ordered to line up in rows of five. As the hours passed, the sun began beating down on our bare skulls. Girls fainted from the heat. Whenever that happened, the others were not permitted to help her. We had to stand still, sun or no sun. The sweat ran down our faces and over our bodies. Our lips became parched from the heat. Finally the SS arrived and the counting began.

When the Germans appeared, the blockalteste shouted loudly, "Achtung, achtung!!", and we stiffened up straight as statues. Sometimes women SS came to count us. They were usually worse than the men. They beat us more often; wanting to prove worthy of their uniforms since most of them were criminals released from prison to be in charge of the Jews.

The zahlappell killed many people: Those who couldn't survive the long hours in the blazing sun, those who developed blisters and rashes on their bodies and those who fainted from exhaustion, were all dragged away and were never seen again. The counting usually did not take long, but after the SS left we were still not permitted to go back to the barracks. We were forced to wait until the whole lager had been accounted for.

Even when it rained the counting still took place, whether it poured or hailed, even when all hell broke loose. After the whole camp was accounted for we were permitted to return to the barracks. We remained wet since we had no other clothes in which to change. The rags we were wearing had to dry out on our bodies.

When the bread rations were handed out at roll call it caused a great deal of friction. Fights and arguments erupted. Four people received one small loaf of bread and were supposed to divide it among themselves. The fifth person in the row received a pre-cut ration. The noisy quarrels usually involved the four who had to divide the small loaf among themselves. Some one always would claim that one of the others had taken a larger share. The fights were so fierce that some of the girls would go to the blockalteste to ask her to intervene in behalf of the cheated. Her blows usually quieted every one down for a while.

However, as time passed the hunger became so acute that even blows on the combatants' heads would not stop the fights from erupting. The blockalteste finally decided to have her aides pre-cut the bread into individual portions for every one before it was given out. In that way it was sheer luck who received the larger ration. I can attest to the fact that the portion I usually received would look so pitifully small that I would want to cry bitterly, while a ration that someone else received always looked a little larger.

This also happened with the "soup". Toward the late summer, the "soup" finally began to improve enough to become edible. No matter where I was, either at work or in line for the "soup", the other person's bowl seemed to be fuller and the contents thicker than mine. When I stood at the end of the line I was afraid that they would run out of soup when my turn came. Sometimes this did happen and there was nothing one could do, except to starve a little more until the next day. This didn't always happen. On several occasions the blockalteste sent to the kitchen for more to give to those who had not received any. It was supplied to her, provided the kitchen still had some left. Not every blockalteste would do this. Some of them just didn't care about the others. If I happened to be in front of the line, I was sure to get soup but that wasn't always the best. Those up front frequently received watery mixture, and after I swallowed it, I would envy those at the end of the line because they were sure to get thicker mixture.

Those girls who were at the beginning of the soup line on rare occasions received a bit of extra soup provided that everybody had received the fixed ration and there was still some soup left in the vats. When I was in the front there was never any soup left. I was never lucky enough to receive more of the precious soup.

When the soup was finished, lucky girls were selected to return the empty tureens to the kitchen. That was a treat. Before they did, they dipped their hands into the vats and licked them for whatever soup was left. They wiped the containers clean and sucked up every bit of soup they could get. Those who had a spoon ladled out whatever they could. There were fights about who should return them. I never had a chance.

Birkenau-Auschwitz was a bleak and desolate place, nothing but colorless barracks and sand. The C-Lager was barren too, with its thirty drab barracks made of wooden planks which were located on each side of a wide, dusty promenade called Lagerstrasse. The barracks were identical. You couldn't tell which one was yours unless you saw its number. When we marched, twice daily, in our rows of five, to the latrine and back, clouds of dust rose from under our feet.

The toilet was at the far end of the C-Lager. It had no number, unlike all the other barracks which were numbered from one to twenty-eight. (The other un-numbered barrack was the washroom.) It was located in a barrack about the same style as the one we lived in. It consisted of three rows of wooden planks con-taining holes with a trench underneath. The Germans called it the "scheiss haus." The SS guards usually ac-companied us to the toilet, but remained outside when we entered. The blockalteste did go in with us. We were always ordered to hurry. When a girl sat down, there was always some one waiting for her to finish. Nevertheless, we were able to exchange information with other girls from different barracks. We told each other who we had seen in the camp adjacent to ours, as well as any news about the war we might have learned.

One day when the latrine was being cleaned a baby was found there. The camp authorities instructed the bar-racks supervisors to find out who had given birth to the infant. No one admitted to being the mother of this poor innocent, a baby that was born at the wrong time, in the wrong place and to the wrong mother. The woman who gave birth to the little one cheated Dr. Mengele of his evil practice; sending both mother and child to the gas chamber, as he usually did. Children under the age of 16 were not considered "ar-beitsfahig" (capable of working), and were automati-cally sent to their deaths. We used to wonder why they didn't save the young mothers. They were capable of working. Why then were they gassed? The explanation was that Dr. Mengele decided that when small children are separated from their mothers they

133

cry along with their mothers. Dr. Mengele, the feared god of Auschwitz, did not like such annoyances. He therefore sentenced the mothers and the children to die without much ado. Another specious reason for sending both to die together was Mengele's malevolent belief that it would be unethical and inhuman to send a child to the ovens without permitting the mother to witness his or her death.

The C-lager was being built. At one point I was selected to work on the square at the entrance to the camp, and there to lay a pavement. We were supplied with large iron hammers and were ordered to smash big rocks into smaller pieces and place them contiguously. This was a back-breaking job, but fortunately it didn't last long. After a few days they brought in a crew to complete the job.

In those early days in C-Lager it was extremely hot and humid. During the day there was no shelter from the heat. We were rarely permitted to lie down in our berths in the daytime. They didn't want us to mistake this place for a rest station. The block leader told us repeatedly that we should have any no misconception about Auschwitz. It was a "vernichtungs lager," an annihilation camp and only that. Work was only an adjunct byproduct.

Birkenau or Auschwitz 2 was the worst of the four divisions of Auschwitz. That was where all the gas chambers and the crematoriums were located. The other ancillary camps were Auschwitz 1; Auschwitz 3, or Buna; and Auschwitz 4. Auschwitz 1 was the first camp in the complex and it was somewhat better than Birkenau. The gas chamber at Auschwitz 1 was not used any longer and the living quarters were better. Auschwitz 3, Buna, was where they produced synthetic oil and rubber. They employed thousands of male and female prisoners on these projects. Auschwitz 4, or Manowitz, included explosive plants operated by such firms as I.G. Farben. Other "respected" German corporations also established factories there to produce war related products, such as explosives for the German war machine. They enriched themselves on slave labor while thousands of the workers died from the beatings, hard labor, disease, hunger and cold.

There was not a tree or a blade of grass in Birkenau except for the flower beds that beautified the areas surrounding the five gas chambers. These were planted to delude the doomed Jews about what awaited them in those buildings. One never saw a bird fly over the camp. The putrid odor of burning flesh and the thick smoke kept them away from Birkenau.

Soon after I arrived in the C-Lager, we received an important visitor. It was at the ritual zahlappell. Needless to say, we were ordered to stand at a most rigid attention and warned not to even blink an eye. The blockalteste told us who the great man was. Some had never heard his name before. I was one of them. The blockalteste laughed at us when some one asked her who he was. I saw him. It was Adolph Eichmann, he had come to visit us. After all, he was the one who had delivered us to our new life. He was dressed in a well tailored uniform and was accompanied by pretty young ladies and a large dog. He carried a large whip.

Everyone in C-Lager was given a red enameled tin bowl for the midday soup. As soon as we received the soup we drank it from the bowl. Spoons had not been given to us. Some, however, had "organized" a spoon or a knife. To possess these utensils was considered a treat. I never had them. I swallowed directly from the bowl. It was good. When I finished the soup and the bowl was empty, I scraped it with my forefinger to get every last bit from the bowl. Then I licked my finger for every last drop.

Because we were forced to stand for hours in the zahlappell exposed to the sun, many of the girls developed blisters from over exposure. There were others whose bellies became bloated from hunger or who suffered from rashes all over their bodies. These, along with the ones who fainted from standing too long in the humid, sticky atmosphere were all taken away and never seen or heard from again. Where? Everybody knew the answer to that question.

In Auschwitz it was not God who decided one's fate. Here He had no control over who should live and who should die. This death camp had its own god. He was dressed immaculately in an elegant uniform, highly polished black boots and white gloves. He carried a leather riding crop and exuded an air of superiority. He seemed very sure of himself. Handsome, tall and slender, he would flick his fingers to the right and to the left. Right or left, one always meant death. He was none other than the infamous Dr. Josef Mengele, known as the "Angel of Death" and the "Devil of Auschwitz". Every one of us, the victims in Birkenau-Auschwitz saw this devil incarnate in action, many times.

There were two zahlappells in C-Lager, one in the early morning and one in the afternoon. After the morning roll call when we were permitted to disperse, we would sit on the ground or walk between the two barracks. We talked with friends. The major topic of discussion in Auschwitz was food. The Hungarian women ruminated over the delicacies they had eaten at home. Perhaps our talking about food alleviated our craving for it, and helped us to cope with the harsh reality of camp life. It certainly occupied our minds and diverted us for a while from the cruelties rampant around us. Food was a favorite topic of the inmates, because everyone was starving. In real life we were deprived of everything, a home, family and nourishment. All that was left to us was a fantasy of a better future, and fond memories of the past when we lived as normal human beings.

People who have never been starved cannot possibly imagine the agony a hungry person experiences. It is difficult to fathom how painful it was to wait until the soup was finally brought to us. Everything else was blocked out from our minds. We also suffered from sleeplessness and fatigue. Lack of food would make us listless. The Germans constantly kept us hungry and thirsty so that we would concern ourselves only with our animal needs and not dwell on what they were doing to us. They invoked science and psychology to destroy us, and thus achieve their goal. We stopped caring about what was happening around us. When we heard that some one had been condemned to the gas chamber, it no longer shocked us. We got used to it. It became a normal everyday occurrence.

Prisoners talked and dreamed of food. Each one told whoever cared to listen, what sumptuous meals had been eaten in her house. One could actually describe the various menus from hearing them so often. Those who descended from wealthy families remembered the roast chicken and other delicacies; the poor ravenously recalled the boiled potatoes. There was one belief we all shared in common, and that was that we would never again condemn any food as bad. We would savor even those meals that we had previously considered unpalatable. We all wished that there would come a time when there would be such an abundance of bread that we would not be able to eat all of it. No one really believed that there could be that much anywhere. We had a very negative opinion about the soup since it was our major staple. We promised ourselves that if and when we were liberated we would never have soup again. We would eat only solids, a treat we hardly ever received here, except for the piece of bread which had been mixed with sawdust.

Since the hunger was so severe in camp, people used different methods for devouring the small ration of bread that was doled out. Some would eat the bread immediately upon receiving it. This was very practical. It satisfied the worst hunger pangs though only for a short while, and it also precluded this precious staple from being stolen, as this was a common occurrence in the camps. Others, including myself, preferred to divide the ration and save some for later. I was convinced that other people somehow bore their hunger better than I did. It seemed that those who were physically weaker endured the harsh conditions of the camp better that the strong ones. Maybe it was their inner strength which did not show.

We also suffered from an inferiority complex. This was occasioned by looking at the handsome, immaculately attired and well fed Germans who held the power of life and death over us. When we compared ourselves, the difference was staggering: our heads were shaved, we were clad in rags, and looked liked skeletons instead of human beings. Once we were "somebodies." Now we were treated like dirt.

Prisoners identified with their captors to such an extent that very often they would behave as cruelly as the Germans. Inmates were constantly witnessing, if not experiencing, beatings from their sadistic tormenters. As a result, when opportunities presented themselves many prisoners would beat others at the slightest provocation and sometimes without any reason at all. Generally, the tendency toward violent behavior increased so greatly that even those who did not engage in terrorist behavior became so used to it that it didn't bother them any longer. It had become a way of life.

We washed and slept in large groups. Even private needs such as using the lavatory were done publicly with guards always present. One's privacy was nonexistent. As a result, everyone craved some time for themselves. We promised ourselves that after liberation each one of us would retreat to some secluded place bereft of people.

The only people who ever talked and dreamed about liberation were the new arrivals. The oldtimers never mentioned the subject. Most of them derided the Hungarians for believing that they would ever be free. The veteran inmates said that no one leaves Auschwitz alive, let alone free. They behaved accordingly. Since they didn't believe in ever getting out of the camp they tried to live as best they could in it. Most of them cooperated with the Germans.

The old-timers lived quite well in the camp. They had good clothes and enough food. The clothing came from "canada", the depot where things were sorted out after the arrival of each new transport arrived. Newcomers were ordered to leave all their belongings in the train. Some of the abandoned possessions were stolen

139

by the workers in "canada". The veterans paid for those things with bread and margarine that they stole from our rations. The Germans knew about it, but they didn't object, as long as these prisoners tortured the newer ones.

It was common knowledge that the gas chamber was geared to function twenty-four hours a day. The people who were brought in were usually those who had just arrived in the transports. Whenever they did not arrive from the outside, inmates from Auschwitz were gassed instead. By this time we had become experts on how the German system in Auschwitz worked. The Germans, however, would always devise new variations to catch us off guard. During the early days in Auschwitz Those who were to go left meant death, and the right, life. By the time we arrived, the procedure had been changed. Left was life and right, death. They would also ask "volunteers" for what was supposed to be a "good job." But that failed to succeed a while: No one would volunteer for anything, because it only led to the gas chamber.

Once, they tried to round up a group of girls, supposedly for a transfer to a "good work camp," but no one would stand in line. They beat us with long whips to force us to queue up for this assignment. Everyone pushed to the rear. Blood flowed, but no one remained in the front to form a line. Each one would try to hide behind another to escape the selection and the blows. No one wanted to be included in the "good" transport because in most cases the gas chamber was the ultimate destination. The few elegantly dressed business men who came to examine and choose the "merchandise" were forced to leave without a group of slave laborers. We stopped believing the Germans. They were always lying, and were masters of deceit.

That time they abandoned the project, but not for long.

One day after zahlappell we were not told, as was usually the case, that we could disperse. Instead, we were ordered to march, in a straight line. "Ruhe." No talking. Armed guards accompanied us. When we reached the gate every one felt that this was the end, that we were surely going to the gas chamber. Some one near me expressed her fears that we were approaching death. We were apprehensive, as we marched in the direction of the gas chamber. However, there was still hope. The showers were there too, so it was still conceivable we were just going for a bath and a change of clothes. They might also be transferring to another work location. Transports left C-Lager almost daily. We were finally led into the showers, and we breathed a sigh of relief. We were saved, that is, for the time being. We undressed in front of the guards. We no longer cared that they stared. We knew the procedure. We washed quickly to remove any residue of what might be soap left on our skin when they turned off the flow of water. Each time we went to the showers we would undress in the anteroom. When we were finished we would exit at the other end, where we would receive another pair of pants and a different panty and a different dress. The clothes we wore were put through an "entlausung" (delousing process) and were later given to other girls.

Outside, we lined up in fives quickly and quietly. What now? We were ordered to march outside the barbed wire fences and we were heavily guarded. We passed several camps that were separated by powerfully electrified barbed wire fences. Armed guards were everywhere along with snarling dogs. We came to a halt at one camp where we were counted. The gate opened and we were admitted to yet another camp. It was similar to the first, except that this one was called B-Lager and it was a work camp as opposed to C-Lager. C-lager was considered a transition camp.

We were assigned to a barrack, in which the berths had straw filled mattresses in a rough sack. These would irritate our bodies. It was, however, much better to lie on the straw than on the bare boards as we did in C-Lager. This time I had an upper berth which was considered better than one on a lower level. Here one could sometimes sit up straight without having to lower one's head as was necessary on the lower levels.

On that first day in B-Lager, when I lay down, I felt something in the straw. I hoped that it would be a potato or a beet. Another girl was fortunate to find a few potatoes in the straw mattress. I reached under mine, and found a book printed in the Czech language. It had been a long time since I had read anything in Czech; it seemed almost a lifetime ago. I opened it at random somewhere near the center. It stated that one had to be grateful, no matter what. Even if one's foot is broken, it could still be worse; he could have broken both. I closed the book. I very much doubted whether there was anything for which I had to be grateful in this living hell called Auschwitz, except that I was still alive while so very many had already perished.

The previous occupants of the B-Lager were Czech Jews who were brought to Birkenau from the so called "model" ghetto, Theresienstadt. They were brought there in families and kept for a while in B-Lager. Later, they were all condemned to the gas chamber. I saw a few of them when I arrived at the C-Lager.

After zahlappell we would look for people we knew. I found my sister-in-law, Lenke, from Ungwar. She was my brother Baruch Bendit's wife. She was in a very fine commando unit, the "scheiss commando." Their job was to clean the "scheiss haus," the toilets. Five or six women would fill a tank with the filth that was pumped out from the toilets. Sometimes they would send in two or three men with hoses to help out. The tank was mounted on wheels. It looked like a horseless wagon. Women were used as human draft horses. They would push the wagon outside of the camp where they emptied the tank. Their long journey with the tank outside the camp gave them an opportunity to "organize" some food. This also allowed them to meet men and hear the news.

Lenke brought us the story of a man who had lived in Bistra, which was five or six kilometers from Berezov. He was brought to Auschwitz before his family, since he was serving in the work battalions. He was assigned to stand guard at the gas chamber entrance. (This was usually done by an SS man.) One day his wife and two children were among a group taken off the transports brought to the gas chamber. His wife was terribly frightened. She asked where they were being taken. He answered that it was just to take a bath. This was the usual German ruse which was used to deceive the Jews. They wanted them to die quietly and orderly and not cause any disturbances. They loved order. This man felt very guilty afterwards and felt as if he had killed his own wife and children. As a result, he became insane.

Lenke could also obtain additional food, such as a carrot, a beet or a potato. We would gladly eat those vegetables raw, if only we could obtain them. I would sometimes go to her barrack to talk with her. When I

143

first met her in C-Lager, she saw me in my baggy brown dress in which I looked deformed and made me feel very badly. Soon afterwards I found a piece of rope and tied it around my waist as a belt. When she saw me attired this way, she warned me not to try to look pretty in Auschwitz. The pretty girls were not fortunate, she said. They were being used to satisfy the sexual pleasures of the German officers.

On one such visit I complained that I had contracted pneumonia. My upper back and sides ached severely. She comforted me, assuring me that it was only a bad cold and gave me a red beet which was supposed to "cure" my "pneumonia". She also advised me not to trade scraps of horse meat which were sometimes said to be in the soup, for bread. She needn't have worried. I never found even a trace of meat in my soup.

Soon after I arrived in B-Lager a few other girls and I were assigned to clean and prepare the last block of the camp. It was being converted into a hospital. We were supplied with buckets, brushes and chlorine, and were accompanied by an armed guard, who also supervised our work. Of course, he didn't help. He just stood there smoking and enjoying his superior status. It was our job to scrub the place clean and disinfect it. We were not given gloves, and had to work with the chlorine on our bare hands. By the time the filthy barrack was scrubbed clean our hands were bleeding. We were lucky that it was only a one time job.

When I was taken to clean the barrack for a hospital I wondered at the German paradox. I thought sadly: Who are they going to "cure" in that hospital barrack? Countless, healthy people were being sent to the gas chamber every day.

144

In my barrack, two sisters presented a pair of beautiful slippers that they had made out of straw, to the block-alteste. They were woven by hand. The block leader proudly showed them to the rest of the girls in the barrack. She rewarded the two girls handsomely with bread and soup. It was profitable to have some skill. Even in Auschwitz, having a special talent could be fortunate. The Germans were always asking for girls who knew English or had a popular trade.

After a few days in B-Lager I was assigned to work in the "weberei," the weaving plant. We wove various materials, mostly hair and cellophane. After working there for a short time a few of us were chosen to move some necessary equipment over to our camp from one that was located a long distance away. We were ordered to carry large wooden boards and other parts. That day all hell broke loose. A storm was raging. The sky was black with dense clouds, the wind was gusty and huge pieces of hail kept falling. The gale-like wind turned and twisted, and together with over-sized hail propelled by the wind, seemed as if all the components were pantomiming the dance of death.

As we returned with the equipment, we couldn't see where we were going. Our eyes were blinded by the wind and the teeming rain. We just placed one leg in front of the other and hoped that we were advancing a step. The load on our backs was heavy, and we were bowed under by its weight. We bent our heads toward the ground to avoid the wind-driven pellets from hitting our faces. If somebody lagged behind, she was urged to proceed with the butt of an SS rifle. He swung it right and left, and brought it down on the heads of the poor girls who were forced to march in fives in this hellish weather. When we finally reached the camp we were soaking wet, cold and shivering, we had no dry clothes to change into, so we remained wet. We weren't permitted the luxury of resting either. We had to sit down at our assigned places and resume our work.

I was so preoccupied with the thought of how cold and wet I was feeling, that I had not realized that the capo, our work supervisor, had given coffee to those girls who had carried the equipment. Another girl near me told the capo that I was one of those who performed extra work. The capo then wanted to know why I hadn't come forward to ask for coffee. "Isn't this coffee good enough for you?" she yelled at me. She lashed out at me with her whip across my back a number of times for not having asked for coffee.

I didn't care too much for that black viscous liquid that the Germans called coffee. They served it to us mostly in the early morning. We never had the time to drink it because we were rushed out of the barrack to line up for the zahlappell. This ersatz coffee had no nutritional value and tasted as bitter as hell. However, had I been aware that they had been offering coffee, I would have asked for some. Any hot liquid could have warmed us a little. But this concoction wasn't even hot. It had probably been left over from the morning.

They never gave us coffee or any other liquid we really needed as when we had been baking in the hot sun for hours on zahlappell. Those who fainted were left to lie on the ground. No one was allowed to help with a little water, even if we had it. At those times we could have quenched our thirst with any liquid, even that foul coffee. Or on those cold winter days in sub-freezing weather we would have gladly swallowed any hot liquid. But then it was unavailable. I tried to find an excuse for the capo who had just hit me without provocation. Whoever had spent time in Auschwitz even for one day could not be judged by normal human standards. The capos and the blockaltestes of Auschwitz had been prisoners themselves, most likely for a long period of time. They helped the Germans to operate the camps. They were given total authority over us. Some were Jewish, some Gentiles. The higher ranking capos and lageraltestes were Germans who had been released from prison. Among these were thieves, prostitutes and murderers. Those in the lower ranks were Jewish. No matter what their nationality, they were always cruel and heartless. If they weren't, they would not have been suitable for the job, and would soon have been replaced by others more willing to execute the German policy of cruelty to the inmates. A capo who lost his post became an ordinary prisoner, suffering from hunger, thirst, cold and hard labor with very little chance for survival. A capo or blockalteste received more and better food, good clothing and they did not work hard. Capos were not cold in the winter as we were. They slept in better quarters with enough blankets. He or she learned rather quickly where their loyalty should lie.

The longer a person spent in the camps, the more cruel and indifferent to the suffering and deaths of others, he would become. We lived in an atmosphere of arrant brutality, and witnessed it daily as the Germans made us the recipients of their inhuman treatment. We in turn identified with them and often imitated them. Prisoners became cruel, especially those who served as wardens or foremen. They treated others as parsley; using the same methods employed by the SS. Sometimes they were worse since they were supposed to be doing the dirty work for the Germans.

147

But unlike the SS, they acted that way for their survival. If they failed they would have been exchanged, and other prisoners would eagerly covet their duties. No one wanted to be among the downtrodden or "out group," those who were at the bottom of the heap. It was more desirous to be in the "ruling class" group rather than to be a faceless, nameless prisoner without rights or privileges. Those wardens who didn't act like beasts lost their positions and, later, in most cases, their lives. They then were lowly prisoners, suffering from hunger, cold and fatigue from hard labor, becoming a prime candidate for the gas chamber.

The Jewish capos and blockaltestes all had terrible stories about how they were initiated into the concentration camp. They all agreed that at present the Germans had mellowed a bit and were not as unrelenting as they were in the past. Some capos, however, beat and tortured prisoners to satisfy their sadistic cravings. After a short period of camp life we too became indifferent to the beatings. Our sensitivities were numbed. We were unmoved when others were tortured or dragged away for whatever reason.

As for the German guards it was common knowledge that the Nazis selected them from among criminals and murderers. Rudolf Hess, the commandant at Auschwitz, was an ex-convict. Not only were the German guards heartless but they were, in most cases, extremely vicious. In all my experiences with them I never met even one German guard who was remotely humane. All of them were bloody killers.

Other European nationalities, as the Hungarians and the Poles, were also involved. It was not by chance or coincidence that all the major death camps were located in Poland. Hitler's Germany had a faithful collaborators and allies among the Polish people who were eager to eradicate the Jews. There were some, however, who saved a few Jews by hiding them in their attics and bunkers and who, in doing so, risked their own lives. The majority, however, agreed most heartily with Hitler's final plan for the solution for destroying the Jews.

As for the German people, in general, they were so hardened by hatred and so dedicated to implementing Hitler's resolve to annihilate the Jews, that when the allies stood at the gates of the camps they forced the Jewish inmates to evacuate to prevent them from being liberated. Even when the Germans could use the transportation facilities for their own war effort, they assigned them to transfer the inmates instead. When they could not obtain necessary transportation for the doomed Jews, they marched them to a place where they could be exterminated before the Germans were finally defeated.

Soon after we arrived in the B-Lager we were ordered to line up in single file. The queue was endless. I didn't know what was happening at the beginning of the line, but I was slowly advancing. It was a warm summers day and the sun was bright. It could have been a magical day if you weren't a Jew in Poland or in Germany. I soon learned that we were being tattooed. A rumor spread that those who were being subjected to this process were becoming the property of the German government in which case the Nazis would be proscribed from hurting us. In other words, they wouldn't be sending us to the gas chamber. Otherwise, why would they bother to tattoo us? I really couldn't understand the distinction between what the German government and the Nazis. For me every German was a Nazi and every Nazi a murderer. The tattooing was a slow process.

When the line was about half its original size, a number of airplanes appeared in the sky. The allies, our saviours, had arrived to bomb the allegedly invincible supermen. We heard the explosions and saw smoke rising not too far away. It came from the vicinity of Auschwitz. I prayed: God, send these planes by the millions. Let them completely darken the German sky, and drop bombs on every square foot of German soil. Let them hit me too, as long as they devastate the Nazis in the process.

As soon as the air raid alarm sounded, the Germans who guarded the square disappeared. They ran to the shelter. The tattooing, however, continued.

When I neared the square I noticed two young women in white coats. They had some bottles on a tray on a small table. After a while I was called by one of the two women to step forward. She then greeted me in a friendly manner, something that was very rare and unexpected in Auschwitz. "Little one, you are the last one on the line," she said to me. I was instinctively frightened by these women's doctor-like appearance. There was a well known admonition: "Beware of the doctors of Auschwitz." I was well aware of the experiments on human guinea pigs that physicians were conducting there.

She saw that I was frightened and told me not to worry; that she would make the tattoo so small that I would be able to wear a watch on my wrist, that the number would not affect the attractiveness of the watch. After I bared my left arm, she etched the number A-10981 on the inside. As she promised, the digits were very small indeed, and not too easily visible. The others had their numbers placed on the outside of their arms, with much larger numerals. Having large numbers proved to be a disadvantage on selection days; they were easily visible and could be written down quickly. Inconspicuousness was an advantage in avoiding selection for the gas chamber.

That was the one and only time during all my concentration camp experiences that any one in authority had a kind word for me.

My wearing of a watch actually did occur some 14 years later. However, at the time when she mentioned it, the eventuality of wearing a gold watch was farthest from my mind. I could never have imagined it.

We were ordered to memorize our numbers. We were told that from that time onward each of us would be identified only by that number. The same digits were also printed on a piece of white cloth, on which a yellow triangle had been added. We were all ordered to sew this piece of cloth on to the left side of our outer garments. This was done on the following day while we were standing on Zahlappell. We were instructed to turn to face our partners in line and then to sew the patches on the left side of each other's chest. While I was busy attaching hers, she in turn did the same for me. Needles and thread, like many other supplies, were not readily available; they had to be "organized". Mostly they came from "canada".

I remember another woman, an inmate, who was also nice to me in Auschwitz. One day, after having finished my midday soup, I walked around the alley between the two barracks looking for something to eat. I knew that we wouldn't receive any more food until the following day, and I was still just as hungry.

Having consumed the small portion of watery soup, my stomach started to throb as before. I don't know what I hoped to find, but I searched like a caged animal, circling the alley between the two barracks. As I passed I noticed two women sitting on the dirty ground, conversing, one of them held out her red tin bowl with a little soup in it to me. She asked me in Hungarian whether I wanted the soup. I nodded and she let me have it. I could not believe my good fortune. I hungrily swallowed the soup and thanked her, as I returned the empty bowl. The poor soul must have been a newcomer in Auschwitz. She had not yet become used to the camp's diet. The Hungarian women called this Auschwitz soup "moslek". This, in Hungarian means dishwashing liquid, which, in fact, was what the soup looked like and tasted.

As the summer progressed, the soup began to improve. It would sometimes have pieces of cabbage and scraps of potatoes in it, and it tasted delicious. The problem was that we got too little of it. It was never enough.

Our days started very early, perhaps five A.M. or even earlier. The morning was the most difficult time of the day. After sleeping and perhaps dreaming of a better place and a better time, we were awakened to the harsh and cruel reality of Auschwitz, along with thoughts of what the new day might bring. No one was certain of living to see the next day.

Fear, anxiety and beatings forced us to hurry and to get out of "bed." It was not supposed to take more then a few minutes between "aufstehen," (arising), and leaving the block. We slept in our underclothes, having removed our dresses, which we placed under our heads, lest they be stolen. There was no problem about getting dressed; we didn't have much to put on. We did have to make the "bed" and fold the blanket (whenever we had one) in a certain way. If any one was slow, leaving the block, she received a number of lashes on the back from the blockalteste, who stationed herself at the door. To prevent beatings, people pushed each other while hurrying to get out.

It was especially bad in the winter because of the severe cold. We were rushed out of the block only to stand for what seemed to be interminable periods of time lined up in the alley between the two blocks. The black and bitter German ersatz coffee was placed at the door, but we were pushed out so quickly that we seldom had time to drink it even in the event that someone wanted it.

Zahlappell was a nightmare. As we stood in our rows of fives, the blockalteste first checked the line to see if we were standing properly. Then she counted us. After that there was the endless waiting for the SS man (sometimes woman) to come and count us to make sure that no one had escaped through the electrified barbed wire fences. If the count wasn't right, we were required to continue standing until everyone had been accounted for, dead or alive. Whether it was hot as hell or freezing cold, we were forced to stand until the count was correct.

Once, when the zahlappell was not right, we stood for two whole days. We were counted and recounted repeatedly. Ferocious looking dogs and many armed SS men arrived, and tallies went on and on. We knew that something was wrong. The Germans had told the lageralteste, who was German, that unless the roll call was correct we would stand without food or drink until we all dropped dead. If it turned out that somebody was really missing from our camp we would have to pay for her escape. Anyone who survived the prolonged standing at roll call would be subjected to a punishment called decimation, in which every tenth girl in the line would be shot.

We were finally told that a girl was missing. I could hardly believe it. How could anybody escape from Birkenau with its highly charged barbed wire fences, its watch towers with powerful floodlights, and its roving patrols of guards with killer dogs that circled each of the camps? Nevertheless, one girl had not been accounted for. I thought that they were more intrigued by the fact that someone could escape through these virtually fool proof alarms, rather than caring whether one Jew escaped. They might have been afraid that she would tell the world what was happening in Auschwitz. They needn't have worried. Information was available to anyone who wanted to know what was happening in Auschwitz, but most people didn't care to find out.

Note

What was happening in Auschwitz leaked out through Nazi channels at the very beginning of the gassing. A high ranking Nazi official conveyed the information to Switzerland. From there the story was sent to the Allies. Two Jewish prisoners, Rudolf Vrba and Alfred Wetzler escaped from Birkenau-Auschwitz on April 10, 1944. A second pair, Olsa Mordowicz and Rosin fled on May 27, 1944. A Polish major was also success-

ful. Each group presented a detailed report on what was happening in Auschwitz. The above named escapees came in contact with other prisoners; the Sonder commando who worked in the gas chambers and crematoria and knew about everything that was happening in Birkenau. Their combined reports were sent to the Allies. The Vrba-Wetzler data was 33 pages, the Mordowitz-Rosin one was 7 and the Polish major's information consisted of 19 pages. They were all published on the front page of the New York Times on November 26, 1944. Vrba who was a 19 and a half year old Slovakian, had memorized the number of Jews put to death by gas in Birkenau from April, 1942 to April, 1944. The chief reason for their escapes was to alert the outside world to the dreadful reality of Auschwitz.

The SS checked and rechecked the barbed wire fences. Then they looked for tunnels underneath them. They brought blood hound dogs that were kept in Auschwitz solely for this purpose. There were a total of two hundred of them there. Nothing was disturbed. The fences were not tampered with anywhere. We silently prayed that the mystery would be resolved soon. Otherwise we would all be lost.

After two days of standing at roll call with just one very short break, the missing girl was found. She had come in on a recent transport from a ghetto in Poland, and had been traveling in an overcrowded box car for days. Her group shared the transport with a load of equipment used in a workshop. The Germans had dismantled it and were now bringing it to Auschwitz-B Lager where it would be set up again. After the equipment was unloaded, the girl had fallen asleep under one of the machines. She slept for two entire days. She woke, feeling very hungry. After she crept out from under the machine she began looking around for some food. The Germans found her as she was rummaging through the garbage. Everybody else was on line under strict observation when she was found.

The Germans brought her to the square where we were standing. The SS officers all gathered to see the creature who had given them such a scare. They took revenge, by making her kneel in front of them and kiss the gun that was going to be used to shoot her. They made her crawl from one SS on one side to another on the other side. They made her beg for her life. After she did everything they ordered and had suffered a great deal of humiliation in front of the whole camp, they led her away. The roll call was over. The mystery was solved. We were permitted to return to our blocks half dead of fatigue, hunger and thirst. We finally received some food and drink, and were relieved. No one thought of the poor girl any longer. We all knew where she had been taken.

Usually, we were led directly from the zahlappell to our work, which started at six in the morning and did not end until eight at night. We were given our midday ration of soup. When the tureens were brought the capo would distribute the contents to us. Sometimes the soup would arrive as early as ten A.M. We were not permitted to stop working while the soup was being distributed, but we could put down the materials with which we were working when we had the soup in our possession. As soon as the bowl was empty, we had to resume our work. The fact that our hands were filthy and foul smelling from the tar did not matter.

We had the soup anyway. We were not granted the luxury of washing our hands.

The "weberie" (weaving) was set up in Block Five. Previously it had been located in a different barrack. When the Germans decided to move our work location, we carried all the equipment over to Block Five.

We were weaving human hair into cables. The hair was delivered to us from the gas chamber. Occasionally there were other items mixed in with the hair, such as spectacles or dentures. A girl once found a spool of yarn and ten American dollars under the thread. The hair was shorn off the heads of the dead women who had recently arrived on transports to Auschwitz, and who were immediately gassed. Their gold teeth had also been removed at that time. We dipped the hair into black, hot tar and wove it into long braids. We were shown how to do this using six bundles of hair. The job was difficult. We had to twist the hot hair to tighten and strengthen it. When it cooled, it became as stiff as metal. We worked seven days a week, fourteen hours a day, and were urged by blows from the capo's club to produce a great deal more. She made sure that we worked at maximum speed. The capo wanted to keep her job.

Our labors for the Germans improved their war effort. The cables that we made were used on their ships. The woven hair (without the tar) was also converted into sleeping bags for submarine personnel, and clothing for German railroad workers. They would also stuff mattresses with the hair. We realized that we were contributing to our own destruction. The more we produced, resulted in a stronger Germany. If they became more powerful they could fight the Allies for a longer period of time, which of course, would prolong our agony.

We could not refuse to work, even though it militated against us. We continued against our will, we hated slaving for the Germans one bit. The hair assignment was especially disgusting. For one thing we were well aware of the fact that the hair came from the heads of dead women, and our hands became black, sticky and dirty. We couldn't even scratch ourselves with our filthy hands that smelled so badly.

In addition to the hair job, we also worked with cellophane. The material was cut into long strips and woven into long cords. This task job wasn't as bad the one with the hair. We alternated between the two. One day I was selected by the capo, a middle aged Jewish woman from Poland, to work in the front room, directly across from her "private" quarters. We were called the "zuschneiders" (cutters). There were eighteen of us. We cut the sheets of cellophane into long strips which were then carried to the weavers who arranged them into long braids.

We were closely supervised by this capo. She was quite bitter. Her whole family had been shot before her eyes, including her husband and children. She frequently told us that we didn't know what a concentration camp was really like. We should have been there three or four years earlier. Our people had died easily, she said. They were simply gassed. Previously, the Polish Jews and those from other occupied countries were subjected to unbearable tortures before they died. Many were buried alive. What a comfort, I thought bitterly, that my parents and two sisters had died even quicker by a more advanced system, poisoned gas.

Once she gave me a blow with her hand. Someone said something that made me smile. I hadn't noticed that she had been looking in my direction. She hit me across the face as hard as she could and promised that more would follow if I didn't behave. "Where do you think you are anyway," she yelled. I never knew what offended these people to such an extent that they kept beating inmates for no apparent reason.

One Sunday afternoon, we were allowed to stop work a little earlier than usual. We were ordered to line up for roll call, which we always did after work, no matter how tired we were. After we were counted we were told to remain on line. Olga, our Slovak block-alteste distributed blue uniforms to each of the workers of the weberei. She threw the same length of blue rope to each girl in line, regardless of her size. The piece she threw to me was torn. Afraid that I would be accused of sabotage, of not taking proper care of German property, I reported it to her. She immediately struck me viciously on my head. These people were only too eager to implement their right to hit their underlings. She never explained why she struck me.

As a zuschneider I worked with two sisters who came from a town near Berezov. I had known both of them previously. They used to travel from Manesterits to Berezov to visit their uncle and aunt, the Kahan family. I had attended school with the Kahan's eldest son, Mendel. He and I were the same age and we graduated together in 1938 shortly before the Czechs were forced to leave Carpathia, when the Germans invaded Czechoslovakia. Mendel was the one who came out of hiding to join his family in the ghetto. He had claimed that they needed him since he was the oldest. We were on the same truck that transported us to the

159

ghetto.

These two sisters were very "tuchtig" (capable). They knew how to obtain additional food by "organizing." One day I saw them eating a raw potato which had not been distributed. They told me that they had a friend who worked in the kitchen. I envied them for being resourceful enough to sneak things away from under the Germans' watchful eyes.

One day, as we worked at our respective tables where, as always, we were not permitted to talk, the two sisters said in a whisper to me that their cousin Mendel was in the men's camp adjacent to B-Lager. He had been transferred from a labor camp that was especially bad. The entire group of men had been forced to toil in a quarry using heavy tools. They were brought to the adjacent men's camp to "recuperate" for a short while. I went to see him. We spoke briefly across the double barbed wire fences. I presented him with a gift; half my ration of bread. The two sisters, his cousins, told me that it was our "duty" to help him convalesce. He was indeed in poor condition, terribly undernourished and worn out from the hard labor forced upon him. I had to throw the bread very carefully across the two high electrified barbed-wire fences. I had to be on the alert for the German guards who, with dogs were patrolling between the two fences, about one and a half yards apart. I also had to watch out for other men in his camp who would throw themselves on the bread.

I did not realize how powerfully persuasive those two sisters were, and they convinced me. I gave up half of my meager allotment of bread a number of times and tossed it to Mendel through the wire to help him recover. In Auschwitz he improved, not only because he wasn't forced to work, but also, the extra food he received from his cousins and me certainly helped.

Mendel fared much better in Auschwitz than he did in the labor camp where he had been. He said that the work he was forced to do was extremely difficult. They suffered beatings and other indignities on the job. The quarry in which they worked was far from their camp and they had to march to and from work over a rugged mountain trail. The food was meager; one bowl of soup a day and one small ration of bread which was no more than we received in Auschwitz, even though he worked much harder.

Mendel liked being near us and that cost him his life. After he had been there for two weeks a selection took place in his camp. On that day, the doctors were choosing those who looked healthy to return to work. Those who had not improved were left in the camp to await gassing. He had been ordered to go back to work. He was not aware of the usual fate that awaited those who were "selected" to stay. They were those who became useless to the Germans and deemed unworthy to live. He foolishly sneaked in the line of those who remained in the camp. When his cousins and I learned what he had done we were frantic. They told him what a grave mistake he had made, and what the consequence would be. He tried to correct his grave mistake. He told the authorities what he had done, and said that he was capable of working. It didn't help. Two days later he was sent to the gas chamber. He was not yet twenty years old.

An inmate in a concentration camp learned first not to be conspicuous and not to volunteer for "good" jobs. For one thing, these assignments were never what the Germans said they would be, and the volunteers usually ended up in the wrong column, the one which was destined for the gas chamber. Instead of volunteering we adopted a "let the chips fall where they may" attitude. At least then they would not have to blame themselves for the fatal consequences. Mendel Kahan was a good example. Had he remained in line where he was supposed to be, he might be alive today.

In Auschwitz, it was always beneficial to look healthy, but not too much so. We had heard that the strong men were picked for very unpleasant jobs, such as serving with the "sonder command." The unit that hauled the bodies out of the gas chambers and into the crematoriums. Quite often a son would have to place his own father into the crematorium. Only men were recruited for the sonder command; however, the women worried about their brothers and other family males being recruited into this unit.

I met a young man, right after the war who looked, even to the untrained eye, to be mentally deranged. Someone told me that he had worked in the sonder command unit in Auschwitz, and that was supposed to have explained everything. It did. I watched him on one occasion, take out a hundred pengo bill, and light a match to it. With that money he could have bought needed food.

The life span of a member of the Sonder commando was three to four weeks. They either committed suicide or were gassed by the Germans when their nerves were shattered. They wanted no one in this group to survive bear witness against them. However, occasionally, some did survive to describe in detail the dirty ruses the Germans used on the unsuspecting victims to lure them into believing they were going to take a shower. If any suspected foul play, they would use force. They wanted the Jews to die quickly, quietly, without noise or commotion.

In Auschwitz we were not accorded the luxury of observing any of our holidays. Because we had no calendars, we had to estimate, on our own the time, when a particular holiday would take place. We always knew exactly when each observance took place, even though we could not celebrate it.

On Tisha-ba-av, most religious Jews fasted to remember the day the Romans burned the second temple in Jerusalem. On this occasion most of the girls in my block in C-Lager did not line up for the soup as they usually did as soon as the whistle sounded. The block-alteste did not know why suddenly the starved wretches were no longer hungry. Some girls acquainted her with the reason behind the fast. The Blockalteste then told us that in Auschwitz we were permitted to eat and that we would be able to fast when we were outside of the camp. Many girls were not persuaded and still refused to eat. She sent for the Lageralteste who said that the soup could not be saved until evening. The tureens had to be sent back to the kitchen.

In Auschwitz one could not afford the luxury of not eating, she said, since we were given the absolute minimum for our survival. By fasting we decreased our chances of survival. To fast, while in Auschwitz, in order to commemorate the destruction of the temple two thousand years ago struck me as being unreasonable. Besides, abstaining from food helped the Germans destroy us more rapidly. In my mind the destruction of the Jews by the Germans was far greater than the havoc wreaked by the Romans. Jews everywhere fasted for the last two thousand years on this day to remember that first tragedy. Who would fast for us in remembrance of our holocaust? The Germans were exterminating us so rapidly that I began to worry that soon no one would be left alive to remember the bloody hell of Auschwitz.

The lageralteste persuaded some of us to eat the soup, but others clung tenaciously to their beliefs and continued to fast. The soup was returned to the kitchen. I was hoping that those who decided to break their fast at noon might get an extra portion, but it did not happen. They preferred to return the food to the Germans instead of giving it to us. They were faithful slaves to their masters. They had to prove time and again that they were worthy of maintaining their position.

However, on "Yom Kippur", the Day of Atonement, we all refused to eat, mostly out of habit rather than for religious reasons. It used to be such a special day.

On the eve of Yom Kippur we had nothing to eat. We were never given anything for supper. We refused to eat our ration of bread on the following morning, it being Yom Kippur. At noon time when the soup was brought out we didn't want it. Maybe two people in the entire weberei took soup. The rest fasted. The Polish capo in the weberei was furious. "Stupid Hungarians," she yelled. "You are given a little bit of food and you don't eat it. After you have been in Auschwitz for two or three years you will gladly eat, if only you had some soup."

It was very difficult to work from early morning until late in the evening without eating or drinking anything. Since we were fasting we were not given a noon break. The last time we had any food was the

164

previous day at ten in the morning. After that, some 33 to 34 hours passed until late in the following evening when we had our ration of dry bread that we received in the morning and which we had saved. We did not even get some tea or coffee. Nothing. Yom Kippur was the only holiday that some of us observed. We would just mention Rosh Hashana, the Jewish New Year, to one another in passing. On Yom Kippur I carried my ration of bread in my bosom all day. It was the only place where it was safe.

We could never forget our holidays. The Germans were the ones who reminded us of them in their own perverted way. They always knew when there was a Jewish holiday. They would always prepare something "special" for us. Sometimes it was heavy labor or longer zahlappells in bad weather. At other times they conducted a "selection" for the gas chamber, even if it was on the most sacred day of the Jews. On Yom Kippur we were worked as hard as ever. Our capo made sure of that. Suddenly the whistle blew, and when that happened at an unusual time in the morning, in the evening or for soup, it always meant big trouble.

The "selections" were the horror of every inmate in Auschwitz. When the word passed through the crowd every one turned pale. Since we were all undernourished and overworked, none of us had much confidence in being lucky to "pass" the selection on Yom Kippur.

We were ordered out of the barracks that housed the weberei and were told to line up in single file. When I was outside I noticed that not only our barracks but the whole B-Lager and other camps as well were gathered outside for the "special" event. We were than

165

told to undress completely right in the camp, and to hold our clothes under our right arms while keeping our left ones high above our heads. Girls in the line started pinching their cheeks to get some color into their pale faces. We were all starved, but on this day of Yom Kippur we even delayed eating the ration of bread and drinking the bitter ersatz coffee. We also refused to eat the small amount of midday soup.

It was rumored that Dr. Mengele, in addition to selecting the weak ones for the gassing, was asking each girl about her occupation. It was decided that the best and safest thing to say was "schneiderin," dressmaker. Even those who never held a needle in hand said "dressmaker." He couldn't possibly have used that many dressmakers.

It was also wise, if at all possible, to pass him by very quickly, to deprive him of the chance for a close examination. That tactic was not always successful. He was always accompanied by a few SS officers with ferocious dogs. He would flick his finger to the right or to the left. We quickly learned which was the good side, since those who were doomed looked emaciated or suffered from other rash or skin blemish diseases.

Mengele hated skin disfigurements. I saw two sisters who were cruelly separated this way because one had blemished skin, and was ordered to one side, while the clear-skinned was sent to the to the other side. Those that were going to the gas chamber were guarded very closely, but occasionally someone would get away. Once I noticed a girl sneaking away to join the lucky line of those who would remain alive. I also saw a woman in the healthy looking line cross over to the condemned group to share the fate of her sister in the gas chamber.

Having one or more sisters in Auschwitz had its good and bad features. It was good in that sisters would share their food with each other, particularly if one of them was able to obtain a little extra. They would also help each other when standing in the endless zahlappell lines. They would exchange places so that the one who stood on the outside and was exposed to the cold and to the blows of the SS, could switch to the center where she was somewhat protected from both. The center girl was also sheltered a bit from the eyes of the SS men who conducted selections at every roll call. The center girl was not always noticed. She might have had a cold, a fever or she just may not have looked too well. Strangers weren't always willing to change places, even when asked. It was also better to share a blanket and lie next to your sister than to a total stranger. The bad part about being there with a sister was the possibility of having to witness the selection for death of one of them without being able to do anything about it. The alternatives were to suffer in silence or to join her.

Those who were doomed to die were kept secluded and locked in Block 25. They were sometimes kept there for many days without food or water which prolonged their agony. This happened when transports from the ghettos were arriving and there was no room for them in the gas chamber. At other times they were forced to wait in Block 25 until a sufficient number of them were accumulated, so as not to waste too much gas on a small number of victims. Others who were brought to be asphyxiated were those slave laborers whose bodies had been reduced to skin-covered barely mobile skeletons and from whom the Germans could not get any more work. They had become useless and good only for fuel to keep the ovens burning twenty four hours a day. When victims were led, under heavy guard, to the gas chamber, the whole camp was under, "blocksperre" (enclosure of the barrack). No one was permitted to go out or to look out.

The "lucky" ones who were kept alive had to cope with the terrible reality that someone you knew, a family member, a friend you had grown fond of, was doomed by Dr. Mengele because she was pale or thin and was dragged away never to be seen or heard from again.

If I lived a thousand years, I could not forget those "selections" and how they affected us emotionally and psychologically. Those whom the notorious Dr. Mengele sent to the wrong side knew that they would soon to die. Some offered such fierce resistance that one wondered where they got the strength. I once saw a slim girl who was selected for the gas, fight the Germans like a true story book heroine. She kicked, bit, scratched and fought them tooth and nail, but they would not surrender to a Jewish girl. We watched them in horror, dragging her until they reached the gate. She battled them all the way to the camp gate and quite probably all the way to the gas chamber.

In this way, sisters were separated from each other. The cries from these siblings was heartrending and nerve-wracking, but not to the Germans. They kept composure. It never bothered them. They were expert, professional murderers.

The inadequate diet affected us adversely. Almost all of the women lost their menstruation cycle soon after their arrival in Auschwitz. The reason for the loss of our periods was the starvation diet from which we all suffered. In a way, we were fortunate to lose our periods, because we were in no position to handle menstruation in a concentration camp. We had no sanitary napkins or even an extra pair of panties.

I had my period once during all the time I was in the concentration camps. As I was standing on zahlappell, two months after I arrived in Auschwitz, I felt a sudden warm stream running down my legs. I was greatly surprised since no one had periods while in camp. As the blood flowed, I had to remain standing at attention in my place in the line. It was an awful experience, but I had nothing with which to stop the flow. I had to remain standing for hours while the blood was streaming. After the zahlappell a girl gave me a piece of rag to use for a napkin. I could not wash my panties. They remained dirty until we were taken to the latrine and I sneaked into the washroom where I inconspicuously washed my panties in cold water with a scrap of Auschwitz soap with the letters RJF stamped on it that some one had given me.

We all thought that the Germans had laced our soup with bromide and that had caused our menstrual stoppage. It was said that we would never be able to bear children even if we eventually did leave the camps. The Germans were killing the present and future generations of Jews. Some of us believed that even if we did give birth, the children would be deformed as a result of the bromide or whatever it was that they put into our soup. As a result, a few women stopped eating soup, altogether, or tried to swallow as little as possible. But hunger triumphed, and they ate whatever was offered to them.

We also lost weight because of our poor diet. This resulted in a shrinking of our breasts as time passed. After a few months in Auschwitz, we became virtually flat chested. Our sex urges disappeared too. We became feminine in gender only. Our sexual drive was lost for most of us, even in our fantasies. It seems that under extreme traumatic conditions such as hard labor, starvation and constant fear of imminent death, sex is no longer a necessity. Perhaps it persisted among those who had experienced sex before they arrived at the concentration camps, but for those of us who had never been married, it did not exist at all. We saw so much nudity that it no longer awoke any sexual desire. Not that a lonely inmate was able to indulge in any physical intimacy in the camps anyway.

However, those who could obtain more food than the rest of us like the lageraltestes, the blockaltestes and the capos, did, on occasion, engage in sexual activity. Some of them would sell their amorous favors for food.

Others who dared to have sexual encounter soon learned that the German order prohibiting such activities were to be taken seriously. One Sunday, after returning from the weberei a bit earlier than usual, we were ordered to line up for zahlappell. Olga, the blockalteste, selected a girl whom she chose earlier, from the lot of us, to be a stubendienst. The stubendiensts did not go to work the way the rest of us did. Their duties were light. They helped the blockalteste to see that the barrack was kept clean, helped her distribute the soup, and cut the bread. They also were rewarded with privileges. They were assigned the best bunks and received the most blankets, they got more soup and they did not have to work as hard as the rest of us. As a result they were better nourished and were healthier than the others. This also meant that they were less likely to be chosen during a "selection". They were not required to line up as the rest of us did for that ritual. They participated only in special "selections". Everybody wanted to be a stubendienst.

On this day, however, one of Olga's own stubendiensts committed a grave sin. Olga found her in the barrack on a bunk bed having intercourse with one of the men who had come to help the women drain the lavatory in B-Lager. Olga was furious. She waved her finger, insulted her, and shouted obscenities. What if a German had entered the barrack instead of her, she cried. She dragged her out of the line and forced her to stand alone in front of everyone. This girl was quite pretty. She was tall, with jet black eyes, short curly dark hair, and a swarthy complexion. She stood there her face flushed, the poor soul. She had committed a major "crime" and she was paying for it.

After the zahlappell was over and Olga could not think of any more insults to hurl at the poor girl, she was sent away from our block. Where to? No one knew. She was never seen again. Maybe she joined the ranks of the overworked and the starved in the concentration camps. Or perhaps she was sent to that place from which there was no return. But Olga was not German; she was Jewish, a prisoner herself. She could have ignored the incident and not have made such a pitiful spectacle of the poor girl.

We also encountered SS women in Auschwitz. They wore army jackets and culottes, black shiny boots, and each carried a pistol in a leather holster, the same as the SS men. They were usually worse than the men, if that was possible. They had to prove that they were sadistic enough to be worthy of their SS uniforms.

One of these SS women has remained in my mind ever since. She was an "oberscharfurerin", (platoon sergeant). She wore a silver pistol and an immaculate uniform, and was usually accompanied by a large dog. When this woman came to count us we were so afraid that we would stand as motionless as statues. We even held our breaths until she passed us. Everything about her body was ideal. She was blond, blue eyed, with an angelic face. I think her name was Erma Grese. Once when she arrived to count us, she emerged from behind the barracks. She tried to surprise us and catch us off guard, as an excuse to beat a few girls. She started counting the groups of fives from the rear. She found nothing amiss this time. She completed her tally and reluctantly left.

There were rumors that this woman wore an iron glove when she came to conduct the roll call. I once saw her beat a girl a few lines from where I stood. The girl had waved a fly from her face. The SS woman struck her in the back with such power that the girl began to cough up blood.

The rumor was it that this pretty, cruel bitch was Dr. Mengele's mistress. What could one expect from a close associate of the devil himself? No matter how much one rejects the belief in the existence of the devil, I can swear that Dr. Mengele and this amazon who was probably his cold-blooded mistress, were both devils incarnate. How else could one explain their behavior? She, Dr. Mengele and the rest of the Germans seemed like creatures from some pre-historic era. They definitely did not act like human beings. Their business was death and their chief occupation was murder. We would cringe with fear whenever we saw them.

Every once in a while we were ordered to stop our work and march out of the camp. We might be going to the omnipresent gas chamber or just off to take a shower. We only felt safe when we actually saw the water pouring from the holes in the ceiling.

Once, when we were leaving we saw a long line of malnutritioned, worn out men. They wore the concentration camp uniform, striped pajamas which draped over their shrunken bodies. The yellow star of David with the word "Jude" printed in black was sewn onto their uniforms. They were marching towards the gas chamber and in fact they were almost there. We all recognized the signs that marked them for asphyxiation; they all looked like barely breathing skeletons. The Germans had literally worked and starved them to death. Now they were trudging in a long line in fives to death.

One of the men in this column was hugging a loaf of bread under his arm. A girl from our line jumped on the unsuspecting man and seized the bread, depriving him from his only possession in this world, the bread. When she returned to our column with the loaf, we severely reprimanded her for her dastardly act. She defended herself by rationalizing that the man would not have had the time or the opportunity to eat the bread. He was already too close his poisonous destination. "Why waste the bread?" she said. She could still satisfy some of her own hunger with it. Auschwitz logic.

The Germans treated us as animals. We, in turn, reacted as if we were. The girl had taken from a dying man his last possession on earth. I did not approve of her behavior, although I too was very hungry. I could not have been so callous and unfeeling. In addition to our trips to the bathhouse, we occasionally went out to bring materials to the weberei, items such as cellophane and hair which were used in our work. We were closely guarded on all these trips. Once, as we crossed the little wooden bridge over the murky pond I looked into the water. It was thick with a viscous-like substance and the stagnant water hardly moved. A girl from our column said in Hungarian (she hoped that the guards would not understand) "You see, the Germans are dumping the ashes of our parents into these waters." Somebody else said (also in Hungarian), "holgos" (shut up). She did not want to be reminded of these grim stories about Auschwitz. Or maybe she still harbored the illusion that the gas chamber did not exist and that it was just an ugly rumor the oldtimers had spread to frighten the newcomers.

Some of the recent arrivals, especially the Hungarians, did not believe the stories about the gas chamber. They thought that it was a camp for old people and children. They said that the asphyxiations did not take place. When the veteran inmates pointed out the huge chimney with the black smoke emanating from it, the newcomers said that it must be a factory. They felt that the Slovakian and Polish Jews just wanted to scare and torture us because they were jealous.

However, I realized from the very first day, that the stories about the gas chamber were true. I recalled what my cousin, Chaim Hersh, said had happened to the transport from our region in early 1942. All those who were supposed to be "relocated" were shot in a ditch and covered with a thin layer of soil. Those who's dying was slower were also buried in the ditch. One man from a town near Berezov said that he trembled so violently when they started shooting at everyone, he fell into the ditch before they shot him.

Later, after the German butchers left, he climbed out of the mass grave and ran from Poland to the Carpathians, just as my cousin had done.

At that time no one wanted to believe all the horror stories that were making the rounds. They were just too repulsive for human minds to lend them credence. At that time we could "walk away" from these unpleasant stories by simply disbelieving them. But we couldn't do that in Auschwitz. With the ever present pervasive order of burning flesh, one could hardly deny the oldtimers reports of the ghastly events that were taking place. We saw for ourselves the flames and smoke belching out of the huge, red chimney. Seemingly endless long lines of human beings disappeared into that building. What further proof did one need? One night, while every one was sleeping I was awakened by an urgent need to urinate. I did not know what to do. It was strictly forbidden to walk out of the barracks alone at anytime, especially at night, but I had little choice. I finally decided to risk it. I left through the back door, knowing that the front one would be locked and guarded. As I stepped out into the night, the sky above was red, aglow with the hellish fires emanating from the tall chimney. I wondered whose parents, sisters, brothers or entire families the flames were consuming. I watched the horrifying scene as if I were under a hypnotic spell. Reluctant to push my luck any further, I returned to the barrack. Later I learned that there were buckets at the front door that I could have used.

On another occasion, I saw the Germans pour kerosene on a barrack in C-Lager filled with gypsies. Then they ignited it. The heartrending screams of the human torches could be heard far into the distance.

Sometime in July of 1944 we heard that an attempt had been made on Hitler's life. The archetype of evil might already be dead. I held my breath. Please, God, make it happen. Let it be true, not a rumor, I thought. I started to fantasize about what it would be like to be free, not to be enclosed by electrified fences and surrounded by armed guards with vicious dogs; to be able to eat all the bread I wanted, to go to the toilet unescorted by a captor, and to breathe air that was not saturated with burning flesh. But life in the camp continued as before. Nothing eventful happened. The assassination attempt had failed. To our great sorrow, Hitler survived.

We were so closely watched and supervised that it was impossible for any of us to do anything to stop the gassing and cremating of humans. We needed major help from the outside, from the Allies. But they did not bomb the gas chambers and the crematoriums. They did not destroy the railroads that led to Auschwitz and Birkenau, they did not halt the Germans from bringing in new trainloads of victims.

As I lay on the hard boards during the nights, I heard the cattle trains coming in. They arrived during the day and night. When the train reached its final destination, Birkenau-Auschwitz, it emitted a mournful sound, a loud cry, a sort of wailing, heard in a funeral procession. I remember that plaintive sound from the time my family and I reached Auschwitz.

I looked towards the sky hoping to see the Allies. Where are you? I even fantasized that the Allies would drop food packages for us, but as usual nothing good ever happened in Auschwitz.

Later in July the Sonder commando, whose job it was

to remove the dead bodies from the gas chambers and transfer them into the ovens which converted them to ashes, planned a rebellion against the Germans. It was done in a very primitive way. They had no high-tech munitions. They did destroy one of the gas chambers. Their success, however, was very limited. The Germans executed all those who survived the uprising. But gas chamber #5 was destroyed. It exploded with a loud noise. We didn't know what had happened. Suddenly whistles started to blow and cries of "blocksperre" were heard. The Germans immediately forced everyone back into the barracks and those inside were not allowed to leave. The entire camp was covered with thick black smoke. The oldtimers in our camp said that the Sonder commando uprising was senseless. No one had the slightest chance of waging a successful rebellion against the Germans who had plenty of ammunition and the capability to retaliate quickly. Although one crematorium was destroyed, the Germans had four more that they kept functioning day and night.

The Sonder commando had made a desperate attempt to end the gassing. They had a good reason for attempting what they did, since theirs was the most horrendous job of all. In addition to removing the bodies from the gas chamber and burning the corpses, they had to use pliers to extract the gold teeth from the contorted bodies. They had to search for jewels in noses, ears and all bodily openings.

Their time to be condemned to the gas chambers was imminent and they knew it. After their extermination, a fresh group was brought to replace the dead teams. Tragically, they were helping the Germans to exterminate their own brethren. Any strong young man could be picked to work in the Sonder commando. There was a great deal of burning to do. Each day some twenty thousand people were poisoned by gas with no traces left behind. Since they couldn't dispose of all the people they killed in the crematoriums, despite working day and night, they ordered inmates to dig large pits in which additional bodies were burned. The Germans didn't stop there, they threw live children into the flaming pits.

When I heard about the Sonder commando I shuddered. To force Jews to help in exterminating their own was unspeakably evil. Only the German appreciation of coldblooded and diabolical irony could conceive that. How fortunate that they didn't use women for this horrible job. But I immediately thought of my young brothers. How terrible. Then I rejected the thought. They were not strong looking, and always thin.

Most of the suicides in Auschwitz occurred among the Sonder commandos. There were other cases as well. It was very easy to end ones life in Auschwitz. All a contemplating suicide had to do was to run into the electrified barbed wire and all the persecution and torment would be over. The tortuous concern over Dr. Mengele's selections would no longer threaten ones sanity and hunger would no longer be a problem. Shivering in the zahlappell or broiling under the blazing sun without shelter and water would be over. All misery would be over. Freedom would be attained at last.

That summer of 1944 was extremely hot and humid. Added to that, was the heavy smoke from the chimneys that we inhaled and the presence of the cloyingly sweet, choking stench of burning human flesh. We felt faint most of the time. That was what our summer was like.

Sometime during the month of August, we were ordered to line up. In the middle of the square was a structure resembling a swimming pool. Most of the camps had these, but I had never seen anybody using them. We were ordered to undress and go to the pool. We obeyed. The muddy water in the pool was no more than two or three inches deep. It was the accumulation of the last rain. We could not understand why they were suddenly treating us so well, allowing us to swim. There must have been a reason. We knew the Germans only too well. We soon learned. Planes appeared overhead and took pictures of us, probably to show the Red Cross how well they treated their Jewish captives. One could have taken a swim in the hot and humid weather, but the closest thing to a pool in Auschwitz was a muddy puddle.

Sometimes, when we were outside the camp, we encountered pretty Gypsy girls working on the road. They lived in a family camp not far from ours. They had been in Auschwitz for quite a long time. One night during the month of October, all the Gypsies, except the young ones, were herded into trucks and transported to the gas chambers. They knew where they were being taken. That night twenty thousand of them died. The next morning all we saw was a deserted camp and thick, black smoke rising from the tall chimney.

The interminable standing at zahlappell twice a day during the hot summer months was tortuous. People fainted from the sweltering climate. However, when autumn came and brought the torrential rains with it, we had to contend with the deep mud in the alleys between each of the two blocks, the place where we would line up for roll call. It was difficult to pull my feet out of the slimy, sticky mixture that clung to my clogs. Trudging to and from the latrine was also unbearable.

Our travail worsened when winter arrived. The zahlappell took place even in subzero temperatures. We were forced to stand for what seemed to be endless periods of time, waiting to be counted. During this procedure we were not allowed to move our feet. In the cold this was numbing. So we would try to move our legs whenever no one was watching. This was easier for the girl in the center who was hidden by those on either side of her.

To make matters worse, the barracks were never heated. Although we were given "winter" clothes, they offered very little protection against the Polish winter. The barracks were cold. The bitter wind blew through the openings in the walls.

The so-called "winter" clothes that I received consisted of a little black coat without a lining. This was one of those items which wasn't good enough to be sent to Germany. My good red coat had been taken away from me when I arrived at Auschwitz, and was probably among the other better clothes that were shipped to Germany to keep a German fraulein warm. In the meantime I shivered and my teeth chattered from the biting cold. I had no shoes either. I had received wooden clogs but no stockings. I had no underwear and had not received anything to cover my hairless head. My hands were also exposed to the cold without gloves or mittens.

In order not to look too civilian in my little black coat, a square piece of cloth had been cut out of the back and a square of prison striped material was sewn into its place. In addition, a large cross was painted on the back of the coat in bright red. We were lined up for the occasion. A woman performed the job. In the front of the coat, on the left side, I had to sew my identification. It was large and black on a white background, along with a yellow triangle so that I could immediately be identified as Jewish. Every prisoner received a different symbol: The political prisoners wore red triangles, the criminals, green ones, homosexuals pink, gypsies brown, and the shiftless, had black.

It was during this harsh fall and winter time that I complained to sister-in-law, Lenke, of a severe pain in my upper back and that I was certain I had contracted pneumonia. She assured me that my symptoms were the result of the harsh cold and that they would disappear. It was then that she gave me the red beet to "cure" my pneumonia. I took it and returned to my barrack where another girl loaned me her knife. I cut some slices of the beet and ate them slowly, savoring every bite. After much suffering, the aches in my sides and upper back seemed to disappear.

During the winter we were also given blankets. That is, six of us who slept on one side of the tiered bunks received one for all of us. Soon after receiving it, and during the night when we were asleep and covered, the blanket was suddenly pulled off us. I awoke immediately sat up and looked around. Everything was quiet and every one seemed sound asleep. But the blanket was gone and was never returned. From that time on I had to use the little black coat as my only protection against the cold.

In spite of the gloom, the freezing weather, and the

hard labor, there was a ray of sunshine in Auschwitz that we awaited eagerly. The bombardments of camp and the proximity by the Allies had given a semblance of hope. The allied planes targeted for the munitions factory and the synthetic rubber plant. They didn't attack often enough, as far as we were concerned. We wished that they would come every day. We wanted them to blast Auschwitz to smithereens. We could actually hear the bombs exploding. The louder the noise, the happier we became. When the planes appeared and the alarm sounded, the German guards would disappear. They would run to the air raid shelters. Not us. There were no shelters for us. We remained in the weberei. To commemorate the occasion we would stop working. During the bombardments we were left unsupervised. Even the Jewish capo retired to her room.

As the walls of the barrack shook we cheered. We were not afraid. I preferred to die in an Allied bombing than at the bloody hands of the German butchers. The more potent the explosions the louder we cheered and screamed with delight. We released our repressed emotions; those we would never allow to surface the Germans were present.

The sounds of bursting bombs was like music to my ears. It made me feel good, unlike the concerts to which we were subjected in Auschwitz. The Germans had organized an orchestra of highly qualified Jewish male musicians. (There was a female orchestra as well in Auschwitz, but I never heard them play). This group was ordered to play beautiful music on the plaza near the gas chamber when they herded two to three thousand people into the gas chamber at one time: another example of the Germans' devilish sense of juxtaposition. The music would also muffle the unworldly screams of the dying. The Germans, of course, would amuse themselves by listening to fine classical music. After all, they are repeated to be a very cultured people.

I adopted the bombardments as my personal revenge. Somebody was paying back the Germans for what they had done to us. We were told that the aerial assaults in and around Auschwitz were being launched chiefly by the Russians. I was so grateful to them for battling the Germans that I pledged them my eternal love. I promised, that no matter what they did in the future I would never hate them.

I shall always remember with affection, those exhilarating moments of listening to the detonations. Those were the only times that we could permit ourselves to overtly enjoy the luxury of expressing the anger we harbored against our oppressors. We were never able to do this in their presence. During the bombardments we cheered and sang. The Germans were finally getting their just deserts. We weren't even afraid. "Towarishi" (comrade) up there, let them have it, the bloody bastards. They were the exemplification of evil. One more bomb, towarishi, for me and for my family.

We had heard rumors that the war was going badly for the Germans. However, in Auschwitz, the Germans were still strong. Our lives were still in their hands, and they treated us as they damned well pleased. The continuation and intensification of the bombings meant that the war was wreaking havoc, and that it would eventually end with the downfall of the Germans even if we did not live to see that day. We knew that they would be executed before we could be liberated. They wouldn't want witnesses to their crimes.

December of 1944 was coming to an end. The Christmas holiday was supposed to symbolize "peace on earth, good will toward men." The Germans had no "good will" for Jews. There aim was to kill as many of us as possible, if not all, before the war ended. They knew that the conflict would end soon and that they had little chance of winning it. Now, getting rid of the Jews would compensate for their failure to win the war. The closer the Allies came, the more frantic they became to dispose of the remaining Jews.

All through the war, it seemed to me that it would last eternally. Each day in Auschwitz was an eternity. It appeared that no one was in any great hurry to see an end to the conflagration except the trapped and doomed Jews, who could do nothing to accelerate its end. The Germans realized that the dead could not testify against them. So all they had to do was kill us to assure their postwar safety.

Christmas was minimally observed in Auschwitz. I expected something, at a day's rest off from work, or perhaps a cancellation of the zahlappell. Since, on the Jewish holidays they intensified their torture, I thought that maybe on their holiday they would treat us to a better soup, or something else to mark the occasion. But nothing happened. We stood endlessly as usual at the zahlappell, and received the same meager bowl of soup. We worked as we did every day, Christmas or not.

When the new year of 1945 arrived we received some holiday treats. For one thing, the zahlappell was postponed from early in the morning to 11 o'clock. Until that time we were allowed to stay in the barracks were permitted to talk. It was bitter cold outside. Although the barracks were not heated, it was far better indoors. We also had our midday soup at 10 o'clock, and the soup was different and much better than it ever had been. For the first time we were given soup that was recognizable and not just a colorless mush. It was yellow split pea which was hot, thick and delicious. Each one of us received a second helping. Even the blockalteste's mood was better; she was friendly and spoke like a normal human being.

The spirit of the holidays was definitely in the air. When we received our second helping, the blockalteste warned us not to save any soup for later. Some girls who slept in the upper berths, and could hide things without being noticed, did not listen to her, and saved a bowl of soup. Later I hated myself for having obeyed the order. While others had the soup a second time after the zahlappell, I had nothing left. We thought to ourselves and whispered to each other wishes that the new year would find us released from German bondage.

Soon after the new year, on January 6, after the morning zahlappell, instead of returning to the block, we were marched out of the gate in the direction of the general area where both the gas chamber and the bathhouse were located. Which destination was it going to be this time?, I thought. Only God and the Germans knew and neither was telling us. We were always scared when we were marched in that direction. I was relieved when I saw that our line was being directed towards the showers; I could see water coming out of the holes in the ceiling.

We took showers, as we had done in the past, but this time after we had lined up in the traditional fives, we were not marched back into the camp. Instead, we remained standing outside for several hours. The cold was unbearable. The freezing, gusting wind pierced our bodies. The thin clothes were totally inadequate for the Polish winter. We shivered and our teeth chattered. We were not been able to dry ourselves after the shower. We did not even have towels. We always placed our clothes directly on our wet bodies. This made us feel even colder. I thought: This is it, if they don't let us inside soon, we will all freeze to death. We had been outside in the frigid air since very early in the morning for the traditional Zahlappell. We were freezing at the Zahlappell as usual and then we waited to get back into the barrack to warm up a little. Instead, we were marched away and now after the shower there was more standing in line, more waiting and more freezing. We jumped from foot to foot in a sort of improvised dance, a mad one. We placed our arms around ourselves and rubbed our shoulders, all while no one was watching. In Auschwitz winter started in October and it was January now and we were cold the entire time. The blistering wind penetrated the light clothes we were wearing. It felt as if we were naked.

Finally, some additional SS arrived. They started to distribute small packages wrapped in brown paper. They weighed about a pound and were the size of a large book. No one had any idea of the contents. Each of us also received a small loaf of bread. We surmised that something serious was about to happen. I thought that we were probably going on a long journey. We never received a whole loaf of bread at one time. Our portions were about a quarter of a loaf for the entire day. We were counted and recounted. Finally, we were ordered to start marching by the SS who guarded us. It was better to move than to stand in one place, but we did shift our weight from one foot to the other, we stamped our feet on the ground to prevent numbness from setting. We marched, but not towards the camp from which we came. Instead we headed in the opposite direction, away from the B-Lager. We realized that they were moving us away from Auschwitz, but we didn't know where. We were going in the direction of the railroad station; about a thousand girls marching to a new destination. I was roughly in the center of the long column. We were going to the same station at which we arrived. We were very apprehensive. Every change in the concentration camp was always for the worse. The place was deserted. It was bitter cold. There were no inmates to be seen when we passed the short distance from the bathhouse to the station, just many armed SS guards and snarling dogs. I glanced towards the camp we just had left. I felt hungry and scared, familiar feelings by now.

I thought of my dearest family and friends whom I had left and would never see again. They were all dead. My mother and father, my two sisters and all those relatives who were the wrong age; they were either too young or too old to slave for the Germans, so they went directly from the train station to the gas chamber. I wasn't sorry to leave Auschwitz. Nothing could ever be worse than that hell hole. I hoped I would never see that place again, but in my mind's eye I would always see Auschwitz and remain there until my dying day. I was happy to leave, but was apprehensive of the one to which I was going. What would it be like?

As we marched on, the tall metal gate of the camp came into view. Above this gate, a curved arc of black metal letters formed an inscription which read,

"Arbeit Macht Frei" (Work will liberate you). We saw this sign when we arrived at Auschwitz. The words were cynical and mocking. No one in Auschwitz was free, except the dead who could not be exploited, humiliated and mistreated. All the reward for the hard labor for the Germans in Auschwitz was to turn the victims into "mussulmaner", skeletons, the walking dead. Once that state was reached death was the liberator.

We marched past sites we had previously: the gray barracks, the watch towers manned by ever present and vigilant guards aiming their machine guns at us. The cold was unbearable. The ground was covered with a layer of ice and snow. It was extremely hazardous. The snow cracked under our feet. We marched in fives. The wind howled. A great number of SS were marched along on each side of the column. They were clad in warm coats, hats, gloves and shiny boots. They even had earmuffs. Our feet were wrapped in rags for a little warmth and to prevent them from freezing. I, however, had difficulty marching. Soon after I started, the snow stuck to my wooden clogs, and they became very heavy and slippery. I knew better than to stop and scrape the ice from the clogs. I would lose my place in the row of five and the girls would have trampled me, or worse, I would have been beaten with the SS man's rifle butt for spoiling the symmetry of the column. We continued trudging. I couldn't stop to clear my clogs. They wouldn't tolerate such infractions. On these marches when the Germans evacuated the camps that were soon to be liberated by the Allies, those who lagged behind, usually the sick and feeble, were shot on the spot and the corpses were left lying in the road.

We travelled on the same rough road that was dusty in

the summer and covered with ice and snow in the winter, and upon which thousands had marched to their deaths in the gas chambers. After what seemed like an interminable length of time the slippery road in the bitter cold, we reached our destination. Actually, it took only about 20-30 minutes. It was the railroad station at Birkenau-Auschwitz. This was where all the trains brought in their human cargo literally to a dead end. We were quite familiar with the place. A long cattle train was in the station, waiting. It was the same type of train with the box cars that my family and I boarded at Chust to take us to Auschwitz. But that seemed like a century ago. I still had a family then. Now I was alone. Not even one girl from Berezov was with me. We were all separated and scattered. The Germans didn't want families or friends together. Each person would be a lone witness to their atrocities.

The "station", many tracks leading to a platform, was heavily guarded, and covered with snow and ice. There were SS men and barking dogs exposing their fangs all around us. Machine guns in the towers, at the station and in the nearby camp, were poised to fire at the slightest hint of a disturbance. We went through the same procedure as we did when we boarded the train in Chust. The Germans assigned out eighty of us to one box car. There was no ramp. We helped one another to get on the train. This time we had no luggage to take up room.

As the box car filled, the doors closed. But before this happened, we were given the now familiar two buckets, one with water, the other empty. This time three armed guards were posted in our car. They remained seated at the door, secluded from us. The door was locked from the inside. These were not the usual SS guards. They were part of from the Wehrmacht (the regular German army). We were told to move away from them. They didn't want us near them. Well, we were just as discrimination. We huddled to warm each other. The air was so frigid that we could hardly breathe. Our clothing was light and unsuitable for this kind of weather. The only small window in the box car was covered with barbed wire, so that we couldn't escape. The barbed wire unfortunately could not prevent wind from entering. This was the end. We were sure of it. No one could survive in this sub zero weather without adequate clothing. When all eighty of us were jammed in, we sat down very close to each other on the floor of the dirty car. The only warmth we felt was generated by the close proximity of our own bodies. Not that there was any room to stretch out. The guards occupied a lot of space.

As soon as the doors closed, the train slowly moved away from the station. Night was approaching and we were freezing. I thought we would be dead before we reached our destination, wherever that might be. Some of the girls started to eat their bread. They wanted to do this, to have one last satisfactory feeling before they died. Some one suggested that we open the little packages we received in Auschwitz. One woman did. We could not believe our eyes. It contained a piece of paper, a folded, brown, ribbed piece of paper. What could we do with it? We all examined it closely and then one woman shouted that it was a paper sleeping bag, an example of German ingenuity. Many of us had never seen such an item before. Some one demonstrated how to use it. We all crawled into our paper bags. It was certainly better than nothing. It helped somewhat to alleviate our condition.

In B-Lager I became a friend of two nice girls, Roszi and her companion. They were both about my age, 19 - 20. I had met Roszi quite by chance while roaming through the alley before I was assigned to the weberei. When she told me that she came from Ungwar, the capital of Carpathia, I mentioned that I was there once and that I had two brothers who lived there. When I mentioned who my brothers were, she told me that she used to date my brother, Shmuel Moshe. We became friends instantly. Roszi was tall and slender. She had short, curly, ash blonde hair and nice, green-blue eyes. We were both in the same barrack. We didn't talk much about our homes. The memories seemed too remote. We just told each other about the places we came from. We didn't want to remember our homes although we never really forgot them. It was too painful to recall. We didn't discuss our past lives, just a few things occasionally. We were together for about three months, assigned to the same work, but not near each other. We communicated only after work, before we took our respective places in the berths.

After we met, we stood together in line at the endless zahlappell, twice daily. We would switch places when either of us was standing in the front rank, with too much exposure to the Germans and the other officials of the camp. In the front it was also much colder. Roszi was a very smart girl. I was very fond of her. She had a nice voice and would sing song. I heard her rendition of a Hungarian gypsy song, which I liked. She sang it for me several times. I learned the words and memorized the melody but my voice left a great deal to be desired.

When it was very cold she continued to take a cold shower whenever possible. When we could sneak away after work, I would accompany her. "It is very important to keep clean here", she would say. In the beginning it was extremely difficult to undress in the open barrack because of the icy weather. There were only two walls across from each other and wide, completely open doors in both the front and the rear of the barrack. In Auschwitz it turned cold very early in the season. The showers were located in that virtually open barrack.

As I opened the faucet and the frigid water started raining on me, my heart would skip a few beats and I would momentarily stop breathing. I was sure that I would contract pneumonia or turn into an icicle. Later Roszi taught me a trick to use when I took a cold shower. First, I would get wet, then step away from under the water, and rub my body vigorously with the small piece of soap available had. I worked very quickly. After soaping myself I stepped back under the water to rinse off the soap. We had no towels to dry ourselves so we used an outer garment and then dressed quickly. We would save the wet garment for the last to allow it dry out us. Sometimes we would hold it in our hands until it was dry. After a number of cold showers, I got used to them.

Now we were huddling on the dirty floor to keep from freezing. Here we had no room to move or stretch our legs. We were jam-packed like herring in a barrel, but this time we didn't mind it too much. The closer we were, the warmer we could feel.

Every one of us was very lonely and felt alienated. We had been torn away from our families, homes and friends. We formed alliances with other girls resembling like surrogate families, since the Germans destroyed our real families. These affiliations helped alleviate some of the loneliness. We helped each other whenever we could. It made life a little easier and a bit more bearable. Now the three of us, Roszi, her Ungwar friend and I huddled to keep warm.

Our armed guards, who kept their distance from us, stayed together too. They were not as cold as we were. They were dressed warmly. They talked quietly so as not to be heard. Throughout the entire journey which lasted three days we received no food. Our guards, however, were very well fed. We watched them as they ate their salami, cheese and slices of bread, not the concentration camp variety which was mixed with saw dust that was given to us. But we had nothing after we finished our small loaf of bread. We could not easily take water from the bucket, and we had no cups. We had to drink from tip the bucket. We really weren't very thirsty, but we were very hungry. We even missed that little serving of watery soup we used to get in Auschwitz.

On the second day of our trip the impossible happened. One of the guards while eating threw a slice of bread, and I caught it. My friend Roszi insisted that the guard had looked at her and had thrown the bread to her. I was too hungry to give up the whole slice. I offered to share it with her, but she claimed that the whole slice belonged to her.

The German bastard, out of sheer malice, had thrown us the bread so they could all watch the hungry wretches fight over it. She was very angry and never forgave me.

Starvation is a torture that is very difficult to explain to someone who has not experienced it, but it is arguably the worst thing that can happen to a human being. More than forty years have passed since that time and to this day I cannot bear to see food wasted or thrown out. I still remember how hunger can affect a person. It drives people out of their minds. Hunger was so terrible that some stopped at nothing to obtain food. The cruelest act was stealing from another prisoner.

The cattle train zoomed on to the unknown. What awaited us? We didn't know. We knew what we had left behind and that we would never be able to forget it. In Auschwitz we were subjected to deprivation, hunger and hard labor. We were allowed to move only with permission, and forced to inhale air that was tainted with the acrid, sickening odor of burning flesh. We watched the never ending fires of hell rising to the sky.

As the train sped forward, I looked through the cracks in the wall. I saw a very strange scene not too far away. I saw people walking, without escorts of armed guards and dogs. They were dressed in ordinary street clothing. What was most surprising, I noticed a lady in a nice black coat, a dark red hat and a pocketbook. I could not believe my eyes. I thought that no one wore this "finery" any longer. Even more striking was the fact that these people were walking freely in all directions. After only a few months of camp life I could not recognize the outside world. It seemed almost non-existent, that no one lived outside of a concentration camp.

On this journey, as on the previous one, we had to satisfy our human needs in front of all those present, men and women. To do this before the girls, no longer bothered us. We learned to live with this in Auschwitz. Hundreds of us would go to the latrines at one time. Now, however, our audience was the male guards.

To solve this problem girls volunteered to stand in front of the girl who was using the toilets to hide her from the view of the guards. We had no blankets as we had when we came to Auschwitz. The meager bucket of water we received in Auschwitz was hardly enough, but we did not suffer from thirst as much as we did on our first trip, since it was not hot as now as it was then. When the train stopped somewhere the guards unlocked the doors and ordered the girls to take down the foul smelling bucket. Others went to fill the empty one with water.

After three days of our journey to nowhere in the crowded cattle car was halted. I looked outside and saw only a deserted, snow covered terrain. I realized that this was where we would be getting off. We had arrived. By this time our paper sleeping bags were in shreds. We didn't leave a scrap of paper behind. Instead, we made good use of them. Some one suggested that the paper wrapped around our stockingless feet would keep them a little warmer. We received an order, "Alles heraus." (Everyone out) We left the train, a strange mass of emaciated, worn out, and hungry humanity. My feet hurt when I tried to straighten them out. We could hardly stand. We had kept them bent under us for lack of space for too long and they became stiff, and they hurt. It was painful when I tried to get out of the train. I sat for three days curled up like a fetus. We helped each other down from the box cars. There was no ramp, as usual.

We lined up in fives. We were experts at this procedure. We did it quietly and quickly to avoid being beaten.

As soon as we alighted I noticed a familiar face at the head of the long line. I recognized the hated one surrounded by other SS officers. He smiled coldly and sneeringly. He knew that we were not happy to see him. He had come to "welcome" us. He left his post as commandant of Birkenau (Auschwitz) to supervise another camp. It was none other than the feared lagerfuhrer of Birkenau-Auschwitz, the brutal and merciless, pig-eyed Josef Kramer. He knew that we hated him. He and Rudolf Hess, who was the commandant of all the divisions of Auschwitz, loved it very much. Hess and his family lived in a villa near Auschwitz.

No other camp was as efficient in exterminating the Jews as Auschwitz. Rudolf Hess boasted that the facilities at Treblinka could gas only two hundred people at one time. With the improved technology at Auschwitz two thousand could be annihilated in one gas chamber. Justice was partially meted out when they granted Hess the choice of being hanged in Auschwitz, his favorite place on earth, but not before he, Kramer and Dr. Mengele exterminated three and a half million people, mostly Jews. Josef Kramer left Birkenau when the Russian Army was approaching and the Germans started to evacuate the Jews to prevent them from being liberated. He became the Commandant of Bergen-Belsen. Now we had returned to his domain for a second time, but we hadn't learned yet where we were.

As we started marching the recent snow stuck to my wooden clogs. My instinct for survival drove me on. Lagging behind to scrape the snow from the clogs was risky. I learned in Auschwitz that if you couldn't walk, rise in the morning, or work hard you were a likely candidate for the crematorium. I learned in Auschwitz that as far as the Germans were concerned they had only one commandment, not ten, and that one was, kill the Jews, the more the better. They obeyed it faithfully. We marched on.

After a long while, we reached the outskirts of what seemed to be another concentration camp. At the gate was a large poster which pictured a soldier in a foreign uniform straining to listen to a German soldier. Under the picture the caption read: "Don't talk! The enemy is listening." By this time I knew quite well who my real enemy was.

As we entered the camp we were met by a familiar site. The same painfully thin, starved and over-worked inmates we saw previously in Auschwitz, and those who were sent to Birkenau to end their miserable lives. The same rows of drab, colorless barracks on each side along the path of our march. We passed a few gates secured by armed guards. We noticed the same watch towers occupied by additional armed sentries and equipped with floodlights. The huge chimney of the crematorium loomed ahead of us. Thick, black smoke soared to the sky. But this time it did not leave a shocking impression; instead, we barely noticed it. Finally, we were led into a barrack.

Roszi, her friend and I climbed to the top of one of the berths. We had learned that the top level was better than the lower one. In the top berth you could sometimes sit up straight, without lowering your head. Also, there was no danger of the berths crashing down and killing the occupant below as often happened. We found out from other girls that we were now in the concentration camp called Bergen-Belsen, which was located near Hanover, in Germany. We also learned that Bergen-Belsen was a dumping ground.

The German thousand year Reich was crumbling. They were evacuating the Jewish occupants of other camps that were about to be liberated by the Allies. They transferred the Jewish inmates and dumped them in Bergen-Belsen. The air here too was fouled by the odious odor of burning flesh, and black smoke rose rapidly to the sky as it had in Birkenau. We were quite familiar with it.

Bergen-Belsen was an extremely large camp. It encompassed roughly six square miles. It was originally established in 1943 as a transit camp to allow Jews with the proper papers to emigrate to Latin American countries or to Palestine in exchange for Germans returning from Allied countries. Only two exchanges took place. In some ways Bergen-Belsen was better and in another it was worse than Auschwitz, if anything in this world could ever be worse than that. The only advantages of Bergen-Belsen was that there were no gas chambers and no selections for them were conducted out by a Dr. Mengele. There was no need for selections. People died "naturally" of hunger, disease and mistreatment. The worst feature, which I soon found out for myself, was the lack of regular distribution of bread and soup. A little watery soup was doled out randomly, sometimes to one camp and at times to another one. After three days I still had not received any food.

Auschwitz and Bergen-Belsen were both horrible places. Auschwitz was a death camp. Bergen-Belsen was a dumping ground. The Germans had lost territory in the East, especially in Poland. They emptied the camps of their Jewish population to preclude their liberation. They gathered the starving, sick and overworked Jews from all four corners of Europe, many arrived on foot, others in cattle cars like the one that transported me to Bergen-Belsen. All this was done in the dead of the harsh winter, without adequate clothing and without food. In this way thousands upon thousands were brought to Bergen-Belsen, if they did not die along the nightmarish way.

As mentioned, I spent the first three days in Bergen-Belsen without any food. There are no adequate words in any language to express exactly how one feels when one is starved for many days. In addition to the hunger pangs, I had no strength left. I was listless and apathetic. I could hardly walk. My stomach made loud noises. All I thought about was food. Except for the small loaf of bread, I had not eaten in six days.

Roszi, however, did receive soup once during this time. She happened to be outside in front of the barrack when the vats containing the watery concoctions were delivered. The blockalteste did not blow her whistle to announce to everyone that soup was available as was the custom in Auschwitz. Since there was not enough soup for everyone in the barrack, the blockalteste told no one about its arrival. We were perhaps two thousand crammed into one barrack which could barely house five hundred. I asked Roszi why she did not bring me a little soup. She said that the blockalteste who distributed it refused to give her any more. Roszi and I shared a berth for some three or four days in Bergen-Belsen. The barracks in Bergen-Belsen were similar to the ones in Auschwitz except that the center structures resembling an oven were not present in Bergen-Belsen units. There was no limit set for the amount of inmates occupying a barrack. They squeezed in as many as they could. I also asked Roszi why she didn't call me to get some soup. She said that it was too late, that the entire distribution took only a few minutes. I am sure the blockalteste did not believe that she intended to give the soup to someone else. I immediately rushed outside, hoping to get some. There was, however, no sign of any soup.

When the tureens of watery soup were brought out from the kitchen which could take place anywhere from ten in the morning to one in the afternoon, those who happened to be nearby received a little, while people inside the barrack did without. That meant that many would starve to death. And that is what happened in Bergen-Belsen. People die of starvation. They still kept bringing many more people into the camp. After a few days without food I felt that this surely was the end. I became desperate.

None of the girls in our barrack were working at this time. The population of Bergen-Belsen was already reduced drastically. Hard labor, lack of nourishment and beatings took their toll. Wraith-like figurines could no longer work. But there were still many who were available for slave labor.

After I had been in Bergen-Belsen for five days a selection took place during which girls were picked for "good work", as we were told by the Germans. I never believed them anyway. I had learned long ago that their promises to the Jews were worthless. They always lied to us. Now, I no longer cared where I was sent, or whether I lived or died. I could not bear the debilitating hunger. I was starved in Auschwitz, too, but there at least I received a small ration of bread once a day and one little portion of soup. It was far from enough, but it was something. Here I received nothing.

I was selected for the purportedly good job. The girls that were chosen were ordered to line up in fives and waited for the Germans to take us to the work site. I was eager to get away from here, to any place, out of Bergen-Belsen. While I was waiting in line with about two hundred other girls, my cousin Riva passed by. The line I was standing in was not very orderly since we were not supervised. Riva saw me.

I grew up with Riva. Her family lived only a few houses from us. We went to school together and we shared the same hut in the Izo ghetto. We lay together on the bare floor of the peasant's home. When I was brought to the ghetto after my unsuccessful attempt at hiding, she removed the lice from my hair. We even shared the same cattle car that brought us to Auschwitz. Riva was of medium height, slender with ash-brown hair. In Berezov I was never able to learn her true identity or to study her personality. In Auschwitz, we were separated on the first zahlappell when we entered the C-Lager. She was assigned to a different barrack. We were not allowed visit other barracks. If one occasionally disobeyed this restriction, it was done at one's own risk. Needless to say, transfer from one barrack to another was seldom, if ever possible. You stayed where you were placed. I was also separated from the rest of the girls from Berezov. I never met any of them, even in the latrine.

Of course, Riva and I were delighted to see each other. She asked me what sort of line I was standing in. I told her to go to it was for a work assignment. Somewhere, away from Bergen-Belsen I hoped. She said that she was just brought in from a labor camp, and that other places were just as bad. More food was not available in the labor camps either, and in addition the work was very hard. Here, at least, we didn't have to slave for them. She also told me that there was another girl, Yehudith, from Berezov, who came with her. I knew her very well. In Berezov the Jews were all acquainted with each other. She was a few years older than Riva and I, who were the same age. She was my older sister Rivka's friend. But since she was not married and had no children she was not sent to the gas chamber in Auschwitz as was my sister Rivka.

I walked away from the line; since we were not guarded. I decided to remain in Bergen-Belsen. Riva and I went to look for Yehudith. We found her in her barrack. We were both happy to see a familiar face from Berezov. We talked for a while and exchanged information and recalled what had happened to us up to that time. I learned that the two of them were close in the labor camp as I was with Roszi in Auschwitz. Riva and Yehudith told me that they had worked extremely hard in the place they were shipped from Auschwitz. They were brought to Bergen- Belsen only a few days before, just as I had arrived five days earlier. I now knew in which barrack they were staying. I promised to come back on the following day to spend some time with the two of them. I returned to my barrack and waited, maybe there would be a distribution of food, but it didn't happen. I was faint from hunger now.

The next day, very early in the morning, I heard a rumor in my barrack from some girls who had been outside to the effect that the Germans were taking girls to work in the kitchen. I immediately went to investigate. Before I could decide whether I wanted to work in the kitchen, I was selected by the SS. They, along with the blockova picked girls from among those who happened to be there at the time. I was ordered to join the group of those who had already been selected. When they had as many of us as they needed, they recounted us several times and marched us off accompanied by armed SS guards. We kept going for about maybe twenty minutes. On the way to the kitchen we passed a few camps and noticed emaciated inmates with dull eyes looking at us. An armed sentry was stationed at each camp who opened it for the SS who guarded us. The camps we passed were quite similar to the one from which I came, drab looking barracks for undernourished and overworked prisoners. We finally came to a long isolated structure. A number of men's camps were located across from it. The kitchen was rather secluded from the camps and surprisingly, was not surrounded by a barbed wire fence. The nearest camp was about five hundred yards from the kitchen. Bergen-Belsen looked very much like Auschwitz. There was one difference, however. The tall fences of barbed wire in Bergen-Belsen were not electrified as it was in Auschwitz. Here one couldn't commit suicide by touching the wires. The kitchen facility was about 200 yards long and perhaps twenty-five yards wide. It was divided into two sections. One for peeling and cleaning the vegetables. The other for cooking them and for making the soup.

When we reached the kitchen, our column was divided into two groups. One marched off to the left. My group entered a large room with a wet cement floor. Later I learned that the left side was for cooking the soup, the right was the peeling kitchen or schalkuche. A short, plump woman with a large face and eyes who looked to be in her thirties was wearing the familiar yellow arm band with the word "capo" in black letters on it. I learned later that she was A Polish Jew and that her name was Emma. The capo motioned to me to sit down at a rectangular table on the right side. There were a number of those tables in the large square room. She handed me a knife and told me to start peeling carrots, because that was what the other girls at the table were doing. I started, but my eyes popped when I saw the carrots. I wanted to stuff all of them into my mouth. I was starved. It was now six days since I had eaten. I watched the other girls and the capo as well.

Whenever she turned away from me I stuffed a piece of carrot into my mouth. I kept peeling and eating whenever I could. Later in the morning we all received a bowl of hot, sweet, barley soup. It was absolutely out of this world. I had never tasted anything so delicious. When I finished the soup and licked the bowl clean with my tongue I resumed peeling the carrots.

The schalkuche was a big, square room with a pool in the center. Rectangular tables flanked both sides of the pool. The door to the main kitchen was on the left. At first I did not understand why there was a pool doing in the kitchen. Later I realized that the beets, potatoes and the carrots were being washed there. I also learned, later, that this was a very wearying, back-breaking job. A truckload of potatoes was dumped into the pool and my job was to wash the soil from them by constantly moving the potatoes in the pool with a long iron fork. Pushing the potatoes around so that they rubbed against each other in the water, cleaned them.

After "breakfast" the capo held yet another selection and sent some girls back to the camp as being unfit for that work. I, however, was chosen to remain on the job. I did not know whether it was good or bad to be told to stay, but one thing was certain: I would have a little more food than I would on another assignment or not working, although I would have to work very, very diligently for it. I couldn't even see in a nightmare how hard I would have to work for the privilege of eating some raw, tasteless beets and potatoes. At the end of the first day I was able to save my bowl of yellowish beet soup. I carried it proudly to Roszi, whom I left in the barrack early that morning. I went straight to the upper level berth, proud and glad that I had something for her to eat. I knew she was starving and I wanted to be reconciled with her and keep her as a friend. I was determined even if I had to steal to bring her whatever I could every day.

When I climbed into the berth I saw strange girls whom I had never seen before. There was no sign of Roszi and her Ungwar companion. I asked the girls how long they had been in that berth. They told me that they had just arrived there that same afternoon. What happened to the girls who were here before?, I asked. They were taken to some other place. Where? They did not know. I kept asking every one but I never found out. I decided to go to my cousin Riva's barrack. There were some scraps of horse meat in the bowl. I fished them out with my fingers and ate it along the way.

Reaching Riva's barrack, I offered her the soup. I told her about my work in the kitchen. She said she already knew about it. She had visited my barrack and some of the girls told her that they saw me being selected for that job. She refused the soup. It contained no meat, only pieces of turnips. She informed me that their barrack had received soup that day, but she wanted better things such as ham and meat, now that I was working in the kitchen. She told me about a girl who worked there who brought a piece of meat for a relative in that barrack. I wanted to give the soup to Yehudith, but since she wasn't there and I did not know where to look for her, I handed my bowl of soup to a lucky stranger and waited until she finished it. I informed my cousin that I didn't work in the kitchen and that I had no possibility of getting there. The schalkuche was something else entirely. We only peeled vegetables and washed and disposed of the leavings. I could only go into the kitchen when I was sent there by the capo or the German Oberscharfuhrer who was in charge that place. I hadn't even seen ham.

At this time my "organizing" power was ineffective. I could not steal. I didn't know how. I was scared. I never got an extra ration in Auschwitz except the red beet from Lenke. I saw that the girls around me ate something other than the turnips I had. But no one told me how they got it. I knew that it came from the main kitchen where the food was being cooked. Later I learned how to obtain some food when I carried the buckets of peeled turnips to be cooked. On my way out of the kitchen I noticed a large, metal vat in which horse meat was being cooked. This vat was located near the door that separated the two kitchens. Near the center of the soup kitchen was the Oberscharfuhrer's private office. One had to be careful because he was constantly watching us from his window. I dipped my bowl into the receptacle and filled it with meat soup which I later ate with a piece of bread when the Germans and the capo were not watching. On another occasion I managed to take a piece of ham from the oberscharfuhrer's table and again, devoured it when no one was around. This ham was not for the prisoners; it was for the Germans only.

On the following day when I returned from work, Riva came to my barrack to check if I had brought her any food. I was surprised to see her. I thought she didn't want beet soup or raw beets, but only meat. She wasn't as particular as she was on the previous day when she received soup. I had some slices of turnips that I had carried out in my bosom. I brought the turnips in the event she showed up. She took them all. I was, in fact, very helpful to my cousin. She needed me to supply her with stolen food for her survival. Every morsel contributed to that end.

They transferred all the kitchen workers, myself included, to a another camp. There were two major women's camps in Bergen-Belsen and these were subdivided into smaller ones. Each consisted of a cluster of barracks surrounded by a barbed wire fence. At least a thousand girls were housed in each barrack. Later on, they crammed in many more. We were awakened at three in the morning, stood on line until the armed German SS guards arrived to count us, then they escorted us to work in the darkness and frigid cold of the night. Our day not only started early, it ended very late. Sometimes until ten or eleven o'clock at night, and sometimes earlier. Exhausted, in the clothes in which I was working, I threw myself in the berth, which had no straw mattress. Just wooden boards and one blanket.

I was not always fortunate enough to work indoors in the schalkuche peeling and washing vegetables. The carrot season was over. A few of us were given pick axes and wheelbarrows and taken to a site not far from the kitchen but very close to the crematorium. The field was quite large, and it contained rows upon rows of buried beets. Long, deep ditches were dug in the fall, and after the turnips were deposited in them, they were covered with a thick layer of soil and some straw. The soil over the turnips was piled high as a knoll in long rows. The turnips or beets were a pale yellow. The Germans called them, "steckruben". They were used to feed cattle. However, in some places it was fed to humans. We had some in our vegetable garden in Berezov. No one liked them when mother served them as a side dish. She eventually stopped planting them.

Now the soil that was piled over the beets to protect them was frozen rock-solid and covered over with snow and ice. We received the order to dig up the beets, load them into the wheelbarrows and push them to the schalkuche, to be peeled, washed and cooked.

We worked in teams of two, each twosome in a different row. One girl dug up the turnips while the other pushed the loaded wheelbarrow to the kitchen. After a time we switched. The winter day did not provide enough light by which to dig until late so they illuminated the area with huge floodlights from the watch tower right in front of us. The lights prolonged our workday. Sometimes the deep ditches filled with water from the melting ice.

I wore the wooden clogs that I received for the winter, in Auschwitz. By this time they were worn out, especially the soles where the wood had almost completely disappeared. My feet got wet, and stayed that way the entire day. There was nothing I could do to exchange the clogs for others. I tried. I asked the capo for replacements. There were none available in Bergen-Belsen. My feet remained wet until I got to the barrack late at night when I removed them briefly. The rags that I wrapped around my feet had not dried completely during the brief night. I had to wear them damp the next morning.

One morning as I tried to rise from my boards, I could not move my back. My spine was stiff and very painful. I became frightened. What has happened to me? I kept trying to raise myself. It was clearly not the right time to become ill. After many attempts I managed to get down from the berth. Fortunately I was sleeping in the lowest berth. I found it very difficult to straighten up. I tried to walk, but each time I took a step I felt a sharp pain shooting down from my back into my legs and up again to my neck, but I put on my clogs and went out to stand on zahlappell.

By the time I was outdoors every one was already lined up. We were counted and then ordered to march. As I walked I experienced excruciating pain. I made it to the work site and kept digging and loading the beets into the wheelbarrow, biting my lips until they bled to be able to endure the pain and still keep working. In Bergen-Belsen as in Auschwitz you either kept working or you died.

My back and legs hurt but I kept digging the beets and pushing the wheelbarrows, sometimes in the mud and often through the snow. I washed truckloads of vegetables with a very sore back. The pain was concentrated mostly in the lower part of the back and in the legs. Ever since that day my back and legs have never ceased to hurt. At times the pain is so severe that I am confined to bed and can only make it to the bathroom with great effort.

Near the digging site, there was an encampment of

young men, surrounded by a tall fence of barbed wire. The men ranged in age between sixteen to forty. They were all Jews from all over Europe. They were housed in barracks similar to those inhabited by the women. They would congregate near the fence and watch us as we worked. Apparently, they did not. They kept asking us for beets. God knows they were hungry, but we were constantly told not to give beets to any one. It was strictly forbidden. The men would also ask the usual questions, where we were from. When I said that I came from Berezov, a young man said that he was from Chust. "If you are from Berezov you must have travelled to Chust many times" he said. I confirmed that indeed this was true. He gave me his name, and asked me whether I knew his family. I said that I didn't.

He noticed my clogs and informed me that he had an extra pair of men's shoes. I could have them in exchange for a few beets. To enforce the rule against giving beets to anyone we were being closely watched from the nearby tower by an armed sentry. Because he was a "landsman" from Chust, and promised me a pair of shoes which I so desperately needed, I agreed to take the risk. I threw him a few beets, and he in turn tossed me the shoes, which I promptly put on right there in the field. They were, of course, made for men and were far too big for me. So I stuffed than with some rags to fill them out. It was much better than the clogs which were by this time completely worn out at the soles and heels. I would throw him a beet on a number of other occasions, and I would have continued to do so.

However, once, when I called out that a beet was for a certain man as I threw it, I noticed that the faces of the other girls with whom I worked paled. There was

210

a deadly silence on both sides of the fence. I knew something terrible had happened. I turned around, and I was face to face with the German Oberscharfuhrer. He seldom visited came to the site as we were watched from the tower. But he came at this time.

He struck me in the face and ear so hard that my head reeled and my ear began to ring. I felt a burning sensation in my head. "I will teach you," he promised, "to disobey orders. As for you," he said to the men who were standing very still, as if stricken on the other side of the fence, "you will not receive your soup tomorrow." He then turned around and walked away. I felt awful, not so much for myself as for the innocent men. I was guilty and ashamed that the entire camp wouldn't get that little life sustaining soup because I got my pair of shoes and the man from Chust had received a little extra food to eat.

When we returned to the kitchen, our capo, Emma, had heard about what transpired at the digging site. She reprimanded me and said that it was foolish and wrong for me to have given beets when we were so closely watched from the tower. "You could have been shot by the sentry. You are very lucky," she said. I felt so guilty, I couldn't sleep that night. I worried about the camp of ten thousand men who would not receive their small ration of soup because of my rash act. I wondered what the Oberscharfuhrer had in mind for my punishment. Would he shoot me? The Germans were killing prisoners for less serious offenses than stealing food. On the next morning, however, at ten o'clock the men in that camp received their soup. A girl from the kitchen rushed to the schalkuche to bring me the good news. I breathed a enormous sigh of relief. Thank goodness they had their little soup. I did not hear from that young man after the incident, but I am certain that he got the message, loudly and clearly, that I would not throw any more beets to him. The other men didn't ask for them any longer after this event.

The Oberscharfuhrer had probably forgotten his threat of the previous day. Or perhaps he had other things on his mind besides punishing me and the entire camp inmates, because he never mentioned it again.

Every day after work my cousin Riva would visit me. I always had something hidden in my bosom for her. In order to smuggle out more food for her, Riva suggested that I tie a cord to the bottom of my underpants. Since the clothes I wore were baggy anyway, I could easily hide potatoes, slices of beets, a carrot or cabbage in my pants. She always brought Yehudith with her, and as soon as they arrived she promptly relieved me of the goodies. I never asked whether she gave any of the food to her friend. At the time I assumed that she did, since they had formed some sort of an alliance for sharing. Later, I became skeptical because Riva proved to be very selfish. She thought only about herself. Forgive me, Yehudith for never offering you anything. You never asked.

One day after work Yehudith alone came to see me. I was rather surprised to see her without Riva. She told me that Riva had contracted typhus, that she ran a high fever and was so weak she couldn't rise from her lying position. I went to visit her, and found her on the floor. Their barrack had no berths. She was so feverish that you didn't need a thermometer was not needed to determine her dangerous condition. Her face was flushed. She asked whether knew a doctor. Some medical men did not reveal their profession to the Germans but worked instead at other jobs. They

212

didn't wish to practice medicine German-style, that is, to help with their "experiments". These physicians often gave advice to the sick. When I shook my head negatively, she asked for aspirin. I had none.

In fact, there was very little that I could do but continue to bring her food. There was no doctor or medication available. Even in Auschwitz there was a sick bay where some of the sick received treatment after a fashion. Those who didn't improve within the allotted time of three weeks were condemned to the gas chamber. There was no medical treatment available at Bergen-Belsen about which I was aware. Not even aspirin for fever was available. A typhus epidemic ravaged Bergen-Belsen. Riva was infected at the start. She was one of the first victims. People in the men's and women's camps came down with the disease. Since none of the stricken inmates received any medical attention, most of the infected died. Some, however, recovered despite the lack of care, although such cases were few. The Germans did nothing to curtail the spread of the disease. As the winter dragged on, more and more people succumbed. Almost 50,000 died in Bergen-Belsen. The lice, flies and the overcrowding also contributed to the rampant spreading of the scourge. It continued until the camp was liberated. After that the overcrowding was alleviated through the dispersion of the former inmates from the infested camp. The sick were sent to makeshift hospitals, while those who were well were moved to different locations.

The winter of 1944 - 1945 was very harsh. I had no blanket to protect me from the bitter cold. As they shuttled me from barrack to barrack trying to squeeze more people into the already overcrowded camp, the blanket I had in the previous barrack had to remain

213

there when I left. I must have developed a bladder infection the icy cold, because ever since I returned from work in the evening I visited Riva, I had to urinate very frequently. I must have appropriated the condition by constantly pulling my panties down outside in the bitter cold. It was simply impossible to go outside every two minutes. I was very tired from a long day's work and I could not fall asleep. Some people were still awake and talking. The lights were still on. I was lying on the boards without straw or a blanket. I was in a berth on the lowest level; I wasn't fortunate lucky enough to have a top one which was the most desirable.

After going outdoors to urinate countless times, I could no longer continue to do so. I moved the two center boards of my berth to each side forming an opening through which I rid myself of my excess liquid. To make sure that I would not make a sound and attract attention when it hit to the cement floor, I held my hand under the boards so that the urine noiselessly hit my hand and then trickled to the ground without attracting or disturbing anyone. I thought I had found a solution to my problem, at least for the time being. But I soon noticed that a stream flowing from under my berth towards the next one, and from there towards the center of the barrack. I prayed that the supervisor would switch off the light, so nobody would notice.

A woman who had not yet fallen asleep noticed the puddle and started to scream: "You will make us all sick." I begged her not to make a commotion. "I can't help it," I said. "The urine keeps running out of me. I can't retain it. I know they will throw me out of the barrack if the blockalteste learns about it. Then I will surely die outside from the terrible cold." That

214

seemed to quiet the woman. The other occupants of the adjourning berths were already asleep and didn't notice what happened.

I was awake the entire night relieving myself every few minutes. I also worried about how I could go to work if I couldn't control my bladder.

I was very fortunate. On the next morning all of the kitchen personnel were taken to the bathhouse to take a shower and to have our clothes deloused. The hot shower seemed to alleviate my problem. From the bathhouse we went straight to work. That day, after work the kitchen personnel were assigned to a different barrack.

The new one was a great improvement over the previous one. We had straw mattresses, and I was in a berth on the upper level. However, I had no blanket. I did have one for only a few days in Bergen-Belsen. On the straw mattress I felt a little warmer. At least more so than on the bare boards. In this barrack every one had a narrow berth for herself. The women's camps were located far from the kitchen. My barrack was only a ten minute walk from Riva's.

After I settled in, I went to visit Riva to let her know that I had moved. I also brought her some food, soup, bread and raw vegetables that ever one in the camps relished when they could get them. In addition to the food, she asked for aspirin. She was still quite ill. Her fever had not broken. She lay on the floor and Yehudith helped as much as she could under the circumstances. She applied wet compresses on her body. Riva had lost weight during her illness. Every one in the camps continued to lose weight, sick or not. Every time I visited she mentioned the aspirin.

God knows she needed it. But that was one item that appeared to be nonexistent in Bergen-Belsen.

In Auschwitz there was always a slight possibility that someone could get some tablets from the prisoners who unloaded the trains that entered from the outside, some of which arrived every day. All sorts of things were found in the unclaimed luggage left in the trains, including aspirin which would be pocketed by these prisoners and later sold or exchanged for bread or cigarettes. In Auschwitz, some medication was also stolen by workers in the infirmary. In Bergen-Belsen no trains arrived from the outside. They came from other camps only. As a result, there was no aspirin. The Germans did not supply any medication for the sick Jews. They preferred us dead. I tried to explain all of this to my cousin, but she kept asking me to try. She thought that I could buy anything in exchange for food. It was possible on rare occasions in Auschwitz. I returned the next day with some food. She didn't realize that her situation was not as desperate as other typhus-infected victims in Bergen-Belsen. She, at least, had some food, occasionally warm liquid and water. Others had only the meager rations. Some, nothing at all.

I walked to work each day, and when I was through I returned to my barrack, and then went to see Riva. I could not go directly to Riva's. We walked to work and back escorted by armed guards. Of course, it was not permitted to visit other barracks, and she was in a different camp, but I went anyway. I made this journey in the bitter cold and all that time I was bareheaded and my back ached. I had no scarf, just my short, bobbed hair. A young girl whom I had never seen before, or after for that matter, approached me. She noticed that I was exposed to the biting cold and probably guessed that I worked in the kitchen. She asked whether I would trade a ration of bread for a kerchief. I immediately handed her a piece of bread. It had not been stolen. I couldn't possibly do this since it was under lock and key in some unknown place. The Oberscharfuhrer personally handled the bread. I was able to save my ration because I ate vegetables instead. She then gave me a red kerchief. What was important was that my head and ears were a little warmer, added to that, it was also very becoming. It was made of cotton and not very warm, but it was certainly better than nothing.

During the entire stay in the camps, only once did I get to see myself in a mirror. A girl I had befriended had a piece of a broken mirror. She urged me to look into it. At first I refused. Everybody looked bad, skin and bones and sunken cheeks, scantly dressed in rags. What was there to look at? But I finally agreed. It was after I received the kerchief. I did not look too bad despite of the harsh conditions and probably because I had been eating extra food. The diet of raw beets and potatoes, I am sure, made some difference.

Riva was sick for a long time. Every time I took something out of the kitchen for her, I risked being apprehended. We were never sure just how the Germans were going to punish such activity. We were constantly warned not to take anything. Every now and then searches were conducted to check for food smuggling. The Germans knew quite well that the baggy clothes we were wearing could be used to hide things.

The typical Bergen-Belsen "haftlinge" (prisoner) wore ill-fitting, baggy clothes, tied at the waist with a cord, attached to which was the red tin enameled bowl we used for the soup which was our main staple. Sometimes a spoon and/or a knife and occasionally a ration of bread was tied to the improvised belt.

One day as we were finished with our work, the Germans decided to conduct a search. They always reserved the right to do this among the kitchen personnel. We were all ordered to stop on the way out, line up in single file, and every one of us was submitted to a thorough search by a number of SS men. An SS man approached every girl and ordered her to remove from her bosom and pants, whatever she had hidden there. One of them removed bread from one girl's bosom by rudely shoving his hands under her dress. The rest of us did it ourselves when the SS demanded it. All the rations of bread that each of us saved and had hid in our bosom or pants and were tied above the knees, was confiscated, as was everything else we carried in our bosoms, such as beets and potatoes. We were all sorry that we had not eaten the bread earlier. Fortunately we were treated leniently; not even a beating. We received a warning from the Oberscharfuhrer who promised that we would be punished severely the next time we were caught with food on our persons.

That day I went to visit Riva to let her know that because of the search and confiscation of food, I had nothing to give her. She was still very sick and weak with no break in the fever.

On the following day, at about five or six o'clock in the evening a tureen of soup was brought into the schalkuche from the kitchen. The capo told all of us to hold out our bowl. We realized that the soup was made from the bread they confiscated. They called that sort of soup "brotsuppe" (bread soup) and it was delicious. It was hot, thick and sweet and I was able to get a second helping. So the bread was not completely lost after all.

The bread soup was the gourmet delicacy of the concentration camps, the most popular concoction of the prisoners. I had savored it once before in Auschwitz. I also once received red beet jam in Auschwitz, another treat. They delivered a bucket of it to the barrack, and the blockalteste treated each girl to a spoonful. The lucky ones in the front of the line received two portions, but I only got one. Since we had no utensils for the jam, the blockalteste told us to hold out one of our hands, into the palm of which she placed a glob. We licked it. It was sweet and delicious, but alas, there was too little, just one spoonful.

On the following day we, the kitchen workers, once again brought food to our friends and relatives in spite of the threats from the Germans. After tasting the delicious brotsuppe in the schalkuche, we promised ourselves that after liberation we would definitely cook this favorite. However, I never tasted it again.

Before going to work one morning, the blockalteste announced that we were going to the showers and that we would be transferred to a different barrack. The block elder usually received the order from the German command to lead us. A few armed guards acted as escorts on our way to the bathhouse. I knew that whatever possessions I had with me would be left in the shower area after I undressed. Our clothes were taken from us for delousing. They were returned, still hot from the machine's shower. I had a few potatoes on me that I had smuggled out the day before. I was unable to call on Riva the previous evening because of inclement weather. I knew the

219

potatoes would be lost in the shower, so I left them in my berth. Some lucky new occupant of that berth would find the treasures in the straw mattress where I hid them.

By this time Riva had recovered enough to leave the barrack and walk over to mine. It had been about four weeks since she first took ill. On the following day when I called on my cousin she told me that since I had not come to visit her on the previous evening, she dragged herself, weak as she was, to my barrack and searched my straw mattress where she had found the potatoes. I was very happy that it was she who found them and not some one else.

That was the last shower I ever took in Bergen-Belsen.

After the last shower and the delousing, the kitchen workers were taken to another barrack which was already filled to capacity. All the berths were taken. They usually squeezed a thousand girls into a barrack this size. Now, however, they crammed double that amount into it. Because there were no berths available I was forced to sleep on the bare floor, without even a blanket to cover myself. My little black coat had to serve as a blanket for the night. When I had a cover I would fold the coat and use it as a pillow. That also insured that it would not be stolen. Sometimes, when it was very cold I would use both the coat and the blanket for warmth.

By this time, as the year 1945 moved on, the German Reich was shrinking rapidly. As a result, the Germans dumped more and more Jewish haftlinge into Bergen-Belsen. They were evacuating the other camps that were in imminent danger of being captured by the Allies. I was moved from Auschwitz only three weeks before it was liberated. Had I remained there I would have been freed on January 27 by the Russians. I learned later that the Adler sisters from Berezov were freed on that date and returned home soon afterward.

Not only were the berths all taken in this barrack, but every spot on the floor was occupied. As nighttime came when the various commandos returned from work, the overcrowding became unbearable. Now another shipment of girls had been crowded into the same barrack. If one needed to urinate during the brief night, which often happened, it became a serious problem. You had to step on, and over many of the girls and risk wetting your pants before you could make it out the door.

It was a nightmare to go out during the night. If you got outside, when you returned you encountered yet another problem. You ran the risk of losing your spot on the floor; some one might stretch a bit and your space would be gone. You either pushed in somehow by partially laying on another girl or you remained standing until daybreak.

When I was brought to this barrack I found a little space in the passage between two units of berths. To be more accurate, the spot I claimed was under a berth. The passageway was very narrow and girls who slept in the back of the two adjacent berths used it to climb up and down. When I got back to the barrack after work the floor was already packed like sardines with sleeping girls. So I looked between the berths. I saw a small area. The girls in the berths advised me not to sleep there. When they descended from the berths they would have to step on me, they warned. But I had no choice, I had to lie somewhere, and they did step on me.

I could not have retained that space for too long if it hadn't been for a Polish, Gentile woman who returned from her work before I did and guarded the spot for me every day until I arrived. She would chase every intruder who tried to take the place. We didn't talk much. We were too tired to socialize after our labors. I don't know what work she did for the Germans. When we did talk she spoke in Polish and I in Czech, both Slavic languages in which we were both fluent. I thought that she was very nice, until she later disappointed me when she chased me away after I became ill.

As people kept arriving in Bergen-Belsen our work hours were increased to approximately eighteen hours a day, seven days a week peeling and washing beets. We were awakened by a shrill whistle at about three in the morning for the regular zahlappell. After the counting we were marched off to work and did not return until late at night.

One day shortly after they brought us to this barrack, I crawled under the berth as usual after work to get a few hours of sleep. The berth over me suddenly collapsed. The whole structure with all its thirty six occupants fell top of me. The moment it happened I thought: This is it. I am dead. The girls who were awakened by the collapse of their berths started to scream. Some were hurt. Girls from other berths yelled for us to be quiet. They couldn't care less about what happened to us and just wanted to sleep. The whole barrack was in a turmoil. Here I was lying under the debris. As I heard the sounds of people calling and crying, I realized that I was not dead. The voice of the Gentile woman called to me anxiously: "Can you hear me? Can you crawl out?" We had developed a liking for each other.

I did not know whether I could get out. Maybe all my bones had been broken. I was in terrible pain. I wasn't sure that I could move my limbs because I was covered with parts of the collapsed berth. As I tried to move, some people helped me by removing the debris, and after ten or fifteen minutes I was able to get out from under the splintered wood. I don't know how I managed to survive without any broken bones, but I suffered only minor cuts and bruises. This sort of accident was fairly common. Many in the camps were killed in this way.

German cruelty towards us knew no bounds. One morning at the most ungodly hour of three o'clock, we were standing in line, waiting for an SS man to arrive for the count. The weather was miserable. Sleet and rain were falling driven by gusty winds. I was cold and wet and we were up to our knees in slush. My uncovered head was exposed as I did not as yet have my kerchief. My little black coat was saturated with the water from the snow and sleet. We were waiting for the Germans to come. We actually looked forward to an SS man's arrived to "liberate" us from standing outside in the foul weather.

After about an hour he finally came. It was no wonder that he was in a bad mood, having been forced to leave his warm bed to come out into this horrible weather to count the "damned Jews." I don't know what triggered his anger, maybe it was because I wasn't standing straight enough to suit him, but whatever it was he turned his rifle around and with the butt started beating me over my head and back. He continued to hit me, and I just froze in place. I couldn't move. While he kept pounding me, the girls from the other lines who were watching this barbaric onslaught started yelling to me in many languages.

"Run," some one shouted in Hungarian. "He will kill you." I remained in my place as if I had been riveted to the ground. He finally tired of beating me and left, but not before blood streamed profusely from my head.

When we were finally allowed to march off to work, somebody suggested that I apply cold water to my injuries, which I did. I had open wounds, several lumps on my head, and my body ached all over. What had I done to deserve such a beating? I could only think that he did it to avenge himself for having been forced to come out at this ungodly hour in the horrible weather; that brought to the surface the cruelty which was inherently present in the "noble" German psyche when they dealt with Jews. They treated their dogs, cats and other pets more humanely then they did us.

Bergen-Belsen had become the dumping ground for those stubborn Jews who were still able to cling to life despite the odds against their survival. The camp was intended to house 10,000 prisoners. By April, 1945, the population was 60,000. Not only were sleeping facilities lacking, there was hardly enough space for everyone to sit on the floors. We were sleeping in a fetal position and parts of our bodies overlapped on other girls as they did in the box cars when we arrived at Auschwitz and from Auschwitz to Bergen-Belsen. The Germans continued to bring more people to Bergen-Belsen. Most came from other camps and ghettos such as the one in Budapest. Some of those entering Bergen-Belsen had been walking for many days. Some for two to three weeks and more with hardly any food or water. They arrived sick and exhausted, mere shadows. Many died along the nightmarish journey. Others expired soon after they reached Bergen-Belsen.

Things were getting out of hand. Even the traditionally efficient Germans could hardly maintain order in the camp with such a massive number of inmates. The camp was never designed for this many people. Perhaps the camp administration neglected the camp deliberately. However it was, the Germans failed to provide even the minimum of essential services. People had not washed for weeks because there were no facilities, not even cold water as there was in B-Lager in Birkenau. There was no soap either. The overcrowding was so terrible that prisoners lay on top of others on the bare, dirty floors. It was impossible to stretch our limbs. As for food, the amount of watery soup that was prepared in the kitchens of Bergen-Belsen was hardly enough to provide the barest of minimum nourishment. No free person would have eaten that soup, it was that bad; a few pieces of tasteless beets floating in a bowl of water. To thicken the liquid, girls in the main kitchen would grate potatoes, when available. On rare occasions some scraps of horse meat labeled "not for human consumption" were added to the soup. Even this ersatz product was not available to everyone on a regular basis.

Since no one washed or was able to change their clothes for weeks, it was a small wonder that almost everyone became infested by lice; hordes of them. They voraciously fed on the prisoners' emaciated bodies. The lice were as large as a grain of rice. They multiplied in our clothes, between the seams, under our arms and in the short hair on our heads. They orgiastically sucked blood from our bodies and we were totally defenseless against them. I didn't wash or change clothes. The rags I wore didn't leave my body, not even for the night. It was too cold for sleeping in my underwear, and I couldn't lie on the bare floor without any clothes. The lice were hyperactive day and night.

The workers in the schalkuche made frequent visits to the latrine which was just behind the kitchen. If I was not busy loading or unloading something, I could go to the facility whenever I needed to. That is, we in the schalkuche had earned that privilege. When I first started to work there, we had to ask our capo, Emma, for permission to relieve ourselves. Later, however, she allowed us to use the latrine without reporting to her, but that we were warned to be careful and not to abuse the privilege. She said that no more than one or at the most two of us could go at any one time and cautioned us not to stand and talk behind the kitchen. She had good reasons for her admonitions. The watch tower was only a few hundred feet from the kitchen and from a well-aimed machine gun manned by the ever present, vigilant guard. We were in his sights whenever we made a move.

Nevertheless, each one of us went to the latrine a few times a day, not alone for the obvious reasons, but also because it gave us a short respite, a chance to straighten our backs, and an opportunity to do our own delousing. We would open our clothes and pick out the lice, killing them between the nails of our two thumbs. Sometimes we removed the dress that we wore for the entire day and night and shook it vigorously to get rid of the lice.

The lice were not only a nuisance, they also presented a serious health problem. They crawled all over our bodies, bit us and sucked our blood, and we scratched until we bled. But worst of all, they made us vulnerable for contracting typhus. No matter how hard we tried, we could never kill all of them. They were with us everywhere. They were even nicknamed "partisans" in Bergen-Belsen. The name partisan usually referred to those who fought the Germans in the underground in occupied German territories. "Now," as the adage went, "one can see the partisans marching in the streets of the camp in Bergen-Belsen."

What we called a "latrine" was nothing more than a wooden shack with a deep hole in the ground. To the left, the guard in the tower would look down upon us and watched our delousing procedure and observed when we entered and left the latrine. However, one part of the kitchen was hidden from the view of the tower guard. That was the side where we kept the pile of peels that were thrown out of the kitchen after we prepared the vegetables. Inmates from nearby camps would occasionally sneak over to the mound of peels in search of something edible. If caught by the German Oberscharfuhrer who supervised the kitchen they would be severely beaten and chased away. Whenever we went to the latrine we had to pass this mound of waste. Once, as I was passing I heard the name "Malka" in Yiddish. I stopped in my tracks, looked up and saw Aaron from Berezov, who was my father's partner in baking Passover matzos for the Jews of the town.

They began making leavened bread three or four weeks before Passover. All the young women of Berezov participated. They rolled the pieces of dough into round, thin layers in which small perforations were made so the matzo would not rise when placed into the oven to bake. The whole process had to be finished in less than eighteen minutes. Ever since I was a small child of about ten, I participated in the ritual. In the first year I poured water for the dough kneader. Later I was promoted to pouring the flour into the bowl. When I was fifteen I started rolling out the matzo leaves by myself. I would use the money I earned to buy clothes for the Passover holidays. I never had enough apparel.

But now, on my way to the latrine, I knew that my father and Aaron would never again bake matzos for the Jews of Berezov. My father was already gone, as were virtually all of the rest of the inhabitants of Berezov. They would never again need matzos for Passover. Now Aaron, my father's partner, was here calling to me from the mound of peels. I knew that he was there looking for something to eat. Everybody in Bergen-Belsen was starving. I told him to remain for a minute behind the wall, and promised that I would be right back.

I returned to the schalkuche where, under a table, I had hidden my bowl of sweet barley soup which we received for breakfast and lunch. I had not had a chance to eat it. I went back to Aaron with the bowl which I gave him. He devoured the soup. I asked him if any of my family, friends, or others whom I knew from Berezov or elsewhere were with him in the men's camp. He emphatically said no.

After liberation I learned that he had lied. Avi was with him in that same camp across from and slightly to the left of the kitchen. Avi and Aaron were well acquainted from home and had mutually engaged in some business. Aaron had not told Avi that I worked nearby because he was afraid that he would come to get food for himself and that I would give all my extra portions to Avi and none to Aaron. His fear was justified. If I had known that Avi was so near I would preferred to give my food to Avi, and some to Aaron. But he couldn't be sure of that. This was a time when everyone looked out for his or her self in the struggle

228

for survival. At that time in Bergen-Belsen, with starvation posing the most immediate threat to our lives, every little bit of food helped to prolong life even for an hour or a day. Aaron was doing his best to stay alive. After that first time, Aaron came to see me on many other occasions. It was difficult to visit, because it was forbidden to leave the premises. Besides, there were guards at the gates of every camp. I don't know how he managed to get out. I always gave him something.

Other men also came to the kitchen trying to "organize" some food, for instance, those who brought back the empty tureens from the nearby camps. After the soup was consumed, they would time their arrival at the kitchen to them afford them a better possibility of received something extra, as a beet, a potato or whatever might be available in the kitchen yard. Camp inmates would gladly eat these vegetables raw if they were obtainable. The problem was that this food was very hard to come by. Sometimes loads of beets and or potatoes that were delivered by truck were left lying on the kitchen grounds while we were busy transporting them in wheelbarrows to the schalkuche. Every man waited for his opportunity to get to the kitchen in the hope of obtaining some of these vegetables. They knew the schedule of who went when to the kitchen to return the empty soup tureens.

Two of the girls from the schalkuche were sometimes assigned to guard the vegetables on the ground near the kitchen. Quite often, I was one of them. I'm not sure why we were given this "guard" duty. Maybe the Germans had run out of SS men to do the job, or perhaps they just wanted us to do their dirty work for them. In any event, it was terrible to have to chase other hungry and starved inmates from the grounds

229

and prevent them from sneaking something to eat.

The German Oberscharfuhrer meant what he said when he ordered us to keep all the intruders away. We were given clubs, told to station ourselves in the yard and guard the vegetables or else! We would be punished if somebody made off with any of the vegetables. While we were on guard duty we were under intensive scrutiny both by the Oberscharfuhrer, who would look out of the kitchen window every so often, and by the sentries in the watch tower, who were only a few hundred yards away with their machine guns aimed at us.

Whenever the men appeared with the empty tureens, they would try to sneak a beet or another vegetable. We would pretend to chase them away. We had to. Whenever that happened we would shout at them to make sure that the Germans were satisfied that we were scaring them off, but quietly we would tell them that we wouldn't stop them if they would hurry and run off with their booty. Those who did not get anything complained about their bad luck and their poor treatment.

In all this time conditions at Bergen-Belsen continued to deteriorate. There was a shortage of food, a lack of washing facilities and disease and overcrowding was rampant. The Germans had extorted from the Jews all their material possessions and later their physical attributes by working them virtually to near death. Most of the inmates had already been reduced to the lowest level of human disparity.

The camp right across and slightly to the left of the schalkuche housed the most horrifying creatures that ever lived on this planet. They were called "mussulmaner." I previously encountered such people in Auschwitz, where they were generally regarded as crematorium fodder.

To describe a "mussulman" to anyone who has never seen one is quite impossible; their looks beggared description. Imagine some one who has lost more than two-thirds of his normal weight. Their skeletal bodies were covered with a very thin layer of skin. Because their bones protruded so much, they stretched and ir-ritated the parchment-like skin, making them vul-nerable to sores and infections to appear on the skin over the bony protrusions. Their eyes were dull and sunken in their sockets. Their cheekbones were very prominent. Their striped pajamas, the prison uniform, hung loosely on them as if they were placed on a scarecrow. When they tried to walk they shuffled. Their energy was sapped. If food was of-fered to them, they would eat, but the food entered stomachs that were unable to digest properly. The color of what was once their faces was yellow or gray.

The camp in which the "mussulmaner" existed in was also horrible. The cement floors were covered with water, the walls with mold and mildew. The poor oc-cupants were forced to lay in water. They each pos-sessed a blanket in which they wrapped themselves, whatever the weather. They carried this blanket, their only worldly possession, with them wherever they shuffled. One day a few of us from the schalkuche, accompanied by a number of armed guards, crossed that camp. We were delivering bread from a nearby warehouse to the kitchen for distribu-tion. As we passed through, these skeletal humans pleaded with us, in many languages, for bread. One begged me in Hungarian, "Edes onyukam odyal neken egy kis kenyeret". (Sweet little mother, give me a piece of bread.) Another looked very familiar to me, but I couldn't place him, he was too emaciated. After liberation Avi told me that it was his cousin from Horinch (Avi's home town). He was interned in that camp, and didn't survive.

Those creatures had once been proud people. Now all semblance of their former selves had left them. They pleaded for a piece of bread, but to no avail. They had been reduced by hunger, hard labor and mistreatment to walking cadavers. The special name "mussulman" was an appropriate one. It was camp jargon for someone frail beyond description. The mussulmen's deterioration was not only physical. It affected them mentally. They had lost all hope.

By the time we met them, they resembled zombies. The camp had so debased them that they lost their willingness to fight for survival. If an inmate arrived at this stage, he seldom, if ever, returned to normality. On the other hand, while under German control, and even after liberation, no individual or group ever tried to rehabilitate them. They were left to die without any medical care.

The Germans were exceptionally cruel to them. In this camp they were ordered, at five in the morning, to rise and leave the barracks. They were not permitted to return until eleven at night. They would spend this time outside, hot or cold, rain or shine. When soup was distributed, they had no bowls from which to eat. Inmates from an adjacent camp would throw some to them.

Some horrible events occurred in Bergen-Belsen. Close to where we were digging for beets, was a tall mound of abandoned shoes; children's, men's, women's, of various types. These came from all over Europe. Their owners' journeys ended here. The shoes were all that remained of those whose last journey ended in the crematorium or the pits, just a few hundred yards away. (All those who died in the camp couldn't be disposed of in the crematorium so they dug pits and burned bodies there also.) Clouds of black smoke billowed out of the huge chimney and from the pits and hovered in the foul air over the entire camp and beyond.

During all of the time I was in Bergen-Belsen I heard no bombings or explosions. No fighter planes appeared in the sky as they did Auschwitz. It seemed as if the war had stopped. It just continued for us. There were many rumors. By this time, however, I leant no credence to any of them. I thought that our guards might know more than we did.

SS men of other nationalities worked for the Germans in the camps. In Bergen-Belsen the non-German SS were mostly Hungarians, who were often worse than the Germans in their cruelty against the Jews.

Once, while, digging for beets, my Polish partner left with the wheelbarrow. I remained alone to gather the beets for the time when she returned. A Hungarian guard nearby sang a popular Hungarian song I had heard many times before. He rendered it loud enough for me to hear and understand the meaning of the lyrics. I thought, at that time, that maybe he was trying to send me a message. I wanted very much to believe in the words as he sang them:

> Minden elmulik egyszer
> Es minden a vegehez
> Er minden December uj

Mayust iger.

All I wanted to hear was in that song; Everything passes eventually. All things come to an end. Every December promises a new May.

Our working hours were very long and our rest periods short. Since we had no more than four or five hours of sleep, it was small wonder that my eyes became very red and painful. When I had to rise from the floor under the berth in the early morning when the shrill whistle sounded, I could open my eyes only with great difficulty. I knew that my eyes ached from lack of sleep, but there was nothing I could do about it. I was forced to walk and work in that condition.

After a while, some people noticed my red eyes. Some one told me that a doctor had recommended dipping a piece of rag in urine, and applying it to my eyes during the night. It sounded ridiculous but I was in pain and had to try anything. My eyes were getting worse. I had nothing to lose. I tried the compresses of urine for a few nights and wonder of wonders, it helped. I felt better. My eyes improved and ached less. But our sleeping periods were still too short, and the relief did not last through the short night, so during the days I would leave the cloth over one eye, and on following days I would alternate the cloth from one eye to the other. No one else was aware that I did this each day. They assumed that something was wrong with just one of my eyes. In Auschwitz I would have been sent to the gas chamber for appearing with such an ailment, even the swollen eyes were enough to condemn me to death, but at Bergen-Belsen I was permitted to live.

Passover arrived while I was slaving in the schalkuche.

I remembered the same previous holiday when I still had a family. It seemed like a million years ago. But I could still remember what a special occasion it used to be. This Passover was unlike any other I had ever known. I wanted to savor it, to make it a little different from the rest of the days. On this celebration Jews are not allowed to eat leavened bread. We eat matzo instead. Needless to say, nobody in Bergen-Belsen even saw matzos on that Passover. Even bread was not too readily available. We received a portion only once during the entire eight day holiday period. I promptly hid the bread in my bosom to eat it after Passover, even though Jews are proscribed from having leavened food in their possession during Passover and the Germans did not allow us to have any food at all. I couldn't convince myself to give it up. When I ate it later it was stale and cracked like a dried mud cake. It didn't matter. It still tasted delicious to me.

On those days when I was assigned to peel the beets instead of digging for them, guarding or washing them, I would be seated with six or seven other girls around a rectangular table. As we cut the peels from the beets they fell to the ground under the table. A girl thought of a way to help us get a little more sleep. Every half hour another girl at our table would slide down under it and lay down on the wet, cold cement floor among the wet and dirty peels. When the German guard approached, the other girls would kick the sleeping girl under the table and she would come up, pretending that she was picking up pieces of beets that had fallen. In this way, every girl at the table was able to get a little extra sleep. We also had a little more food than the others. As a result, we were the envy of the camp. Everyone wished they had a family member or a friend working in the kitchen who would

235

obtain stolen food like beets or potatoes. But no one cared to work there. The work was much too hard.

All of this time I was working with a very painful back, legs, and eyes. When I lifted the heavy buckets of cut and washed beets to carry them to the main kitchen, I was in agony. It was especially bad when I had to haul the potatoes or beets out of the pool, after I had finished washing a truck load.

I was rather conspicuous because of the patch on one of my eyes. To call attention to one in any way in a concentration camp was very bad. The Germans always noticed me and called on me to work harder than the other girls. The Germans preferred every one to look alike, a mass of bodies, mere numbers. If they noticed someone who stood out they made him or her a prime target for cruelty.

My patch even received a special name from the girls in the schalkuche. They called me Jan Ziska, after a Czech hero who had fought for the freedom of his people. Jan Ziska (1376- 1424), was a Bohemian military leader whose success on the Hussite side against the German king Sigismund established him as a hero of Czech nationalism. He was blind in one eye which he covered with a patch. I wish somebody could have foreseen the future and decided to call me Moshe Dayan. I would have liked that better.

I didn't object to being called Jan Ziska. But at the time I was not fighting for any one but myself. To stay alive in Bergen-Belsen for one more day, one more hour was a difficult feat under existing conditions.

We had not changed our clothes for a very long time.

Was it weeks? It seemed like months. I lost count. I was still wearing my little black coat. It served its purpose during the day and I used it as a blanket briefly during the cold winter nights. Whose coat had it been? Where was she now? Alive or dead? And who was wearing my nice, dark red one for which it was so difficult for my father to raise the money? He had to sell a parcel of land to pay for my sister Rivka's wedding and to buy me the coat, which was taken from me in Auschwitz. The Germans used hundreds of inmates in Auschwitz to sort, clean and pack the good things they seized from the Jews. They were sending them to Germany. Was some German Fraulein wearing my red coat? She was undoubtedly warm while I was freezing in my threadbare, dirty rag.

The kitchen and the digging site for beets were near the crematorium, and I could see the carts with the dead as they passed by on their last journey to the ovens. They were just thrown onto the wagons by other inmates. There was a special commando whose job it was to gather up the corpses and deliver them to the crematorium. One would hold the legs, the other the hands. They would toss the bodies on the cart as if they were so many discarded rags or chords of wood. Arms and legs would dangle from the conveyance, eyes were still open, staring out from their sockets at an uncaring world which did nothing, to prevent their destruction. They were nude, since they were stripped of their last shreds of clothing by their suffering comrades. They were carried in what the Germans called "straich wagens," which consisted of a flat bed on four wheels. These carts were pulled by other emaciated prisoners.

If I live for a thousand years, I could never forget or

forgive the debased specimens of humanity for what they did to those on the carts and to all of us in Bergen-Belsen. It is indelibly etched in my soul. I sadly watched these transfers of dehumanized, twisted bodies, from morning until night, day after day. I would think that one of those innocent souls whom the Germans killed in cold blood, but first reduced to a "mussulman", was one of my brothers, cousins or people whom I knew and loved. Hatred of the cowardly killers became an obsession with me.

One day I was washing the beets at the pool with a Polish girl. She told me that she had come from the Warsaw ghetto where an uprising broke out. I had never heard of it, although the rebellion had occurred in early 1943 when we were still free. She was present at the time, and told me that the Jews who fought were outnumbered and outgunned. They could not possibly win. The slaughter of those who were caught was terrible. When the Germans set the ghetto ablaze, human torches kept jumping from the inferno. It was useless and pointless, she said, to fight the Germans in the first place. She told me that many Jews in the ghetto had opposed the uprising. As I listened to her, I thought that it was rather symbolically brave that at least some Jews had the guts to fight the invincible Germans and to kill at least a number of the "supermen."

After a few weeks Riva's fever began to lower, and she started to improve. I visited her every day, no matter how late I worked. With few exceptions I always brought something for her. The extra food certainly helped to improve her health, and quite possibly saved her life.

There was a rather thin girl that I met in camp who

238

was living in Riva's block. I never knew her name and I wasn't her friend. I just happened to recognize her from Auschwitz, working in the weberei. I think she was Hungarian. Whenever I saw her in Bergen-Belsen I would give her something, a potato or a piece of turnip. I had once foolishly risked my safety in her behalf. One One day I saw her when she passed by the kitchen on the main road of the camp as part of a long line of girls who were supervised by women SS. I happened to be guarding the vegetables in front of the kitchen at that time. On a sudden impulse I took a piece of bread out of my blouse which I had saved from my ration and threw it to her. I probably did it because she looked so young and vulnerable. She appeared to be sixteen or seventeen at the most. If so, she was younger than I, and I felt sorry for her, having to struggle in Bergen-Belsen at such a tender age. I realized only later how dangerous it was for me to toss her that piece of bread. Her convoy was heavily guarded and so was I.

When I visited my cousin, that girl recognized me. She was present with some of her friends who were huddled on the bare floor near the entrance. Their barrack had no berths at all, and every one was lying on the floor, pressed closely for lack of space. Her friends asked me to give her something. By that time she had become very thin and was probably sick. I told them that I had very little. They begged for a little bit of sugar.

Had they asked for a beet I would gladly have given them one, but I never got any sugar. I saw sugar only once, when our capo, Emma, ate some on a slice of bread. This was a concentration camp delicacy, which few could obtain. When Riva heard that those at the door (as she called them) talked with me, she wanted to know what they wanted. I told her that they asked for some food, and that one of them was probably sick.

Riva demanded that I give them nothing. "Give everything to me," she said, pointing with her forefinger to her chest. By this time, I had been conditioned to obey orders; from the Germans, the block leaders, capos and the like. I even obeyed my cousin's orders. The Germans had really drilled that into us. So at this time I didn't offer the sick girl a piece of turnip or a potato that might have helped her.

Riva was not the only one stricken by typhus. The disease spread through the camp like wild fire. As the ice and snow started to melt in March, the sun began to shine, although not to our advantage. It looked like this would be our last spring. The few primitive latrines filled up, and were not cleaned out. Besides, the sick could not reach them, so they relieved themselves wherever they happened to be lying. The sun now beamed down on the filth, and huge flies began to gather around the open latrines. The flies and the lice that were abundant in Bergen-Belsen spread the typhus rampantly, killing thousands of people. In March of 1945 alone almost 20,000 perished. Another 17,000 died during the first half of April. They were stricken and expired from lack of nourishment and medical attention. The only well-fed creatures in Bergen-Belsen were the disease-carrying lice, flies and the Germans.

When the beet supply in the ditches was exhausted, a truck arrived at the kitchen daily to deliver beets or potatoes. When it arrived two of our girls were assigned to unload the truck while the German driver looked on. I was usually one of the two who were selected, probably because I was conspicuous and the most easily remembered because of the patch over my eye.

The driver addressed me with the informal "du" as he said, "You come here." If he didn't see me he would ask, "Where is the one with the one eye?" As I opened the tail gate and struggled to unload the cargo, he would smoke a cigarette, enjoying his superior status. He watched me while I worked without lifting a finger to help. After I emptied the truck, he drove away, but I still had to carry the beets on a wheelbarrow to the schalkuche and set them into the pool. That was very arduous, backbreaking labor.

I was selected for another "special" job. A German soldier with a horse and wagon (not the kind used to transport the dead, but one with four sides), that arrived every second day to pick up the beet peelings that we threw out in a heap outside. I would use a large shovel and fill his wagon, while he stood by, humming a tune. The soldier told me that the peelings were used to feed the pigs. I had heard that the SS were fattening them somewhere in the camp for their own use. They were very thrifty, and did not waste anything but innocent Jewish lives.

When the typhus epidemic struck, the long procession of wagons bound for the crematorium increased a hundred fold. I watched them rolling from dawn until late at night. They passed the kitchen on the main road loaded with twisted and tortured bodies on their way to their final destination; the pits. After the bodies were consumed by the fire, not even the Germans could humiliate and further debase them. Those intertwined bodies were so unbelievably thin that their flimsy skin covered only shrunken and broken bones.

241

The hollow unseeing eyes still open wide, seemed to look at the world in anger because it failed to protest their bestial German treatment.

Other painfully thin, dehumanized and deprived souls were pushing those wagons loaded with their brethren knowing full well that tomorrow or the following day they, too, would be in those wagons driven by other godforsaken humans to the crematorium. All those destined to enter Bergen-Belsen were forsaken by God and man.

The ghastly parade of the wagons continued all day. It seemed endless. The Germans poured gasoline over the corpses in the pits and cremated them. When gasoline became scarce the Germans proved their ingenuity again. They ordered inmates to dig up roots of trees cut long ago. They burned the roots with the bodies in the ditches.

One morning, at about the end of March, I tried to rise from the floor when the whistle blew, something I did every morning. This time I could not get up no matter how hard I tried.

In the past I was always able to will my body to rise, even when suffering severe pain as I had done months earlier when my back and legs started to ache. At that time I forced myself to get up and go, bend, lift and push the wheelbarrows. It was hell, but I did it. I knew only too well what happens when one refuses to try. The next phase was to deteriorate into a "mussulman," to be spiritually dead. After that, the final destination was the crematorium or the pits.

The gentile woman who lay near me in the berth saw my futile struggle to get. She told me that I was

242

flushed. And so she touched me on the forehead to however unscientifically, check my temperature. When she found that I was running a high fever she told me to get away from her because she was worried that I would infect her with my disease. This was the same woman who had saved my place on the floor earlier. At that point I realized that I had contracted typhus. I was burning with fever.

Now I was really afraid of her. I didn't want her to report me so I crawled away to a different spot, and stretched out on the bare floor. I did not report for work. By then not only was food unobtainable, but water was also not available. The Allies were getting close, although we didn't know it, and the water supply to the camp had been completely cut off by the Germans. I had no medicine with which to treat myself and no food or water. Riva and Yehudith came to my barrack on the following day to pick up the food that I usually brought. They came because I had not gone to their barrack to make my regular delivery to them. Instead of finding food for them, they found me on my "death bed".

They helped me to a berth which was vacant because its occupant had gone to work. All Yehudith could do for me was to fan me with my kerchief. During the night I had to get back on the floor and lie wherever I could find a place. Then, in the morning, when the other girls left for work, I moved into a berth. I didn't even have a drop of water to wet my parched lips. After a few days, my coated tongue was sticking out like a mad dog's. One morning Riva and Yehudith came to visit me and brought me a little muddy water that they had scooped out of a puddle formed by the accumulation of the night's rain. I couldn't drink the dirty water, but I could wet my lips and mouth. Yehudith also wet my kerchief and applied it to my burning body. The cool compress felt good.

Riva and Yehudith came by once at noon and they told me that they had gotten soup outside the barrack. I asked Riva why she didn't bring me also a little bit of soup. She answered that the blockalteste who distributed the soup wouldn't give her a second portion. It hadn't occurred to her to bring me some soup from the first portion. After that she didn't come anymore. I had nothing to give her.

One evening, after many days of languishing on the floor, ravaged by the fever with no food or water, the Jewish capo Emma, who supervised the schalkuche, entered the barrack. When she saw me on the dirty floor, she shook her head sadly. "You too, Monci?," she said. She looked at me with sorrowful eyes. She was the only concentration camp official who addressed me by my name and the only capo who didn't beat me. Emma brought a bowl of hot coffee with her. She handed it to me and told me to drink only a little. As my lips touched the warm, sweet liquid, I thought that I had never tasted anything so delicious.

She started to say, gently at first, that I should stop and return the bowl to her, but I couldn't keep from swallowing the coffee. She had to take it from me by force. In a loud voice she was telling me that she also wanted to give other sick people something to drink.

One day, late in the morning, the barrack was almost empty. Only those whose job it was to take care of the barrack were left, except for myself. I had moved in to a berth as I would usually do during the day so that I would not have to lie on the floor. It was the third berth from the entrance on the left. I chose the lowest one. I knew that in a higher berth I would be better protected from the camp officials, but I couldn't reach the higher one. That day, as I was lying there, a German SS officer entered and started to walk through the barrack very slowly, frequently turning around to stare at me. I, too, looked at him. I I don't know why. But since he looked at me so intensely I stared back. He finally continued on his deliberately paced stroll to the other end of the barrack. Then he came back to where I lay.

As he returned he kept looking at me then walked to the door and left. I was frightened when I saw him, because SS officers would not usually enter the barracks of the Jews which were by now not only filthy but infested with typhus, lice, and dysentery. We were considered highly contagious, vermin, suffering from all the diseases common in such an environment. We were to be avoided at all costs. It was not clear why he had entered, but he certainly had the authority to order the sick evicted from the barrack which was supposed to house only those who were able to work.

When the girls returned from work I told several of them about the SS officer who entered the barrack and looked at me with seeming intent. They told me not to stay in the same barrack with the working girls, since I was no longer able to work. I was worried that I would be removed from the barrack and put in one of those wagons bound for the crematorium. The Germans didn't have to wait until I was dead to send me there. The girls helped me get into another barrack where the sick women were left to die without food and water. In the new place I lay on the floor during the day and night. All the berths were occupied by others, and no one left for work during the day.

To make matters worse, in addition to the fever, I
suffered from diarrhea. It got so bad that I lost all
control over my body. Gallons of dirty water gushed
out of me. I could not raise myself or walk to the
overflowing latrines. In the beginning, since I lay
near the door, I ventured out on very shaky legs and I
relieved myself against the wall of the barrack not far
from the door. After a few days I couldn't even reach
the door. So I rolled over and relieved myself only a
few inches away from where I was lying. I needed to
defecate every few minutes. Even crawling a few
inches away soon became impossible. I wound up
lying in excrement. The stench was horrible. My
clothes were filthy. All I yearned for was a drink of
water before I died.

I was parched. The girls told me that water would not
be good for me anyway. I lay for days in the reeking
feces without food, water or medicine. Riva did not
come again. I had nothing to give her, and she was
probably worried hat she might contract the disease
again.

Once, late at night as I lay in the filth, I heard a commotion in the barrack. Somebody let me in on the
guarded secret that a hidden room had been forced
open, and that a supply of water had been discovered.
The blockalteste had secreted it for herself.

Girls, desperate for water, had broken into the room.
Now people were running back and forth from the
little room. I mustered all my strength and crawled to
that room, not really believing that I would find
water. When I entered the room, to my happy
surprise I saw a big barrel filled with water. I lowered

246

my head into it, and drank the cool water for a long time. I filled my belly to its capacity.

However, I could not retain any of it. As soon as I swallowed the water it rushed unimpeded right out of me. But it had turned green. I concluded that drinking water must be bad for me, and that I would surely die. At least my wish was granted. My life hung in the balance for about eight days. Gallons of green urine were flowing out of me, but by then there wasn't even a drop of liquid left to replace it. I craved water again but none was available.

The days dragged on. The only question left in my mind was how many more days would pass before I would die. The fever and the diarrhea were consuming me.

But then, after what seemed an interminable length of time, the diarrhea stopped, and the high fever of fourteen days finally broke. The disease, however, had left me very weak. I hadn't eaten in more than two weeks, and all I had to drink was the little coffee that Emma had given me and the water from the blockalteste. Small wonder that I could not remain on my feet. My tongue was so badly coated and painful from the fever that it would take a long time to heal. Ten years after that horrible time I would still suffer from scars on my tongue.

Now that I was recovering, I decided to visit my cousin. I thought she would welcome me with open arms. There, at least, I would be with a friend and relative whom I had known in my previous life. I reached her barrack with great difficulty. I had to crawl under a fence that separated the two camps. The walking itself accomplished with great exertion. I had to stop and rest after every few steps. I succeeded by sheer will power only. The girls at the door noticed that I was sick and that I hadn't brought any food as I did previously. Now I was just like one of them. My cousin was not too happy to see me either.

I stayed the night. On the following day my cousin informed me that the girls at the door wanted to vengefully repay on me for not bringing them sugar a while back. They threatened to turn me in to the blockalteste, informing her that I was staying in that barrack "illegally". It was a serious offense, and the blockalteste would mete out punishment before disposing of me. Or maybe she would turn me in to the Germans. I didn't know, but I was scared. Now I was "homeless". I did not belong in any barrack. My cousin told me all of this, but now I was not so sure that they really would have gone through with it. She may have been lying just to get rid of me. I was about to leave for some other place. I didn't feel like going back to that filthy barrack in which I had been so ill. I didn't dare to return my former "working" barrack. I thought that I would just walk into any barrack and find a spot on the floor.

My cousin wandered away the next morning, and I waited for her return. I was weak and lay on the floor with Riva's two blankets, contemplating how quickly things change. I was a valuable relative while I had some largess to offer. Now that I had nothing I was worthless.

I just hoped that if I got well again I might be able to go to work. I lay on the floor in my cousin's barrack. Every one huddled there. My cousin returned with a bowlful of red sauerkraut. I mistakenly thought that she intended to share the cabbage with me, since I had brought her food the day I began working in the peeling kitchen. I foolishly risked being caught by stealing the food I brought to her. And I was also in danger of contracting the disease from her. The food I brought probably saved her life. However, my cousin had other ideas. She told me that I would find it hard to imagine how difficult it was for her to obtain the cabbage. A group of desperate inmates had broken into a cellar at a time when the German guards were not present. Everybody wanted to get some food. By that time that necessity in Bergen-Belsen was virtually nonexistent.

Although the cellar was filled with huge barrels of cabbage, it was almost impossible to get to them. The pushing and shoving was so insistent that people were killed in the struggle for a bowl of cabbage. Some fell to the ground and were trampled by others who tried to reach the barrels. My cousin told me that when I brought her food, it was not as difficult to get it. "You just took it," she said. "Besides," she said, you shouldn't be eating cabbage anyway. It is not good for you. And beware of the blockalteste, she already knows about you. You'd better leave before she comes after you."

I tried to find another block where people wouldn't mind if I joined them as they crouched on the floor. I was never sure whether the girls at the door had actually threatened to turn me in, or if it was just a story conjured up by my cousin to make me leave. If it really was true that they wanted revenge, she was not even a little sorry for having caused me all that trouble. They only saw me when I brought her food, and she was the one who insisted that I give them nothing. "Give everything to me," she said. Now that she was well and I was ailing and didn't have anything more to give her, I was of no further use to her.

At about this time, in April, at the height of our misery, death, hunger, thirst, filth, disease and lice, we heard a rumor that we would be receiving bread. I had heard that story when I lay sick in the barrack. I hadn't seen bread or soup since my illness precluded my working. As it is true about so many rumors, this one did not come to pass. Thank heaven for that. Later I learned that the bread we were supposed to receive had been baked with poison. It was planned for distribution to us before the British arrived so that we would all die just prior to our liberation. Our saviors would have found a gigantic graveyard. There would have been corpses on the ground or on the floors of the barracks.

As it turned out, even without the poisoned bread, when the liberators arrived they saw something so ghastly, they would never forget it. Mounds of corpses were wildly strewn about, and those who were still alive did not look much better. When food was supplied it was so meager that people died from malnutrition. In the two weeks before freedom, from about the beginning to the middle of April, no food was rationed to most of the inmates. Maybe some of the barracks near the kitchen did receive a little watery soup, but in my barrack there was nothing.

Small wonder the sick and the starved had died. Surprisingly, they did not kill us as they had intended, and as I later learned they did in many of the other camps. In those cases they murdered the Jews sometimes only an hour or less before the Allies entered the camp. The Germans were that dedicated to the extermination of the Jews. Losing the war was secondary to wiping us out. The bread had not been distributed because the commandant, Josef Kramer, apparently wanted to save himself, to become a righteous German in the eyes of the world and the Allies and to receive a reward for being so noble.

The British arrived in Bergen-Belsen on April 15, 1945. It was a beautiful spring day, but no one in the camp noticed. Thousands of men and women were lying on the floors, sick with typhus.

There had been no water in the camp and no food distribution at all for a very long time. People were dying by the thousands from starvation and typhus.

Those of us who were not already dead had little hope for salvation. For the previous three days no order had been issued for the removal of the dead to the crematorium as was the custom, so no one bothered to do it. They were just tossed outside to make room for those of us who were still alive.

The dead accumulated by the thousands. Those who were able to walk ventured outside of the barracks, and when they returned they said that there were no guards at their posts. Of course, none of us believed them. How could the guards not be at their posts? It wasn't possible. More people said that they saw no. My cousin Riva said that there were no guards at the cabbage cellar. The Germans had just vanished. Unbelievable, but true.

After a while, someone else came in and said that there were British soldiers in the camp. In the past, the rumors had never been so hopeful. Although it was still incredible; I had not heard any shooting. It couldn't be true. The girl who reported that the British were in the camp must have made a mistake.

251

She probably saw some Germans and mistook them for British. I decided that I had better check this one out myself. I longed to see at least one uniform that didn't belong to a bloody German.

I ventured out of the barrack on shaky legs, weakened by typhus, hunger and thirst, and finally saw, a blessed British soldier. It was a sight that I had yearned for, for so long.

I continued walking, looking around warily. There were no guards. Impossible! Then I came to the center of the women's camp. I saw British medics disinfecting barracks and transporting the sick in ambulances. This was in a different part of the camp, quite a long distance from my cousin's barrack. I did not care to return to her place to visit with my loving cousin. Although now I was no longer afraid of being turned in to the blockalteste. I had difficulty in walking and I was very weak from lack of nourishment for at least two weeks. Reaching the center of the camp to see the British was worth the exhausting effort. Going back wasn't.

We became delirious with joy when we saw our liberators, who finally freed us and put an end to our nightmare. One thing was very strange: we could walk out of the gate with no guards to stop us. We could go wherever we pleased. People found friends and relatives. We looked at each other with eyes that said freedom, but we could not yet fully grasp its tremendous import. We had suffered in bondage for too long to adjust ourselves to our liberty so suddenly. I returned again and again to see the British medics, to convince myself that the German reign of terror was finally over and that their retribution had also come. I had hoped and prayed that I would live to see and rejoice over their downfall. The desire to see them on their knees as we had been was so strong in me that it kept me alive. I couldn't tear myself away from the medics. I was afraid that if I didn't continue to watch them, they might disappear as in a mirage.

Now it was a beautiful experience to stroll out in the sun. Previously the sun had hurt us. It would heat the filth in the overflowing stinking latrines. But now the sun was pleasant; it was warm and resplendent. I walked slowly of necessity. In the distance I saw my friend, Roszi. I called out to her. She turned to see who was calling her. When she realized who it was she wouldn't speak to me, but continued to walk. She was extremely thin and her sunken cheeks resembled two holes. She never forgave me for eating the piece of German bread in the box car.

I hate and despise the bloodthirsty Germans even now after so many years for starving and degrading me to such an extent, that I refused to surrender a small piece of bread to a friend. I was that starved.

Roszi never knew that I had been looking for her, and that I had wanted to atone for taking the bread, no matter to whom the German bastard had thrown it. I wanted to give her my bowl of soup on the first day I worked in the kitchen. I would have made it up to her a hundred fold, had I found her.

I also met Udel, the girl with whom I hid in Berezov what seemed a century ago. She was with two other girls from Berezov. One was named Golda, and the other Udel's niece, Frida. Golda and Frida had both been my friends a long time ago. The three of them had managed to stay together all the time and were never separated even when they were transferred from camp to camp. They were brought to Bergen-Belsen just a few days earlier. Golda and Udel were inseparable, although Udel was much older. Frida was very sick. Her body had shrunken so much, she looked like a little girl of ten instead of a twenty year old. She could not even talk. Golda told me that Frida had not eaten anything in a very long time. In their previous labor camp Frida lost the desire to eat. The meager rations she received she gave to her aunt, Udel. All she did was swallow water, a lot of it, which gave her an extended belly. Her entire body had indeed become swollen. Even now she eschewed food but continued to drink water.

On the first night of liberation I wandered into another barrack, close to the British medics, no longer afraid of being reported to the blockalteste. I found a place on the floor between two berths and I lay down. I remained in that barrack for a few days. The British started to distribute bread. I took the rations and placed them under my head to safeguard from thieves. I accumulated a number of portions and guarded them zealously. I could not eat anymore. I was only extremely thirsty but not hungry. I saved the bread because I was afraid that the British might be forced to retreat and that the Germans would return, in which case, I would still have a supply of bread. I did not think that I would go with the British if they retreated. All I could think of was the bread I had craved for so long and which I could no longer digest. I had been starved for too long.

In my new barrack, the girls who had berths appeared healthier than I did. They partook of some delicacies from cans I had never seen before, and was unable to identify. I was told that these girls worked in the kitchen. One, who was sitting in a nearby berth offered me some of the canned food she was eating.

But another girl in the top berth said that I should not eat anything from the can if I had typhus. I could not swallow any food even if I wanted to. Instead, I was craving tea, but it was not available. All I had to drink was water which was made obtainable by the British. But they gave us no tea or coffee which I wanted so urgently. On the second day they brought vats of warm milk into the barrack. They placed them near the door. Everyone was asked to come forward for a bowlful of the milk. I hadn't tasted any since I left the ghetto. It seemed so long ago. I did not take any milk. I was just unable to drink it. A girl from the upper berth called down to me and asked, "Why don't you go for milk. It's good for you." I did not move. My insides were burning, and all I wanted was warm tea or coffee. As we, the few girls from Berezov, wandered outside, Golda collected some leaves which had started to sprout. She placed her bowl on three stones, made a fire with some dry twigs, and boiled water for improvised "tea" and offered some to me. I wanted to drink more of that concoction, but she took the bowl. She wanted some for herself. The British came each day and asked for volunteers for kitchen duty. I would have loved to work there, but I was too weak and sick.

My cousin Riva came along to see the British who were stationed mostly in the center of the camp. She had explored the entire area and found a hidden warehouse used by the Germans to store clothing they seized from the Jews. She brought some dresses for herself and a packet of men's shirts for her brother, Yankel, who she was certain had survived. She was wrong, unfortunately.

255

I, too, wanted some better clothes for myself instead of the rags that I was wearing. I still had the little black coat with the red cross on the back and the striped square set in. The tattooed number on my arm was still visible on the left side of the front of my coat. I did not bother to remove it. It became an integral part of me. I still wore the same dress I received in Auschwitz. I asked my cousin to tell me where she found the clothing.

She tried to give me directions of the warehouse, but I knew I wouldn't find it, so I asked her to accompany to the place. She reluctantly agreed.

There were a large quantity of clothes in the warehouse, all gathered in a large heap of unsorted varieties for men and women. I found three dresses which I thought might fit me after I gained some weight. I was extremely thin now, having lost a great deal of weight. My mussulman-like complexion was a yellowish-gray and I could hardly propel my feet when I walked. There was one dress that I liked very much, but I never got the opportunity to wear it. When I lived in the barrack I hid the dresses, together with my bread, under my head for safekeeping. I asked a girl nearby to look after them for me when I went out, but there was no longer any need for stealing.

As I was walked from one camp to the next, on the third day of liberation, I saw corpses everywhere I went; mounds of them, decomposing in the sun. I arrived at the kitchen where I had previously worked.

I noticed two mussulmaner near the entrance, still wrapped in their blankets despite the fact that the warm sun and rising temperature. Each one had seized a case of conserves (There were no guards now),

and they carried their booty to the horrible mussulmaner camp across from the kitchen. However,
before they reached their destination a cruel irony intervened, they dropped dead on the cases of food of
which they had been deprived of for so long. Now
that they finally had their food, albeit too late for
them to enjoy it.

I saw a number of Germans, some still wearing their
uniforms, and others who were already attired in
civilian clothes. They were employed to clean,
remove and carry away the thousands of corpses strewn
everywhere. The British arrested the SS ad-
ministrators including the camp commandant Josef
Kramer. Most of them were put to work burying the
thousands of decomposed bodies.

People were still dying and adding to the tremendous
total of those who had already expired. (Another
14,000 of the survivors died after liberation. Almost
all the rest needed medical attention.) Previously,
they had died from lack of food. Now their lives were
being ended by the food that they were eating. Their
shrunken stomachs could no longer digest what they
ate. To rehabilitate these skeletal beings more than
food was needed.

During the three day interval between the period of
the Germans abandonment and disappearance, and the
British arrival, Bergen-Belsen hosted more dead bodies
that an thousand grave diggers would ever see during
their lifetimes.

A putrid odor permeated the camp. The British used
bulldozers to move the huge numbers of rotting bodies
into one place. Then they ordered the few captured
Germans to dig a common grave for all the remains. I

deemed it unfair in the least, that so many, who had lived through sheer hell, did not survive to celebrate the end of their suffering.

We walked from camp to camp. Mingling with men; the sexes no longer segregated. I looked for my brothers, friends or other relatives, but found none.

All of us from Berezov talked about Frida going to the hospital, since she was so sick, a mere shadow of her former self. All one had to do was walk up to one of the medics who were busy placing girls on stretchers. As soon as the ambulances returned, they were placed in them and rushed away.

Many more girls, perhaps hundreds, were waiting on stretchers in the sun. The whole plaza was crowded with them. The medics sprayed disinfectant on everything, including the girl's heads. The girls from Berezov decided that I should be responsible for having Frida transferred to a hospital. I took her hand and approached a medic. I pointed to Frida and said "krank," which means "sick" in German. He understood, although I could not say it in English. Just looking at her face and body it was quite obvious that she was gravely ill. He sprayed her with disinfectant and asked her to undress. He placed her on a stretcher, and I returned to the girls who were waiting. I was also very weak. I was a long way from total recovery from the typhus. My friends convinced me to go to the hospital also.

I approached a medic once again and tried to let him know that I wanted to enter the hospital. I pointed to myself and said "'spital," and then I touched my head. He sprayed D.D.T. on my hair. Then placed a pair of scissors at my neck below my chin, and cut my clothes through the center all the way to the bottom. The lice infested rags that I was wearing, which never left my body during the day or night for the past several weeks, fell to the ground. I was nude. This time, however, I had my hair, and I did not care for the clothes I had been wearing. I looked at the heap of dirty rags. "Goodbye little black coat. I will never see you again, but I will always remember you. I didn't like you at all, but you served me faithfully. You were all I had against the bitter cold during the long days and nights."

The medic placed me on a stretcher, wrapped me in a blanket and placed me in the long line of girls who were also lying on stretchers. Soon, I was put into an ambulance with three other girls.

As it sped away, a girl in the ambulance asked in Hungarian if there were any people from her country there. I was the only one who answered her question. I said that I spoke her language though I wasn't really a Hungarian. Many of us from the Carpathian region spoke Ruthenian, a Slavic language, and most of us spoke Yiddish.

A weak voice in the ambulance said "Is that you Malka? Are you here too?" It was Frida. She had recognized my voice. Although she had been placed on a stretcher earlier, we were in the same ambulance. We had not been riding very long when we stopped. Two medics removed each of our stretchers, and we were brought into a large room, placed on a table and German nuns began to wash us. I was afraid of them. No German could be trusted, including nuns. I thought about the red cross ambulance in which the Germans had delivered the Cyclon B gas in Auschwitz. Now, nuns or any other Germans would surely harm us. I hoped that the British would stop them. As they started to wash me I began to feel better. It felt so good to be cleaned with real soap and warm water. I hadn't showered in the past two months.

They carefully examined my hair. One of the nuns reported to another that I was clean. "No lice here," she said. It was a fortunate coincidence that two days after liberation I had asked Riva to pick the lice out of my head. I couldn't stand them crawling in my hair, the itching and the constant scratching. Riva picked out each nit with her fingers. If the nuns found any lice they would cut off my hair again. They did that to many girls.

After they had finished with me the two nuns wrapped me in a white, clean sheet. This time one of the medics picked me up and carried me to a room on the second floor. I was put into a bed with a mattress and clean white sheets. I was really surprised. Frida was placed in the bed next to me.

There were four girls in the room, which was quite large, about seven square yards. Our two room mates were young girls of about nineteen years of age, and Hungarians. Both had suffered from typhus and were brought from Bergen-Belsen. During the first few days no one talked. Each of us just lay there and enjoyed the beds. It had been such a long time since I slept in one. It was the only "medicine" we received in this hospital.

This makeshift medical facility was not like any other one I had ever known. The only person who came into our room was a Polish, gentile volunteer. She was about five feet tall, and about twenty-five years old. She wore a white hospital robe. She spoke some German and could barely communicate with the Hungarian girls. There was no need to. Her only function was to bring food to each of us, three times a day. No nurses or doctors were available to examine or treat the patients. This volunteer placed our trays on small tables located near our beds. We were free to eat or not what was offered to us. The tray contained very little food. Frida did not eat anything. She was asked rather casually why she refused the food. Frida said that she just couldn't. I expected that the volunteer would report this to some doctor who would then come in and do something for her. No one did.

One of the Hungarian girls in our room, noticed after a few days that Frida's tray was returned untouched and no one tried to do something about it. She asked Frida if she wanted to be fed. Frida declined. I also offered but again she refused. Maybe if I had insisted and forced her to take some food or drink, she might have lived. Since no member of the medical staff administered intravenous feedings and since I had not witnessed any caring in such a long time but only German brutality, it never occurred to me to help my friend, even though she declined nourishment. I took for granted that now after liberation everything would be all right. But it was not so for Frida. She was left to die without any medical intervention. If a doctor had tried to revive her, she might have survived.

We were given very little food and virtually nothing to drink in this hospital, only a liquor shot glass of milk once a day and a like amount of sugar. Also, once a day, at noon time we received half of a small cup of watery soup. We were also given one glucose pill a day. I was still very thirsty. All I wanted was a great deal of tea, coffee or juice. We got nothing.

As I lay near the window every afternoon, I watched the British soldiers drinking tea and milk from large enamel cups. Each soldier filled his cup with steaming hot liquid. I craved a cup of that tea. Why weren't they giving us some, I wondered.

While the three of us in the room started talking after the first few days, Frida never said anything. She was so weak that all she could do was lay in her bed. She couldn't even talk. One night I was awakened by Frida's gasping.

She was breathing laboriously and very loudly. I knew that she was dying. I thought, "What can I do to help her?" There was no buzzer at the beds to summon anyone. And who would come? A doctor? A nurse? None had come to our room previously. What could they do now? It was too late. I went back to sleep. In the morning, when the volunteer brought the tray to Frida, she said, "Ah, she is dead." She went back out. A few minutes later two young men in civilian clothes, probably Germans, entered the room and removed the wizened body of Frida. It was a common sight in Bergen-Belsen, to see dead people. It no longer bothered me that much. Almost all of my friends and relatives were gone. But now I began to think about it a great deal. It was terrible for someone to have lived through that hell and to die just when the nightmare was finally ending.

Two days after Frida died, a tall, middle aged German doctor came into the room accompanied by a woman in her thirties. He wore a civilian suit. She was dressed in a British uniform. They spoke with each other in English. They discharged me along with some other girls. We didn't have any clothes and had been lying in the nude. A man entered into our room and instructed us to go to a different building to receive some clothes. We asked how we could venture outside in the nude. He suggested that we wrap ourselves in our bed sheets. It was not too far. When we were outside, girls who already had received clothing advised us to ask for sweaters. Otherwise we would not get them. In the supply depot, British soldiers were distributing clothes from a large pile. They probably came from the possessions the Germans seized earlier from the Jews and then abandoned. I received two thin summer dresses, two pairs of panties and a pair of mismatched shoes. I wasn't happy with what I was given. I wanted a good pair. I had received the same kind of footwear in Auschwitz. I expected better treatment from the British after liberation. The soldier just shrugged his shoulders. When I asked for a sweater, he said that there were none left.

It was the end of April or the beginning of May. The evenings were still cold. I was inured to being deprived. So I put on one of my dresses, and a pair of panties, made a small bundle of the other dress, and was ready to go. All the discharged girls were loaded on the back of an army truck, and so we left the makeshift hospital.

After travelling for about two hours, the truck came to a halt at a big square in the center of what appeared to be a camp. The army driver opened the tailgate. Since the truck was covered with a tarpaulin I did not see what was going on until I got to the very edge. A British soldier was helping each girl down from the truck. Standing by, beside the British soldier, I saw Avi. Both of them reached up to help me off. I stood face-to-face with Avi, and neither of us could speak. It had been such a long time.

Avi and I had been friends since the day we met for the first time, when I went to Bistra to deliver food for my brother, Chaim Hersh. I had taken the short cut through the forest from Berezov. When I came to the road, a horse and wagon with two teenage Jewish boys came along. They asked whether I wanted a ride. I said I didn't mind walking, but since they had stopped, I would accept their offer. They made a place for me on the front seat between the two of them. When I was seated I asked them, "Why don't we speak Yiddish instead of Ruthenian?" They both laughed. They were a little embarrassed when they heard me speak Yiddish. They thought I was a gentile. They assumed that I was the daughter of a priest. They asked where I was from. When I said Berezov, they were quite surprised. They thought they knew everyone there, especially the girls. They couldn't understand why they never saw me. I said I hadn't been home for quite a while. I had been at my sister's in Tecso. They told me they were both from Horinch. In Bistra I got off and thanked them for the ride. After I delivered the food to my brother, one of them was waiting for me.

It was Avi. He was about 5'7 and slim with light grey eyes which were a bit crossed. He walked back to Berezov with me taking the short way through the forest. Before we made a right turn from the main road, he excused himself and went behind the bushes. I kept walking. A thought crossed my mind. "Maybe I have met my future husband today." It was close. It almost happened. He told me that he came to Berezov quite often to conduct business with Aaron. He also had an aunt in Berezov. She was Esther Mirl Wolvovitz, the widow. As we neared Berezov we walked on a dusty street through cultivated land. Our neighbors, Udel and her sister Mallie, were working

264

in the field. They saw me walking with him. I was quite embarrassed walking alone with a young man, on a side street. Udel later told my sister Rivka and they teased me about starting to date men early.

After that he came to visit see us many times. He befriended my family, as well. Soon thereafter he was referred to as my beau. Once, perhaps a year after we met, we had a serious quarrel about a letter.

At that time the war was raging. About all of the young men had been conscripted into the work battalions. Life in Berezov became very dull and boring. This godforsaken town did not possess a movie or a library, not even a telephone. In medical emergencies we had to walk either to Horinch to find the nearest doctor, or to Chust where there were better ones. The nearest post office was in Horinch. A Ruthenian mailman travelled every day, usually on foot, to Horinch to deliver mail to and from Berezov. The carrier knew everybody in town by their names, even those of us who were young. As a result, whenever somebody received mail, the whole town knew about it. It was easy, when the mailman looked through the small bundle of letters to see whether anyone who inquired, had any mail.

Whenever a young girl received a letter everybody in town made it their business to learn where it came from. I was very surprised that day in early spring when the mailman handed me a letter, since I had not been expecting mail from any one. The only letter I had ever received previously had been from Avi and I never replied because he didn't remember my correct name. Now when I received another letter, I wondered who could have sent it, because Avi was not away.

As I started to read the letter I was shocked. It contained some of the most horrible words ever put on paper. It stated in part, that the writer had observed me engaging in sex with many people in an abnormal way, while others looked on, including the writer and my mother. Some people who saw me receive the letter noticed that it did not have the sender's name or address on the envelope. Every one assumed that it contained something hideous and insulting because of the look of surprise mingled with anger on my face while I was reading. Everybody was curious about its contents. Since I had nothing to be ashamed of, I admitted to a few of my closest friends that it really was a vile missive. The news spread very quickly. Maybe the sender spread the word. I'm not sure why, but everybody asked me about the letter. Now they all had something to talk about.

I decided to reply to that letter, but not to the sender. I honestly couldn't imagine who, in his right mind, would write something so pornographic and stupid. Instead, I wrote to Avi at great length, accusing him of writing the vicious letter, although I knew somehow that he wasn't guilty. I did it mostly to interject some excitement into the depressing atmosphere in which we lived. I felt that people should talk about something besides the war.

On the Saturday evening after I mailed the letter, there was a rumor in town that Jewish girls were being rounded up to work at planting trees, replacing those the Hungarians had cut down. In order to escape the forced labor, several of my friends and I went up in to the mountains where we spent a sleepless night in a barn provided by a Ruthenian friend.

On Sunday morning our friend went to town to attend

church and to do some shopping. When he returned, he told us that there had been no rounding up of girls and that the rumor was just that; not true. After his assurance, we returned home.

That Sunday afternoon, Avi came from Horinch to see me. He confronted me about the letter I wrote. He said that he had come to see me Saturday night right after receiving it, but that I was gone. We argued. He declared that it had never even occurred to him to write something so scurrilous that would trigger such a vehement reply. He also said that he didn't mind at all that I wrote the accusing letter. In fact, he said he enjoyed reading it. He also complimented me on the letter I wrote stating that it was superb. He felt like posting it on the shul wall so that every one could read it. All his friends enjoyed it and were impressed. "Who helped you write it?" he asked.

Now, I was really offended that he thought that I needed help to write a letter. In all the time I knew Avi, he never believed that I did it by myself. The contents were so different from what he was used to. After all, his friends had read it, everyone in Berezov and Horinch knew that I had written something special to Avi, and, even worse, they could recite it word for word. At first I was angry that Avi had virtually published my letter, but later I didn't mind. I received a lot of attention, and it did serve to add some spice to the otherwise dull and depressing atmosphere in Berezov.

Avi accused the young couple who lived in our house of having helped with my reply. The young husband was serving in a work battalion. He had asked to be allowed to work in the woods around Berezov, instead of being shipped to the Russian front. His young wife came along to be with her husband. After they were blamed for helping me, the young wife admitted that it was true, that she had done it. This was a lie. All she did was read some letters to me that she had written to her husband, before they were married, and which he had saved. They were pleasant love notes. I would have been too embarrassed to ask for help with something as intimate as a letter to a boy friend and besides, it was anything but a love letter.

Avi attended my sister Rivka's wedding which took place in the late fall of 1941. Many of our relatives from other towns also came. One of them, a young woman, made up my face. I had never before used cosmetics. She did a terrific job. Every one said that I looked "smashing." Avi was very proud of me. After the dinner and dancing which took place in our house every one went to the only saloon in town for more dancing. At that time, young men and women were not supposed to dance together. Jewish religious customs forbade it, and since every Jew in Berezov was Orthodox, the young people obeyed their parents wishes.

Occasionally, however, there was some close dancing between the sexes. If a young man wished to dance with a girl he would pay a fee to the single musician called a "klezmer" and then request the music he wanted. Then he would invite a young lady to dance with him. At the wedding, Avi asked my mother if he could dance with me.

Mother gave her consent. He paid the fee and asked the musician to play "My Shtetele Belz," and it was for just one couple. He then asked me to dance with him. I was very embarrassed since I did not know the particular dance. Every one looked at me as I stepped on his feet. I was very apologetic. After a while other couples joined us on the dance floor and I felt less conspicuous.

Since the Hungarians occupied our region, they would issue a new decree for the Jews periodically. Often, at midnight, when the authorities were certain that every one would be at home and asleep, they would forcibly enter Jewish homes where some young men still remained. They would drag them away at gun point, and many were never heard from again.

One Sunday afternoon Avi visited us and told my mother and me that the previous night, while his entire family was sound asleep, armed gendarmes banged on their door. As his mother slowly went to open it, Avi jumped out of the back window in his nightclothes. His mother threw his clothes after him before she let the intruders in. He dressed hastily under the window and walked through the night, to Berezov. He said he did not come to us because he did not want to wake my parents. He went to Aaron's home instead. He called on us later in the day. Mother served him a lunch of stuffed cabbage. He stayed at our house until the following morning when his mother arrived. He was still sleeping. She told him that since the gendarmes had not found him, they avenged their loss by jailing his father.

Avi spent the entire Sunday afternoon in our house. In the evening, he went to shul in Berezov. That was where all the news was discussed, analyzed and where information was exchanged. Later Avi returned to us. My parents had already gone to bed. I had saved him some supper. I asked him to remove his shoes and wet socks, and place them near the fireplace to dry. The slush and water were so deep that no shoes could keep out the water. He commented, "How devoted she is to me," upon hearing this all my blood rushed to my face. We looked into each others eyes for a long moment. We were hugging and kissing in our imagination. A good girl from Berezov wouldn't actually do this with a young man before she married him. On Monday morning he left with his mother. He returned home to try to free his father from his detention. I later learned that he was successful. Since his father was middle-aged, Avi was able to bribe some officials. If he had been younger it would have been impossible to get him released.

A few weeks later on one of his visits to us Avi said that he was going to Budapest on business. He promised to visit me when he came back, but he did not return. On the way to Budapest all Jews were taken off the train and taken away. No one knew their destination. It was March 19, 1944. The Germans had invaded Hungary.

Now Avi was standing by the truck. We just stared at each other, not believing what was happening. It seemed that an entire generation had passed since we had seen one another. When all the girls were off the truck, we were led away. He was not allowed to accompany me. He promised that he would find me and he did. We met later in the recuperating place to which we were about to be taken.

It was a convalescent station. The girls who were discharged from the hospital were not sent to the regular camp. This was to be a transition stop. I was assigned to a large room containing six two-layered bunk beds. The other occupants were girls who were also recuperating from typhus.

After we checked in, we were given a pair of men's pajamas in which we felt much better than we would lying in the nude. I learned that we were in Celle, a town near Hanover.

We received a little more and better food than we did at the makeshift hospital in Bergen. We were also given some vitamins and told to take them three times a day. Some ate the sugar-coated tablets all at one time. We were allowed to go outside only occasionally. After lunch we were supposed to lie in our beds and sleep. No visitors were allowed during this rest period. We weren't even permitted to talk with each other during this time. Avi, nevertheless, came daily during visiting hours.

I was still extremely thirsty, because we weren't getting enough liquids. All I wanted to do was drink, drink. I craved liquids. I told Avi that my throat was parched and that I would love to have some borscht (beet soup). He and a friend went into town among the German housewives, and asked around until he finally found one who knew what borscht was, and was even willing to cook it for him. He surprised me the next day with a jar of cold borscht. I was amazed. I didn't think he would go looking for it. I was very thankful to him for his thoughtful efforts in my behalf. I was still burning inside and my thirst had not been slacked, but I did not worry about it. I knew that I was healing and that I would recover. I was gradually becoming accustomed to eating. Others had denounced the newly available food too quickly. Their digestive systems could not function properly because of the abrupt change from starvation conditions to nutritional benefits. Ironically, many died from this new availability of food.

I spent most of the time in the convalescent place resting, sleeping and taking short walks. We talked with
each other and I found out that one of the girls was a
cousin of mine. After ten days, I was sent to barracks
where healthy girls were housed. This camp in Celle
had been a German military one and now the British
had converted it to their administrative headquarters.
Avi and the rest of the men were in the same camp,
on the opposite side from the girls. There was a large
square in the center of the camp. Barracks and stables
were all around the square. The girls were assigned to
the barracks, while the men were housed in the
stables.

We had to go to a kitchen for our food. It was different from the recovery unit, there food was brought
to us. Avi, however, spared me the job of going for
the food. He picked up whatever they were offering
and "organized" the rest. He obtained raw potatoes
which he grated and made into potato pancakes. It
reminded me of my mother who would fry potatoes
called "chramzlech" or latkes, which was everybody's
favorite.

He cooked and baked other delicacies as well. But best
of all were the long walks we took in the near Celle.
We would go there almost daily. We talked a great
deal. We had so much to say to each other. I was
beginning to feel good about life, hopeful that my
nightmare was finally over.

After awhile Avi sent his friend, who was also from
Horinch and whose wife had died in the Izo ghetto, to
ask me whether I would marry Avi. I was offended
and told his friend that since Avi and I had known
each other for such a long time, he could propose to
me himself. Later that same day Avi came over and

apologized for having sent an emissary. He asked me himself whether I would marry him. I told him that I wanted to wait and see. Maybe someone else from my large family had also survived to share this special occasion with me. It was understood, however, that we would get married in the near future. Obviously no one would wed in the camp at Celle. There were no separate quarters or privacy for anyone, and worse yet, I hadn't yet fully recovered from the effects of concentration camp and typhus. My period had not yet returned. (It eventually did just as we were leaving Celle.) Although life was better than it had been for a long time, it was far from ideal for marriage. I was still living with eight girls in one room. The men remained in the stables where the Germans once kept their horses. We took it all in good stride. At least there were fewer worries about food, and we were no longer conscripted for forced labor. Clothes were still a big problem. I owned nothing besides the two summer dresses that were issued to me. I made a dress from a gray army blanket. I had no pattern and sewed it all by hand. I thought it was rather pretty, though not a very professional job. It was the only warm apparel I owned.

The men in Celle were much more ambitious than the women. They weren't satisfied with the British food. They provided a very limited diet indeed. Each man gathered some stones and a pot in the open field near the camp, collected twigs which were in abundance at the site, and cooked. Some of the fare was quite palatable, considering the circumstances. Almost every man had a woman to whom he catered. Needless to say, Avi took care of the food where I was concerned. Since the time I was discharged from the convalescent house and placed in the camp, I never found it necessary to go to the kitchen for the allocated food.

Right from the first day, Avi said that he would bring over whatever was offered.

The British, however, never gave us any meat. What they really liked to cook for us in the kitchen were potatoes but when they reached us they were stone cold. We all expected something better after liberation. We craved meat. In order to obtain it, Avi and a friend went into the meadow where cattle were grazing. They killed a cow and brought the meat to the camp, where they cooked it in an open field. The British learned about this but said nothing.

I did not know where the meat was coming from. All Avi told me was that he had "organized" it. On the second trip to the field, the British army police waited to ambush them. When the two men appeared, they opened fire. One of them escaped. However Avi froze, and could not move. He was captured and jailed. I waited for him to come at the usual time, but he did not show up. I was not overly concerned because anything could have delayed him. Much later, his friend from Horinch told me what had happened. It was very strange. The British were also shooting at Jews? We were used to expecting the worst from the Germans, but we anticipated kinder treatment from the liberators. The smoke where the Germans burned the corpses of the Jews in nearby Bergen-Belsen had not entirely cleared up, and now the British were firing on Jews.

While the Germans were killing millions of Jews, not one nation raised a word of protest, including the British. But when two Jewish boys tried to kill a German's cow, out of desperate necessity, the British fired at them. No one sought revenge on a cow.

They captured one, and detained him in an undisclosed place. We were hungry. Had the British given us sufficient food, this wouldn't have happened. We were without food for such a long time. We suffered unbelievable tortures and degradation at the hands of the German's. They should have been made to pay dearly what they did. Now the British were protecting them from two harmless Jewish men. Where could I lodge my protest? Maybe, I thought, it was the rule of nature for everyone to persecute Jews.

Avi's friend encouraged me to seek help. But first Avi had to be found and that was not easy. I put on my blanket dress the next morning and went to a nearby British army camp. If knew how to speak English, my task would have been much easier. Since I couldn't I had a hard time locating him. The German interpreter at the army base told me that no one knew where Avi was being held. He and the other British soldiers looked at one another and shook their heads. The matter was under the jurisdiction of the military police, one of them finally told me where I could find them. I was not too successful with them, either. I was told that he was transferred to the German civil authorities. I wanted to see the burgomeister of Celle immediately, but I was told I needed an appointment. I made one, and when I saw him I explained the situation telling him that he was my husband, and that he should be freed because we had suffered enough. The burgomeister said that he would not intervene on his behalf or even tell me where he was since he committed a grave crime. What did I expect from a German? Killing Jews en masse and seizing all their possessions was not a grave crime, but slaughtering a German cow for food was one. I now regret that I did not tell him that to his face.

After a week and a half of running around from one military base to another, trying to locate him, I finally found out where I could learn where he was. I pleaded my case to the pretty Czech secretary of the high British commander in charge and this time I said that Avi was my brother. She let me see the commander. He told me through her exactly in what prison he was incarcerated. She translated the information to me in Czech. He said that he could not free him. He would have to stand trial and be punished for his offense. He was not as sympathetic as his secretary had been. From there I went to the prison.

Again, British soldiers told me that I could not see him. No visitors were allowed in the first two weeks of imprisonment. I returned to camp with no success.

While I was running around trying to free Avi, I was not always in camp at noon time when they served the boiled potatoes. I could have asked any one of the girls in my room to bring me the cold ones from the kitchen. A Rumanian girl did, in fact, offer to do this. Instead, I chose to go to the other camp where the girls from Berezov stayed were housed. They, too, were brought from Bergen-Belsen to Celle and placed in a camp. Theirs was located about a mile away from ours.

They all slept in a stable which was previously used for Germans horses. The straw was still on the floor. The girls spread blankets over the straw and slept on the floor. Riva and Yehudith were also in this camp. Riva had the dresses which I had found in the heap at Bergen-Belsen. I learned that after I was admitted to the hospital, she had taken my dresses. I felt hurt that in addition to Riva's appropriating my clothing, she hadn't even visited me once while I was there. I hinted that I now had only two thin summer dresses and I was cold. I received no response.

Golda, the girl I met again in Bergen-Belsen on the day after liberation, was also there. I was very surprised at not having seen Udel. Golda and Udel had been inseparable during their entire stay in the camps.

Golda told me a bizarre story about Udel. After Frida and I had been taken to the hospital in an ambulance, Udel didn't feel too well either. She decided that she also needed hospitalization. A few days after Udel's admission to the hospital, Golda found out where she was and walked several miles to visit her. Golda said she spent several hours with Udel who told her that she was feeling better. When Golda was about to leave, Udel asked her to bring some boiled potatoes on her next visit. Golda brought the potatoes a few days later. When she arrived at Udel's bed she was not there. Another girl had replaced her. Golda, was surprised and asked for Udel. No one in the room knew where she was or what happened to her. She was never seen or heard from again.

On one of my visits to the Berezov girls in the other camp, I mentioned that I hadn't received any food that day. Yehudith offered me a little yellow split pea soup which was cold, but I ate it anyway. All of the girls promised to bring me more soup on the following day, and on any other day, if I wished, if I would come again. I wasn't sure that I could, because I was still busy trying to free Avi. My cousin Riva said that she would bring the soup. In the next few days when I came, Riva gave me a bowl of pea soup. After four days, she commented that she was bringing the soup to repay me for the food I stole for her from the Germans in Bergen-Belsen. What a trade off. She took soup openly from the British kitchen, who gave everyone as much as they wanted, as opposed to stealing from the Germans at the risk of being killed.

Two weeks after Avi's arrest, I was allowed to visit him. The British MP's let us talk for ten minutes in the presence of a German guard. I started to speak Yiddish. Avi asked me to converse in Ruthenian so that the German wouldn't understand. I told him that I was still trying to free him and that I would continue to do so. I didn't mention what the British commandant told me about his having to stand trial for his offense. He asked for a cigarette. I had none since I didn't smoke. I felt awful for not having something for him. He said that the food was very bad, and that he had no cigarettes at all. He asked me whether I had received his note. "What note?", I asked. He said that he wrote one when he was jailed. He threw it through the window to the street, hoping that someone would find it and deliver it to me, so I would know where he was. I asked him if he expected a German to deliver the note. I promised to return soon with food and cigarettes. I would do some "organizing." I kept my promise. I had a very difficult time preparing the items. Since I wasn't allowed to see him for another two weeks, I left the package of food and cigarettes in the British office. They promised to give it to him. But they had to check the contents first. They told me it was a routine procedure. I was certain they would give it to him. I learned later that they never did.

The British began to encourage everyone to leave the camp and return to their homeland. First on their list were the people from Czechoslovakia. We were told that our departure would take place in a few days. I became frantic. How could I leave without Avi? I renewed my efforts to have him released. Once more I called on the British High Command but the commandant was not in. After a few attempts I succeeded in meeting with him. I pleaded my case to the same secretary. I said, "they don't expect me to return to my homeland and leave my husband behind in a jail?" I didn't remember that in the past when I spoke to her I had said that he was my brother. She recalled, however, and told me, in confidence, that it really didn't matter whether he was my brother, husband or just a good friend. The important thing was that I be consistent in my story. I was embarrassed. My face turned red as I thought that I had "blown it." Fortunately, she was very sympathetic, and let me see the commander. When I told him that we were planning to leave on the following day, he became quite helpful. It was apparent that they didn't want to keep us if they could help it. He immediately made some telephone calls to the prison personnel and ordered them to arrange for Avi's release. It took a long time to locate all the people that were needed to implement the procedure. Then he called his driver, and together with his secretary and myself, started for the prison.

It took more than five hours to complete all the arrangements for his release. After all the papers were drawn up and signed, the guard went to get Avi. It was after midnight and he was asleep in his cell. The guard told him to get dressed. He thought that he was being transferred to a different prison. As he was brought up to the street level from the basement, he saw me standing at the door. When he spotted me, he later said, he knew that he was a free man. He was escorted into the office, where he signed some papers, and was released at last.

The British did not bother to return Avi's few belongings which they had taken from him when he was arrested, including his shoelaces. The British soldiers knew that he was my boyfriend and they expected to witness a hugging and kissing reunion. They probably laughed when it didn't occur. A good Jewish girl with my background did not do these things before she was married. Those intimacies were saved for the post marital period. But I was jubilant about having succeeded in freeing him.

We walked from the prison to the camp like two joyful children. Along the way, we passed some German houses, and through their open windows we could hear pleasant music. To get to the camp more quickly, we took a short cut through a field. We passed through this route many times before. In the field, Avi suggested that we sit down on his jacket. I suspected that he wanted to do more than just sit. He wished to make love to me. But I was repulsed by the idea of indulging in this intimate act in a German field on German soil which was soaked in Jewish blood.

We were rather young. I thought that we would have a whole lifetime together. I wanted to wait until the conditions were conducive for blissful consummation. When we reached the camp, we discovered that we had both become celebrities. My roommates congratulated me on the big victory. At first, they couldn't believe me when I told them that Avi was free. He went back to his place to wash and shave. Then he came to our room where he was cheered by all of the girls.

On the following morning at five we assembled in the central square of the camp. A long line of army trucks, covered with tarpaulins, was waiting. Many people with their bundles were gathered in the square. Avi was not among them. I went to his place. I thought perhaps he had overslept. But he was ready. I had the feeling that he would have preferred to remain staying in the camp rather than going home. It wasn't such a bad idea. No one had a home any longer, anyhow. Did he want to stay without me? I learned the answer three days later.

The British didn't give us food for the long journey home. We received absolutely nothing. Not even bread. We were told in Celle, before we departed, that we would receive some identification papers at the end of our trip. As it all turned out, these were not supplied at the end of the trip. As soon as every one boarded any truck we wished we were driven away. Each vehicle accommodated from twenty to twenty-five men and women. Every one tried to stay with friends. Riva, Golda, and Yehudith were on another truck which was loaded at their camp. This one carried girls only, because their's was a women's camp. All of the transports met to form a caravan of about twenty-five. We spread out blankets and sat on the floor.

As we drove on, I saw Germany in ruins. Entire areas were now heaps of rubble. In some towns not even a single house remained unscathed, an erect wall here and there, in a sea of destruction. A lone dog walking and sniffing in the ruins, looking for food. In other places, utter devastation. These ruins were mute reminders of bombed out proud towns that no longer existed. The destruction was total with only the smallest cities and villages remaining.

The scenes I witnessed were a source of great satisfaction to me. I relished the sight of desolation. The

Germans deserved the retribution of their wrecked homes. They inflicted much more misery on others. They lost only their houses which could be rebuilt. So many of their innocent victims paid with their lives, which could never be replaced.

At one point the trucks pulled to the side of the road and stopped. We got off to stretch our legs. Some spotted a field of scallions, and descended on it like hungry locusts. The German owner started to shout at them to go away, but no one paid any attention to him. The British drivers said nothing.

I am not a good traveler, especially in the back of a tarpaulin-covered truck, riding over bumpy roads. Avi suggested that I ask the driver if I could sit in front next to him. We somehow made ourselves understood, and the driver opened the door for me to sit in the cab with him. Avi climbed on top of the cover. At least there he could watch the scenery instead of remaining under the tarp with a backward view of the countryside. I liked it much better in the front rather than under the cover. I could not converse with the driver, but I could see the ruined cities as we passed. As we continued to ride it started to rain. I completely forgot that Avi was on top of the tarpaulin until the driver realized that he was tapping on the cabin window. As I opened the door for him he had a hard time sliding into the cabin while the truck was in motion. The driver couldn't stop. There were other trucks behind him. As he made it, I moved closer to the driver to make room for him. There was not enough room for three people. The driver motioned for me to get up and let Avi sit down. I understood what he meant. I gave my seat to Avi and sat down on his lap. It was strange. I had imagined sitting on his lap before, but not in a British transport.

282

At night the trucks stopped in a small town. We were told that we would spend the night there. Every one scattered. Avi went off with some friends and I could not find him until the next morning when he returned to the truck. He said that he and his friends slept in beds provided by a German family. They traded cigarettes for chickens (or maybe they "organized" the chickens). They lit a fire and roasted the fowls. He said that he looked for me, but couldn't find me. But he did give me a chicken leg, my share of what I had missed in the evening.

Instead of eating it, late that night I had climbed into one of the trucks to lie down. I couldn't find the right one in the dark. In the morning, we drove on.

When I decided to eat the chicken leg the driver wouldn't allow me. He said "no good, no good," and threw it out of the window. It had been very hot that day. The sky was bright and the sun was blistering. The driver probably felt that the leg had spoiled because of the heat.

Late on the following night we reached the border of Czechoslovakia. The drivers told us that the trucks were not allowed to cross into Czech territory. We were told to leave them and walk the short distance across the border into Czechoslovakia. There we boarded an open freight train that was waiting for us. That was all that the Czechs had provided for the returnees. We were almost home. Germany was behind us. We would no longer have to breathe the German air.

As we settled into one of the cars, we were elated. Home, how long we had dreamed about it! We traveled the entire night on that train. It was the most glorious night ever. The moon was never so big and bright. Avi and I sat on some blankets and talked while the others slept. My cousin Riva was asleep not too far away. Sometime late in the night she woke and saw us sitting up. She offered me her "bed" but I refused. I enjoyed talking with Avi. However, I was finally persuaded. She sat in my place and I lay down in hers. I did not sleep too well, however. Riva was sitting too close to Avi.

I rose, thanked her, and sent her back to sleep. After all, it was her place. She reluctantly agreed. By late morning we arrived at Prague, the capital of Czechoslovakia. The train stopped at the Masarik station, one of the two railroad stations in Prague. Avi took a small suitcase from a German girl which contained some of her belongings. He put the contents of her bag into mine. I was furious with him for doing this. I said that "organizing" was alright in Germany, in a concentration camp, but not here and not now. We were rid of Germany, forever I hoped, and we wouldn't need to organize for supplies any longer. The girl whose possessions he took reported the incident to the Czech police. They briefly searched for her belongings, but not too thoroughly.

In the afternoon, a young man from Horinch came to the train. After liberation, people were asking everybody they met about relatives, family or friends that might have survived. That young man told Avi that his sister was alive, and presently in Prague. He gave him her address. Avi packed his few belongings and left to visit her. He promised that he would either return with his sister and then we would all continue on the trip together, or he would come back and take me to his sister. He didn't as yet know which choice was preferable. He said that he was not saying

284

goodbye, and would definitely come back soon. I watched him appear smaller and smaller crossing the empty lot.

When he was only a short distance away I thought: I can still call out to him to wait for me. He could still hear me. Now, as the distance between us grew greater he would not be able to hear me. He became a dot on the horizon, and then nothing.

I could not explain to myself why I was so sad and depressed. He said that he would return, I told myself repeatedly. Why do I have the feeling that everything was over between us? Some one in the open railroad car teased me about his departure: "So, 'Itzickle' (Avi's nickname) left, huh?" Very late that afternoon the train started to move again. It did not go far. It stopped at the main railroad station, the Wilson, named for President Woodrow Wilson of the United States.

The train remained there for the entire night. I was silent all of the time. I was not in the mood to speak with anyone. Other trains stopped at the station. Some passengers got off, while others them. Greetings were exchanged, some embraced and left. And then, there was quiet. No more trains arrived. It was after midnight. A lone man with a broom and shovel was cleaning the station. After he finished, he too left. Only the silence remained. My ears were attuned to the stillness. The occupants of the freight train were all asleep. Only I was awake, listening. Maybe my name would be called. But it wasn't. Avi did not come.

It occurred to me to start looking for him. But how could I find him without an address? I did not even have money for fare on the tramway. How would I get around? The city was crowded with Russian soldiers. They were raping anybody on whom they could lay their hands. Besides, a girl of my upbringing did not go to looking for a young man.

Towards morning I fell asleep for a short while. When I woke I was upset. Maybe he had called for me and because I was asleep I couldn't hear him. My cousin told me that no one had called. Was I that obvious? Later that day the train started to move again out of Prague with myself on board. I wasn't brave enough to leave the train to go on a "manhunt". We were going to the Carpathians by way of Budapest. There was no other route to get to Chust, we were told in Bratislava, where we stayed for a few days. We were not given food throughout the entire trip. Even if food was available at the start of our journey, it was long gone. Before we reached Bratislava our open freight train stopped in the middle of a potato field. Some people started to dig up the potatoes. It was most disappointing to go back to eating raw potatoes as we did in the concentration camp. Others had another way. They travelled to the nearest town, which was a long distance away, and went from house to house like beggars collecting bread from the Czech housewives who were willing to contribute a slice to a hungry concentration camp survivor. Some gave, others didn't.

Riva was among those who went begging. She brought back a bag full of pieces of bread. I would rather have died than go supplicate myself for bread. I just remained very hungry and ate raw potatoes.

In Bratislava we were advised to stay indoors because of the Russian soldiers. We were told that they raped an eighty year old widow. And yes, they collected "chasse" (watches). They were fascinated by timepieces. Like small children they liked to hear them ticking. I saw one of them who displayed wrist watches on both his arms from the wrists to above the elbows almost to his shoulders. He exhibited them to everyone he met. All these had been seized from innocent.

We received food for the first time in Bratislava where we stayed in a shelter which contained beds. We stayed in this place for an entire week. From there we traveled in a Red Cross train. It was quite comfortable since it had beds and we were not exposed to the elements as we were in the open freight trains. Once we stopped at a small station. Right across from us was another train filled with Russian soldiers. The girls in our train kept low profiles. We did not want to attract attention. We had heard enough evil stories about them. Only men ventured out boys went out to bring us water.

Nevertheless, a Russian officer did wander over to our car. He approached me and asked who we were and where we were going. I told him that we were Jews and that we were coming from Germany and going to our former homes. He was very sympathetic. He wanted me to tell him what happened in Germany. Although he had already heard all about it, was it as bad as the rumors that persisted? I told him that, whatever he had heard, no matter what, the truth was far worse than anybody could ever describe. He wanted to know if we had food. I said no. He told me it would attract too much attention if he brought something for us. "Are you really sick?" he asked. I answered, "I am weak and recuperating from typhus." He shook his head and said that he was Jewish too, and warned me to watch out for the other soldiers.

No sooner did he finish his sentence, when a group of soldiers entered our car and went on a rampage. Some girls threw themselves on the men and pulled them on top of them. When the Russians saw that every one was "engaged" in sex, they started to curse. I thought it best to stay near the Jewish officer hoping that he would protect me. I even smiled at him to indicate to the others that I was already taken by one of their comrades. A soldier who was on the way out without having raped anyone, passed me and slapped me on the face so hard that my head turned and I banged it on an iron bed. I suffered a large lump and a sore head. He accompanied his attack with the traditional Russian curse "Yep twoyu mats". I asked the Jewish soldier what I had done to deserve that. He said that the other Russian was angry that he couldn't have me because I was with him. He didn't want an altercation with another officer, so the least he could do was to beat me. That certainly was preferable to being raped by him. Not even the fact that we were on a Red Cross train stopped them. Although they could assume that we were sick, and perhaps contagious, it did not deter them. As far as they were concerned we were people under occupation. They did not realize our situation.

They treated us as they would other German Frauleins. They didn't differentiate between a concentration camp survivor and any other female, German or not.

At midnight, when the train moved, we could breathe easier. The next day we stopped in an orchard, and not too far away we saw a house.

Somebody noticed that there were unripe apricots on the trees. It was Tisha-b'Av, and every one fasted.

By three o'clock I was hungry, faint, and very weak. We didn't have much of a supper on the previous day, so I broke my fast and went into the orchard for some apricots. The woman from the house nearby started to yell at us and warned to stop or she would call the police. We moved on.

At the end of the day the train stopped and we were told that we would have to cross the Danube River on foot, over a temporary bridge. The original one had been blown up during the war. Now, instead of a bridge, there was only a narrow, suspended walkway about two feet wide. We were about to enter Hungary.

With all our belongings on our backs we walked across to the other side. When I had left Germany I had very few possesions, but now, in addition I had to carry those pieces of clothing that Avi had taken from the girl in the Masarik station. After we crossed, some ladies on the Hungarian side distributed bean soup only to those who had fasted. They must have been Jewish because gentiles wouldn't have known that it was Tisha-b'Av and that we were not supposed to eat.

I could not honestly say that I had fasted as I had eaten some apricots sometime earlier. As a result I received no soup. Now we had to walk to the nearest station to board another train. This one was a regular passenger one with seating accommodations.

After we boarded, some Russian soldiers entered the car. I tried to look out of the window. I hoped that they wouldn't see me. As the train started to move I noticed that my cousin Riva was struggling with one of the soldiers. He reeked of alcohol and was almost on top of her. I immediately joined Riva to fight him off. It wasn't too difficult because he was frightfully drunk, and we were able to roll him over, away from her. We then moved to another car. After a few hours, we reached Budapest. The main railroad terminal had been savagely bombed, but the city as a whole was not as bad as those I had seen in Germany. Many places in Czechoslovakia had been totally destroyed, especially the city of Pilzen where ammunition factories were located. Prague, the capital, was not seriously damaged.

Our entire group went to a center where arrivals from the concentration camps were provided with shelter and soup. I remained there overnight, and met a young man from Berezov who was a cousin of Avi's. His name was David and he was the son of Esther Mirl Wolvovitz, the widow. David told me that Avi and his sister had been in Budapest a few days earlier with a group of other people and had already left for home. He also said that Avi told him that everything between the two of us had been arranged. I really did not believe him. I had a strange feeling that something was terribly wrong.

I had a distant relative in Budapest. Neither my mother nor my father ever knew how we were related, but his family claimed that we were. They originally came from Berezov and had moved to Budapest many years earlier. I went to see him. He was about forty-five years old and divorced. He had lived alone since that marital breakup. He lived in a large apartment with a walk-in closet filled with packages left by people. I, too, left my few belongings with him. I also included the bundle that Avi had taken from the German girl in Prague.

On the following day I arrived at the station to board the train for Chust. In the terminal I met Lenke, my former sister-in-law who had given me the red beet in Auschwitz to cure my "pneumonia". Now Lenke was going home to Ungvar where she had lived with my brother. I was glad that she had survived, but I thought sadly about what had befallen my brother, Baruch Bendit. When we were still home in Berezov, we heard from a Ruthenian who had seen Baruch at the Russian front. He told us that one night the Germans poured gasoline on the barrack in which he was sleeping and all the occupants perished. My family mourned for Baruch Bendit as we did for Azick when we heard that he died in Kamenits Podolskiy.

Lenke and I talked for a while before we boarded the train. Then she went to a different car. I wondered why she didn't stay with me. Maybe she wanted to meet another man and didn't want me to see it. I don't know exactly why, but she said goodbye and left for a different part of the train. The trip to Chust was supposed to take twelve to fourteen hours.

There were some young Jewish men and women in the car, and as usual they asked one another where each of them came from, and whether any of them had seen any of their family members. As one of the men started to question me, I realized that he was my cousin from Satoraljaujhely, Hungary. Our mother always told us that she had a brother there, but I had never met anyone from this branch of the family, even when there was no border separating us.

I met another one of my cousins in Celle when I was in the convalescent house. She occupied the same room in which I was, but she remained there when I was discharged. She had been in Bergen-Belsen and suffered from typhus and lice. Her head was shorn a second time after liberation when she was admitted to the hospital. From Celle, I learned later, she was transported to Sweden. When I left I promised that I would come to visit her in the convalescent ward. But I never had an opportunity to do so as I was too busy trying to free Avi. Now, when I met her brother, I told him that his sister Chaya was alive. He was delighted with the news, but kept repeating, "Are you sure that she is alive now? Are you positive? You really saw her?" and "Why isn't she with you?". I told him that all those who reached Celle had survived. Nobody had died there. We talked all through the night while sitting on the floor of the train. It was packed. He left the train before I did.

After we passed Uyhely, the scenery started to become more familiar. The mountains had the same kind of shrubs that were prevalent in Berezov. The trees and other greenery were the same. My heart started to beat rapidly. How many times during my incarceration did I picture my returning home? The dream finally came true. When the conductor announced that in one half hour we would stop at Chust I began to get very nervous. I couldn't wait. At last, the train stopped and I saw the big letters C H U S T. How different it was from the time I last saw this sign at the brick factory when we boarded the cattle cars for an undisclosed destination. Who would I find in my house? I knew that my parents were dead, gassed and burned and the ashes thrown into the Sola river. The same fate befell my sister Rivka, who died with her baby son in the gas chamber, along with my oldest sister Alta, who also had a baby boy. Alta was also sent to Auschwitz, but she might have survived had she so chosen. Her previous neighbor, who was my friend, told me that a Jewish long time prisoner who worked by the railroad advised her to give her child to her mother or mother-in-law. She did not understand. She replied, "Why should I give my child to my mother or mother-in-law?" He explained, that if she insisted on being with her child that they would kill her, that they were killing the children. She answered, "If they are going to murder my child they can kill me too." They did.

My oldest brother Azick was the first member of my family to die at the hands of the bloody Germans. He was taken with all the rest of his town, Drahive, to be executed German-style by an SS mobile mass murder unit called the "Einsatzgruppen" who killed every one by shooting them in the temples in an open ditch which the victims were forced to dig just before they were killed.

My hopes were raised for my two young brothers Shmual Moshe and Chaim Hersh. Shmual was two years older than I, and Chaim Hersh was two years younger. They were exactly the right age to have possibly survived, but only a few of the many young men and women in that category were still alive. They comprised the long lines of overworked and undernourished victims, who were brought to Auschwitz from work camps where the sign over the gate read "Arbeit Macht Frei" (work liberates). They were murderously liberated in Auschwitz like Mendel Kahan, who jumped over the lines to his death. However, I still had some hope for my two young brothers despite the poor odds. Some had survived. I did. Why not them? I stepped down from the train. It was Friday noon and I had been in the train for almost twenty-four hours, instead of the twelve the trip should have taken. It was a pleasant, sunny summer day. It was quite a distance from the station to the center of the

293

city, but I didn't look for transportation. I walked and looked around me as I entered the city. Nothing seemed to have changed on the outside, but everything here was different. There were no Jews to be seen. This street used to be bustling with activity, open stores, vendors, coachmen driving passengers to and from the station. Now there was only an uneasy silence. There were also changes in the government. The Russians had overthrown the defeated Hungarians just as the Hungarians had replaced the Czechs seven years earlier. Now the Russians were in full control of this subjugated region.

Everything else was as it had been, as I had remembered it. Not one house was damaged or ruined. When I reached the center of the town I did not know where to go next. I had finally arrived. What should I do now? I looked around, and I saw someone who appeared to be a young Jew. I ran after him. I told him that I had just arrived. "What do I do?" I asked. He asked me where I came from. I told him, Berezov and that I was returning from the concentration camps. He told me to go to a nearby house where some sisters from Berezov were housed. I thanked him and walked there. It was true. The Adler sisters from the Kuzi-Berezov were staying there. They were liberated in Auschwitz and soon after returned to Chust. They were all young and unmarried and I knew them well. I had gone to school with two of them. The house that they were in was their own. They told me that I could stay with them for the night, but that I couldn't eat there. There was a public soup kitchen for returnees.

They informed me that the soup was distributed only at midday and that I was too late for the Friday distribution. I hadn't eaten since Budapest, when I received midday soup on the day I arrived. I was very hungry, but I would just hope to contain myself. I walked out into the street to look around and I met some people that I knew. They told me that none of the survivors really stayed in Berezov. All those who came back were concentrated in Chust. In the evening I went to the Adler sisters for a place to sleep. I was accommodated on a couch with a quilt. I had a restful sleep after my extensive traveling from Celle to Chust, which was quite a trip. I awoke refreshed but also very hungry. The noises in my stomach were becoming louder. I dressed and went to find the soup kitchen. I got there and waited on line. Someone told me that the woman who cooked the soup was from Berezov. I thought that it was great news and that maybe I would get a double portion. I certainly could use it. But all too soon the cook emerged and announced that no one new on the line would receive any soup. She didn't have enough for everyone.

I was told who she was, but I did not recognize her. She was the older sister of Aaron, the man for whom I had risked my life in Bergen-Belsen, and to whom I had quite often given my portion of the barley soup, bread and turnips, the same one who did not tell Avi that I was working nearby. By doing so he had precluded the possibility of Avi getting some food. He was worried that I would stop supplying him with food and instead give his portion to Avi, which was true. But why was his sister acting so antagonistic to me? I walked away hungrier than before, after inhaling the delicious aroma of the barley and bean soup. In the late afternoon, when I tired of walking in the streets, I went back to the Adler sisters'. They asked if I had received any soup. When I answered no, they gave me a piece of bread.

Somehow Saturday passed and it was Sunday. It was a beautiful summer morning. The sun was shining brightly and the weather was warm. It was a day when it felt good to be alive and outdoors. I left Chust and walked rather briskly along Izo Street. After five kilometers I reached the town of Izo where we had been detained in the ghetto. The former ghetto was now on my left. Just a single row of houses separated the main road from the former ghetto. No sign remained there of the Jews who once resided, walked, hoped and prayed for their deliverance. I remembered the hut in which we lived. Should I visit it? There were too many sad memories. I kept walking.

Fifteen more kilometers and I would be in Berezov. My birthplace, the site of my childhood and the home of my ancestors. As I neared Berezov my heart began to beat faster as I quickened my pace. I passed Horinch, Avi's home town. Although I didn't see any one, I knew that he would learn that I was home. After just a kilometer or two, a horse-drawn wagon appeared from the direction of Chust. I recognized the driver; he was from Berezov. He stopped and asked me to join the rest of the people in the wagon. I knew he made the trip between Chust and Berezov at least twice a day and carried passengers for money. I had none. Besides, since I had walked this far, I could make it all the way. After one more kilometer I could see Berezov bathing in the glow of the sun. It was overgrown with trees. Every house had its own garden and an orchard.

I crossed the wooden bridge across the river Rika and now I was almost home. Nothing had changed here. All the houses remained intact, including the Jewish ones. I passed by the shul where pious men and women had prayed, the women only on the Sabbath and on holidays, the men, three times a day. I didn't want to think about them now because the murky waters of the ponds in far off Auschwitz came to mind. After five minutes I could see our house. It was painted bright yellow, with dark red trim on the windows. I could see the yellow part that I had painted when mother asked me to before Passover. The last Passover. It was exactly the way it was when I saw it the last time.

I met a few Ruthenians on the way; our former friends and neighbors. No one greeted me. They acted as if they didn't see me. Chrestina, my childhood friend, with whom I had played and with whom I ate from the same bowl in her grandfather's house or our's, didn't see me when she passed. I still remember how we rolled down the hill in the back of her grandfather Miklush's garden. Now that I had returned, she wouldn't even look at me or say, "hello.", not even a nod of recognition. Others wouldn't acknowledge me either. They passed by as if I were invisible.

As far as I could determine there were no Jews in Berezov. I stopped about fifty yards from our house and just looked at it; then I stepped over the wooden fence that encircled the yard and the garden and walked into Marika's house, our closest Ruthenian neighbor. When I walked in, Marika and two of her three sons were present. When I greeted them, I could barely hear a reply. Maybe they were confused, perhaps surprised, or just didn't know what to say to me.

Good old Marika. After a while she asked whether others of my family had survived. I shrugged. "Mama?" she asked; she loved my mother. They had been very close. I shook my head. She stopped questioning me and instead gave me a bowl of tokan with milk. It was delicious. I was very hungry. I went to our house after I finished the porridge.

Our house was occupied by a peasant. I knew him. He had married after we were sent to Auschwitz and he moved into our house. There were many Jewish houses, free for the asking. However, there was no trace of our furniture. In one of the rooms the wooden slats from the floor were missing. Half of these pieces were removed, exposing the earth and sand underneath. I asked Mihalie, the new occupant, who had removed the boards. He told me that the Russian soldiers who stayed in the house removed them for firewood.

I went into the garden which was planted with corn and looked at the plum trees in the back and on the sides. They were heavy with fruit; I had never seen them bearing so many plums. The first thing I did was to eat a great deal of them. I was still hungry. The small portion of porridge that Marika had given me wasn't too filling. Mihalie became nervous when he saw me eating. "Please don't," he said. "They will blame me for the missing fruit." "What? Who will blame you?" I asked. He said that the garden now belonged to a Ruthenian from the Kuzi, the part of Berezov that was across the Rika. They had raffled the Jewish land off and this man had won our garden, Mihalie told me. I told him not to worry about the plums, that I would assume the blame.

The new owner had planted the corn, but not the plums. I told him that they belonged to me, and kept eating. I hadn't seen a piece of fruit since the summer before I left Berezov. I told Mihalie that when he met the new owner to tell him that I had taken my fruit, that my parents, or perhaps my grandparents had planted the trees, and the fruit thereof belonged to me.

The outhouse had been removed, and Mihalie told me not to satisfy my biological needs between the corn plants. Well, I wasn't going to comply. I stayed in town for the night. Mihalie let me sleep in the second bed in the house. He and his young wife slept in the other one. I didn't feel too comfortable sleeping there in his presence but I had no choice. The next day I visited our neighbors with whom mother had left our most valued possessions. At that time the only important items I needed to retrieve were clothes.

I was still wearing the dress the British had given me when I was discharged from the hospital. I hadn't brought the dress I wore in Celle, the one I made from an army blanket. My room mates advised me not to take it home. It was not suitable for wearing in the outside world. I called Stefan and Antza Balebane, a highly respected Ruthenian family.

My mother, my sister Rivka and her two sisters-in-law, Udel and Mallie, had left the finest things we owned with the Balebanes. I went to see them in the hope that they would at least return my clothing.

I arrived at the gate of their home, which actually wasn't their original one. They had traded it with the Nojovits family for another house on the outskirts of town. As soon as the Nojovitses disappeared, along with the rest of the Jews of Berezov, the Balebanes moved back to the house they had previously traded. Now they owned both of them. I stood at the gate and could not enter. A ferocious dog snarled and barked and strained to free himself from the long restraining chain to get at me. He evidently objected to my intrusion. Well, his masters didn't seem to like it either. Although they could hear the dog bark and could see me through the window, they waited to see if I would tire of standing there.

I was adamant. I stood like a beggar at the gate and waited for what seemed to be an interminable period. Finally Antza came out and asked me what I wanted. I said that I wanted to come in and talk with her. She motioned me inside and held the dog until I crossed the threshold. Inside, she repeated: "What do you want?" I said very humbly that I would like to have some of my clothes, those my mother had left, since all I had was what I was wearing.

"I don't have any of your clothes," she said. "I don't know what you are talking about." I repeated that she was kind enough to have agreed to take care of various household items for mother, my sister Rivka and her sisters-in-law, but that all I wanted, were my clothes.

Her twelve year old son was present while we were talking. He grabbed a knife and walking menacingly toward me said, "If you don't get out right away 'ya tebe zarizsu'"(I will cut your throat). I looked at his mother for her intervention. She said nothing to him. She said that I had it all wrong, that no one had left anything with her. At that instant I noticed something that belonged to me. I pointed at a small, round table on which one of my handicrafts was laid out. I told her that I had made this in the seventh grade. (Two of my pieces were so beautiful that the teacher had sent them to an exhibit of children's handicraft). She answered that her daughter made those pieces at school. She wasn't very original and those

300

who knew her daughter also realized that she never even held a crochet hook, or any other needle for that matter, in her life. The boy came closer to me brandishing the knife, so I rushed out to save my life.

Only a few days later, as I was standing by our house, I saw the Balebane daughter, the one her mother said had made my handicraft. She was going into the fields with a sack and sickle to cut grass for their cows. She was wearing my mother's brown pinstriped Sabbath dress. The Germans had killed my mother and now the Ruthenians were enjoying the benefits of their cowardly conquests. I became terribly depressed and angry. I felt outraged at the terrible injustice of the great manager up there who was overseeing the affairs of the world.

I had two "homes": one in Berezov in the bed across the room from the peasant who lived in our house; the other in Chust where the survivors of the concentration camps from Berezov were gathered. People from each town in the vicinity occupied a different house or two and remained there together. All of these houses once belonged to Jews who were sent to Auschwitz and never returned. The few survivors from Berezov occupied a little run-down house at the beginning of Izo Street. One of these was Riva who came from Budapest a few days after I did.

No furniture was left in that little place except for broken beds that no one wanted. The bed in which my cousin Riva and I slept was badly damaged. The springs, of what once was a mattress, were broken and protruded. The sharp points cut into my flesh. After a bad night I would rise in the morning with new wounds and bruises. I tried, in vain, to shift my body to the edges where the faulty mattress would

hopefully be less intrusive than it would the center.
We lived in a sort of commune, where we all slept
together, but we didn't eat together since no food was
available.

I had not seen Avi since I arrived home. I knew that
he was around, but he was avoiding me. I had already
heard that he was having an affair with another girl,
some one from his home town.

She was literally the girl next door. She was with his
sister in Prague when he went to bring her to the train
to continue the trip with me, and he never came back.
As I walked into the shopping center, in Chust, a few
days later, carts with all kinds of food were on display
for purchase by shoppers, I noticed him. He, too,
had come to see the shopping center. As he must have
noticed me, he turned his head and pretended that he
hadn't seen me. He walked by without even a cursory
greeting. That was another wound to my pride, to
say the least, and a another keen disappointment
among the many I had suffered lately. But I had to
put an act. Girls were not supposed to appear too
pained when it hurt. They were expected to be stoical
and I was. But if he had left me for somebody better
or prettier I would have understood.

One day a fellow from Berezov handed me a note. He
said it was from Avi. At that time I was wondering
whether he had impregnated his new girlfriend and
was being forced to marry her. I was almost right,
but those details weren't contained in the note. He
asked me to write to him with the whereabouts of the
items he had taken in Budapest from the German girl.
He wanted to pick them up. I didn't reply immediately: Let him ask me in person if he could, I
thought. A few days later, while I was staying in the

house that was once my home he came by.

Riva was with me on that occasion. When she was in Berezov she shared my bed in the peasant's house. We saw Avi approaching, as we happened to look through the front window. I had watched for his arrival many times previously through that same window. After he entered, we talked about general matters since my cousin was present. When he left I walked him to the door. Maybe he would say something important. All he asked for, was the silver pen which was among those things he had taken. He wanted to have that pen. I shook my head negatively. I didn't have a pen; I didn't even remember if there was one. Other than that he had very little to say. He mentioned that he came to Berezov by way of Manesterits. He obviously did not want his new girl to know that he was going to Berezov. That was why he took the roundabout route. I was quite upset and I could barely suppress the tears.

When he left and I returned to the house, I found my cousin standing at the window listening. She commented that I showed that I was upset and that I was not brave enough. But I really didn't care. That was not the last time I saw him, but we never talked about the important issues. I, too, had a new "friend". He was a young Ruthenian who had graduated from high school and was working in the office of the township. He wanted to partake of the possesions taken from the Jews. Those who weren't left with Jewish property for safekeeping felt cheated. This young man wanted to make up for lost opportunities. Everyone envied those few who had the foresight to store the valuables of the doomed Jews, despite the ban that forbade accepting anything from the Jews. Now it was all theirs.

This fellow suggested that it would be wise to have a birth certificate in the event that I ever wanted to leave town. He offered to adjust any age on the birth certificate, younger or older, for a good fee. He supplied me with a birth certificate, and said if I needed anything else all I had to do, was just to let him know. Word spread that he was "nice" to me and Avi asked me whether I could get a certificate for him, stating that he had been fighting with the partisans.

That was a very useful document under Russian rule after the war. The partisans were regarded as national heroes and were given many privileges. Not all of the Russian soldiers could read anyway, and they had a great deal of respect for a "bumashka", a paper with a stamp on it. The contents were not very important. A birth certificate could help save the bearer from a great deal of red tape and trouble. The Ruthenian was happy to furnish me with the certificate Avi requested. His fee was five hundred Hungarian pengos for each document. I paid him but I never received the money from Avi, and, of course, I still have the certificate.

My new "friend" made a deal with me. He would cultivate our land and give me a third of the crop. My share would be held for me in escrow until I returned to claim it, even if it took ten years. But he had to have a paper from me, witnessed and signed, stating that I sold the property to him. But since I did not actually sell anything, he also gave me a written document declaring that nothing belonged to him. This document was also witnessed and signed by Marika's two sons. The one that stated that I sold him the property was written on a sheet of paper which he kept. For the second one that declared the property was not his, he had no paper left. He finally found a scrap which he signed and which I promptly lost, as he expected I would.

That was a good year for Berezov and the surrounding communities. The fields yielded an abundant crop. But those few of us who returned to Berezov, having miraculously survived, didn't share in this bountiful blessing. We had very little to eat. I asked our very good neighbor from across the street for the goose feathers my mother had stored with her. These were supposed to be part of my trousseau. She told me that she would keep the feathers in exchange for the two measures of dry beans she had given me when I was cast out by the "friend" who was supposed to hide me. I asked what had happened to all the food in our attic and in all the other Jewish attics? She told me that all the food that was found in the Jewish homes was collected and divided among the town's poor. Interesting, I reflected bitterly; the Ruthenians never had a welfare system. This, of course, was an exception. They could be generous with the foodstuffs belonging to the doomed Jews. While we were starving and dying, others ate our provisions. They, however, didn't have any such arrangement when a few of the Jews returned so that we too should have something to eat.

I went to Starosta Fusier, the new mayor of Berezov. I thought he would have some sympathy for me. How wrong I was. He said that I could have my parents' real estate holdings back next year. He wouldn't ask anyone who worked the field, to give me a share of this year's crop. I decided to turn to the peasant who had planted potatoes in one of our best parcels of land. When I told his wife the reason for my visit, she said that I had to speak with her husband. When he entered, I explained that I had nothing to eat. Would it be alright if I took some potatoes from our lot? After scratching his head and thinking about it, he finally agreed to permit me to dig out potatoes, but I would have to leave two rows for him and take only a third. When a landowner arranged for someone to cultivate his land, he always received a third of the crop. The worker kept two thirds. Now this Ruthenian agreed that I should have my share. I thanked him for his generosity.

That very afternoon I dug out some potatoes with a pick I borrowed from Marika. I had to ask her for a sack as well in which to bring the potatoes home. I boiled them in a borrowed pot. The cooking was time consuming and difficult. I had to gather wood from the fence around our garden. Luckily, my parents had erected the fence, otherwise I wouldn't have dared to take the wood. It was a laborious chore, and I never went back for more potatoes.

That night Riva and I ate boiled potatoes. Riva was always willing to share my things, but I was never able to partake of any of her possesions.

There was no future for any of our survivors in Berezov. Almost all of the Ruthenians definitely wanted to be rid of the Jews and were not happy that even a few of us had survived and returned. One day somebody threw a hand grenade into a house occupied by three young men. Luckily it did not explode, but it was a positive indication that we were not welcome among our former neighbors. All they wanted was our belongings and now they had them. No one investigated the grenade throwing incident.

Two other men were almost killed. They were the Herskovits brothers from Berezov who also returned.

They dug up the box containing some jewelry, their parents had buried. They also recovered some money from under a beam in the house. When the Ruthenians learned about this, they were so furious about not finding these valuables first, they attempted to kill them. The brothers ran to the starosta and stayed the night in his house. In the morning they left town.

It might seem odd that most Jews owned some jewelry, even though they lacked other essentials. It was considered an investment for the future. Most brides received some jewels as part of their trousseau. Later it could be sold, when the need arose. I remember when my older sister was getting married, my mother sold her gold chain, probably to purchase new clothes for her. Mother complained that she had to sell her chain for her first daughter. What would be left for the others?

I braced myself for a difficult task. Before we were herded into the ghetto I carried a small suitcase filled with family pictures to the home of a prominent Ruthenian family. The suitcase contained photos of every member of my family.

The family had accepted and agreed to safeguard the suitcase. I thought that the Ruthenians might have been tempted to keep other Jewish belongings because of their value, but since these pictures were not valuable to anyone but me, they would surely return them to me, my family's only survivor.

I called them to collect my suitcase. I found the lady of the house at home. She was the same person with whom I had left the suitcase. I asked politely for my case containing the pictures. She immediately became

307

defensive. "We had to burn them because the Hungarians were threatening to search for Jewish articles. We were scared." The authorities, in fact, never searched for Jewish property left with the Ruthenians. Had the Jews been hiding they would surely have looked. A few days later I noticed her daughter heading toward the bus station with the suitcase. They apparently were not reluctant to keep anything of any value.

The Germans burned my family and the Ruthenians did the same with our pictures. Not a trace of their existence was left. My family, members if which laughed and cried, had much sorrow and very little joy, but did not want to die a horrible death in a German death camp to be converted into soap and ashes. Now I had nothing left of them.

Every memento of my family had been completely obliterated. And my loss was profound. Although I desperately needed clothes and tried to reclaim them, I mourned the loss of my pictures even more. The clothing could perhaps be replaced, but never the pictures of my family who were no longer alive.

While in Berezov, in the center of town in front of the shul, Aaron, the man to whom I had given soup and turnips in Bergen-Belsen, came along. I hadn't seen him since.

He hugged and kissed me on the cheek. I felt that he was genuinely happy to see me alive. I was glad that he had survived, but I detected a mocking smile on his face, one that I did not like, and it bothered me greatly. Later, I heard that this was a new joke, a post-concentration camp one that boys were playing on girls. The young man hugs and kisses her and tells

308

her that he is so glad that she survived. She realizes that she doesn't even know him, that she never saw him and she tells him so. He mumbles an apology and walks away. I realized the meaning of his crooked smile. I thought bitterly that I not only gave away my ration of soup and bread many times, I also risked at best a thrashing from the SS oberscharfuhrer for giving him food, and at worst being shot from the watch tower. And this ungrateful son of a bitch plays a silly con game on me.

The Ruthenians even made use of Jewish prayer shawls which were abandoned by their owners. They made dresses from the striped shawls called "tallisim". The Torah scroll of Berezov, however, was not desecrated, thanks to the son of Mickula, who was the starosta of Berezov at the time of our evacuation. He was a well educated and brave young man. After the Jews left the ghetto, he went to the shul when it was empty and removed the Torah scroll from the ark. He then hid it in a makeshift barn on his property. When the war ended, and the few survivors from Berezov started to return to the town, he told them about the Torah. He wanted to give it to Aaron, but he could not take it. There was no place in Berezov to keep the holy scroll; Aaron didn't even have a place for himself. None of us did. Marika told me that after we left the ghetto that our good neighbors collected the prayer books called Sidurim and other religious books including, of course, the Bibles, the Talmud and other Jewish writings that were in the shul and in almost every Jewish house. They were brought to the shul yard and burned there. The Ruthenians wanted no trace of us left in town, except for those things they could use.

The synagogue in Berezov had been desecrated. In the sanctified place where pious Jews had prayed to God, others were now storing hay and straw for their animals. The new starosta, Fuzir, said that he would have the shul cleaned out, but the few Jewish survivors could not remain in Berezov. They were not wanted there.

I became more depressed. Since I had come back to Berezov everything was going wrong. The pictures, the clothes, Avi, and then the home which was no longer at home. I was waiting for a number of my family to return, but no one did. I could not find a place for myself. Why had I survived? It was not worth it. Not for this. I had a more optimistic dream of how it would be after liberation, but nothing turned out as I had envisioned it. I had pictured a world far better than the present one. A man from Berezov named Yankel Markovits said that he had seen my brother, Chaim Hersh, in Mathousen after liberation. I was thrilled with the news. He told me how Chaim Hersh had survived a bombing by the Americans. He had been in a camp that the German SS had abandoned. When they vacated the camp, Jewish prisoners were moved in. Chaim had become a "stubendienst", a cleaning orderly, which meant that he didn't work outside but remained in the barrack to keep it clean. One day he left, with the rest, to enter the fields where the inmates labored for the Germans. Others stayed in the barrack to perform cleaning chores.

On that particular day the Americans bombed the camp believing that the German SS were still there. The bombs scored direct hits on the camp, destroying most of it. All those who remained in the barracks were killed, among them the father of my good friend Ilonka from Berezov. Chaim Hersh survived that bombing. I waited for him to return home.

A number of weeks had passed since then and he still hadn't arrived. I knew only too well that many people died after liberation. Their bodies were dead long before that event, they were living skeletons holding on to life through sheer willpower; their starvation and diseases had already brought them to the point of no return.

I remembered that my mother had left a few pieces of jewelry with Marika. I had not as yet asked for them. I was waiting. One day Marika handed me a small package that contained a pair of diamond earrings, her wedding band, a gold watch and another ring. Some of these valuables had belonged to my brother Azick.

I then asked for my sister Rivka's jewelry. I knew that she had also left that with Marika. Jewelry was all that Marika had agreed to hold for safekeeping. She had refused to take anything else. Marika, however, did not return Rivka's jewelry to me. She had given it instead to Rivka's husband who had also returned to Berezov. Among Rivka's belongings was a pair of my mother's diamond earrings. Mother did not give her the earrings. She had just loaned them to her to wear on one special occasion. They were in the bundle that Marika had given to Rivka's husband.

He had been conscripted for the work battalions long before we were herded into the ghetto. He never left the Carpathians. Near the end of the war when the Russians were approaching, the Hungarians were sending the men from the work battalions to the concentration camps. He and another man from Berezov, Moshe Kahan managed to hide out in the house of a Ruthenian woman who lived alone. She threatened to inform on them if they didn't leave. They in turn said that they would tell the Russians that she was a fascist if she evicted them and didn't give them some food. When it was safe, he emerged from his hideout. He was dividing his time between Berezov and Chust just as the other survivors did.

I asked him to return my mother's earrings, but he refused. He told me that he wanted the earrings and, that he wanted to marry me. I had never liked him, and my parents suspected that he was beating my sister. Now, after all that happened, I was talking with him for the first time. I suppose I hoped that he had changed, but he did not. I asked my former brother-in-law to buy me a pair of shoes. He was already established in some business and was making a good deal of money, while I was still wearing the mismatched shoes that the British gave me in Bergen.

No stores were open in Chust or anywhere else in Carpathia. I hadn't seen any conducting business in Hungary or in Czechoslovakia. Some clothing stores started opening in 1946. There was, however, a gentile cobbler in Chust who made shoes to order. So I suggested that we pay him a visit. My brother-in-law kept promising "Yes, yes, tomorrow, the next day, the next week. I'll buy you a pair of shoes." After he continued postponing it for about three weeks I knew that he wasn't going to buy shoes for me. I dropped the subject, but I still insisted on my mother's earrings, not just for their monetary value, but for personal reasons, chief among them was the fact that they had belonged to my mother. He, on the other hand, wanted to keep them solely for their market value. He was not sentimental where my mother was concerned.

He claimed that he had only one earring and that it belonged to his wife. I countered that my mother had never given them to Rivka. I asked if he would consent to a rabbinical arbitration. The judge we called on listened to both sides and then announced his decision. Since the earrings had belonged to his wife they now belonged to my brother-in-law. How he reached such a dictum is beyond me, since neither of us had witnesses to substantiate our claims. Being a male helped my brother-in-law gain possession of my mother's earrings. The arbiter was a concentration camp survivor and had returned to Chust after the war. He obviously hadn't become less of a chauvinist in the camps. My brother-in- law didn't deny that the earrings were my mother's. On this basis alone he should have insisted that they be returned to me.

Again, I lost. But it didn't matter. Knowing him even if I had won my case I doubt whether he would have given back the one earring.

Meanwhile, summer was drawing to a close. The High Holy days arrived, celebrating a new year, and the Day of Atonement. I spent them in Berezov alone and I was very sad. Although I was liberated, there was no joy for me. To make Yom Kippur a better day than Rosh Hashanah, I decided to go to Horinch to visit a second cousin who had survived.

I borrowed a basket from Marika, and filled it up with plums. I had nothing else. I thought that perhaps my cousin would have something we would share.

On the day before Yom Kippur,(Day of Atonement) I walked the five kilometers to Horinch. When the time came for our last meal before the fast, my cousin began to eat cornbread for her dinner without offering some to me. She didn't take any of my plums either, as I thought she would. So I had some of them for supper and still had most of them left. By that time I had eaten my fill. I was living on them; I had nothing else. After the "meal" we went to the makeshift shul for Kol Nidre and the evening services. At about eleven o'clock that night, long after we had returned from the services, she spread some blankets on the floor; the furniture, including the beds and bedding, had been taken away. We lay down on the floor. Before we fell asleep we heard some noises coming from the direction of the door. Some one was trying to open it. We had confidence in the lock and we remained very quiet listening to what was happening.

My cousin tiptoed to the window and saw a Russian soldier tampering with the lock. Fortunately, he couldn't push the door open, so he gave up and left. At least that was what we thought. However, he returned very shortly with a bunch of keys, and we realized that he was trying each key. Our confidence in the lock's security started to wane. We stopped breathing. Our attention was focused on the door. Suddenly we heard a key being inserted into the slot and the door was pushed open. We became frantic.

The house was located on a small hill. The door was only a few steps from the yard. We were in a room which was only one flight up. My cousin quietly opened a window and we jumped out.

I hurt myself as I fell to the ground, but I arose and ran. We crossed the yard and disappeared into the garden, where we hid among the corn stalks. We stayed there for a long time. Because we didn't want to spend the entire night in a corn field, we rose and slowly walked through many gardens, not daring to appear in the streets. Finally, we reached a house where we found a group of young men were asleep.

One of them was her cousin. She knocked on the window and told him what had happened. He volunteered to stay with us. I had met this young man on my way to Bistra, a long time ago, when a wagon stopped and offered a ride. The other rider was Avi.

When we returned, the Russian soldier was gone. Finding no women to rape and nothing to seize, he left. We went back to sleep, but this time with a guard. The next day was Yom Kippur and it passed slowly.

It wasn't the fasting that was the problem. By that time I had become quite used to it. In fact, because of the lack of food, every day was a minor Yom Kippur for me. What was bothering me was that I had not seen Avi. I knew that he was in Horinch and that he was avoiding me. He had sent another message to me with my second cousin. It said: "When one fares very well one goes dancing on thin ice." I could never understand what he meant by this cryptic adage.

On Yom Kippur, the few survivors of Horinch gathered in a makeshift shul which was set up in one room in an abandoned Jewish house. It wasn't that there was no place of worship in Horinch, but nobody could go to one for fear of the Russians who didn't like praying of any kind, not even for the dead. A small number of girls stood in the yard while some one inside recited "Yiskor". There was no cantor, no rabbi and no Torah. We had a few prayer books which were salvaged from the gutter.

Only those who had lost a parent or close family member were allowed to take part in that prayer. For me it was the first time that I was reciting the "Yiskor". It was also the first time for all of the others who were gathered there. I recited those chilling words of the prayer for my parents, my sisters and my brothers. "Yiskor Elohim...may God remember the soul of my father Yisrael who has gone to his repose; for that I offer charity for his sake in this reward may his soul enjoy eternal life, with the souls of Abraham, Isaac and Jacob, Sarah, Rivka, Rachel and Leah, and the rest of the righteous males and females who are in paradise; and let us say amen." And next was the prayer for my mother and father. When I said "Remember the soul of my mother Bila Hendel, who went to her repose", I choked. I suddenly felt a lump in my throat as I had when I left her alone in a field in Auschwitz. Now I could see in my mind's eye as she must have stood there with many others, in the dressing room adjacent to the gas chamber, after they were stripped of their clothes and their last vestige of dignity.

And then they were herded into the large, sparsely lit hall with pillars supporting the roof, a hollow pipe in the center protruding, through which two masked SS Germans dropped the Zyklon-B gas pellets on them from the roof. As the gas spread they started to choke. God, I can't bear it. I am choking also. As the gas filled the room, the stronger ones struggled to reach higher places where there was some air still left. They trampled children, old people and the weak. We were told this in Auschwitz by those who worked in the gas chambers, the Sonder commandos. Mama, did they trample you, too, before you died?

Mama, to me you did not die. You are alive in my heart. You always will be for as long as I live. I always see you in front of me as you walked about the house doing all the chores. I also see you running off in the direction of the gas chamber, terribly frightened and scared of what lay ahead just a few steps away. I can't help it, Mama. I shall always remember what they did to you, to me, to all of us. I will never stop hating them for their crimes against humanity. How can I ever forget or forgive, when I continue to behold your frightened eyes? You knew you were going to die and you wanted so much to live.

Then I intoned the prayers for my brothers and sisters. There was no one left to do this for them. Then I did the same for my uncles and my aunts. No one from my uncle Berel's family survived to recite the prayer. I did not feel like doing this any longer. The Yom Kippur orisons ask God's forgiveness for wronging our fellow men. I didn't want to ask The Almighty to forgive me. Forgive me for what? He should be asking forgiveness from me. He had punished me terribly. And the whole world should also ask me for forgiveness since it had brutalized me along with the six million of us who were wantonly murdered. The world had done nothing to prevent this holocaust. They should beg forgiveness for remaining silent. Their voices were not raised in protest while we were going up in smoke. I should ask for forgiveness from only one person, my mother, but she was dead. "Mama, can you hear me? Please, mama, I am sorry."

While I was reciting the traditional prayers, I thought of how it had been in the past. On the eve of Yom Kippur my parents would visit the cemetery. There they prayed at the graves of their loved ones, and lit candles for every departed relative. This time I didn't even have a candle to light for my departed parents, sisters and brothers. I couldn't go to the cemetery to pray because they didn't even have a grave. I was not given the opportunity to tear my outer garment when they died to indicate that a life was torn away, as is the Jewish custom. Sons were deprived of the oppor-

317

tunity to recite the Kaddish, the prayer for the dead after their departure, and I couldn't even cry at their funeral. My parents who lived in need all of their lives, were even in death, deprived of a burial and a gravesite. They were simply crammed with two or three thousand others into the gas chamber so that the Germans, with their vaunted efficiency, could save gas and space. They dropped the Zyklon-B gas pellets through a hollow tube on the poor souls. When all of them were dead, they were burned in the ovens like wooden logs, their ashes emptied into the murky waters of the Sola. No trace remained of their existence. Just the sad memory indelibly etched in my heart. This is their only memorial and testament, and it too will soon fade into oblivion as the last survivor is no more. All that will remain will be a historical fact. A cold statistic. "In World War II the Germans murdered....." And who knows? Maybe even this will be forgotten or denied when we, the survivors, will not be alive to point an accusing finger at the Germans.

After the prayer for the dead I returned to my cousin's house.

When evening came we returned to the house where the services were held. In the evening, the prayers were ended. Avi was present in the congregation of men inside the room where the services were conducted. The girls remained outside since men and women do not congregate together for services. We stood at the open door so that we might hear the services. I caught a brief glimpse of Avi in the crowded room at the conclusion of the services. I had not seen or spoken with him since he asked for the pen. At the conclusion of the holiday services the ram's horn is blown. Avi was chosen to do this. It signaled the end of the fast. This year it sounded like a mournful wail for the dearly departed.

Every one went home. When I arrived at my cousin's house I ate a few more plums while my cousin partook of more bread. The next morning I went back to Berezov.

On the holiday eve, I told a fruit dealer that I could sell him the plums from our garden. He wanted to know whether they belonged to me, so that he would not have to travel to Berezov only to find that a new owner would not permit him take the fruit. I assured him that it was mine, and that I had sent a message to that effect to the Ruthenian who planted the corn in our garden. The dealer wanted me to leave first. He would follow me to Berezov later.

I arrived at the house, and, a short time later, he appeared, but we found no plums on the trees. They were all gone. Not one was left. The young man who came for the fruit was justifiably very angry. He had driven his horse all that distance for nothing.

I asked Mihalie, who lived in our house, what had happened to the plums. He told me that the man from the Kuzi who had cultivated the garden had come on the day before on Yom Kippur and removed the plums. "Didn't you tell him that they were mine, that he did not plant them as he did the corn?"

"I did tell him," said Mihalie, "but he continued to take them anyway."

I went to the Kuzi to look for this man. I found his wife in the yard cooking lekwar, prune jam, from my plums. I identified myself, and asked her why they had removed the fruit. "You did not invest anything in the plums. The corn is yours but the plums are not." She answered that they had pruned the trees and that everything in the garden belonged to them. She said that they had received everything when the property was raffled off.

"And what about me? What will I eat?" I asked her. To placate me, she handed me a small pot of the jam, and that for all intents and purposes would be all I would get. There was nothing I could do. I walked away defeated. I had lost again.

Now I had no home or even a place where I could stay or wash. I did not have a bar of soap or a bowl for water. I had no towel either, and besides what did it matter whether I washed or not? I could use the little stream that flowed right in the back of our house and along the garden. I could do that only at night, but without soap or a towel, it wouldn't do much good. God, what is happening to me?, I thought.

After a few weeks in Berezov I developed boils all over my body. They were ugly, they itched and when I scratched they because inflamed and painful. If that had happened to me in Auschwitz I would immediately have been condemned to the gas chamber. Dr. Mengele sent many there with less serious maladies.

One afternoon I walked out of the house to wash my hands in the little stream called Potick. I noticed our neighbor Antza, from across the street, talking with Russian officer. After I finished washing and was returning to the house he approached me. "I know you," he said. I shrugged, and started to walk away. I was sure that what he had in mind was the same thing they all did. "I know you from somewhere" was an old line. "I saw you in Bergen-Belsen," he said. I was shocked when I heard that. I couldn't believe it. Had I heard him correctly or was the travail of Auschwitz and Bergen-Belsen so physically recognizable? "I saw you in Barrack Fifteen on the third berth in the left-hand side," he said.

"But the Russians did not liberate Bergen-Belsen," I stammered. "How could you have seen me there?" I wasn't in that barrack when I was liberated. He told me that he was stationed, with a group of partisans, in a forest near Bergen-Belsen. They knew what was happening in the camps. They had been on a reconnaissance mission. Although he wasn't supposed to enter the camp, he wanted to see, at first hand, how the Germans were treating their Jewish captives.

So, dressed in an SS uniform he entered the camp quite easily. "What I saw," he said, "I will never forget for as long as I live. I could not absorb the enormity of the horrors I witnessed. So I decided to concentrate on one scene and to remember it forever. I went into Block Fifteen and I saw you in the third berth, on the left side at the bottom. You were very sick, burning with fever. Your lips were chapped and your tongue was visible. I looked at you very closely and the scene was unforgettable. I did not believe that you could possibly survive under those conditions. I am delighted that you did, and very happy to see that you are well." I could not understand what he meant by my being "well," as I was still hungry, forlorn, and in many ways, quite miserable. But I do remember the SS officer who came into the barrack and looked at me very so intensely. As a result of his visit, I left that barrack. I was too scared to stay there when I was no longer able to work.

I asked why he was interested in us, the concentration camp inmates, although as I was asking the question I realized that I already knew the answer. He was Jewish, too. I asked why he hadn't told me who he was when he visited. I would have been greatly buoyed by the fact that a friend was nearby. He answered that he could not endanger his comrades by revealing his true identity.

I told him how badly the Ruthenians were treating me. Not one of them was willing to return our possessions which were given to them for safekeeping. I had no clothes, I told him. I hoped that now that I had made a friend in uniform, he would help me retrieve my clothes and the pair of new shoes that I never wore and that I really needed. Instead, he said, "Leave the clothes and everything else. Get out of here while you still can. Don't you see that they consumed with hate? Forget the clothes and get as far away as you can."

Now, I had my answer. Of course, I couldn't have remained with the peasant in the same room much longer. But I hadn't been able to face up to the disappointing fact that Berezov was no longer my home, that it never could be my home again.

Yehudith was also sent by the British to her home in Berezov; they no longer wanted to feed the survivors and moved out as many they could. She asked me to accompany her to the home of some good friends from the past, to retrieve the possessions that her family had left with them, that is, what the Hungarians had not taken. They had confiscated most of Yehudith's trousseau before the Germans invaded Hungary. The remainder she left with good friends. Just as my family did, her's also left their possessions with Ruthenian neighbors. Now she wanted me to help her carry her belongings to her house. Of course, nothing was returned, just as the results were for me. The woman who had agreed to hold Yehudith's belongings for her had just finished cooking a pot of tokan, and offered Yehudith and me a little, but she insisted that we eat on the bench outside. Her intentions were obvious. Every one who passed would notice her generosity. We were in no position to refuse the bit of food, so we acceded to her request. The bowl of porridge was all Yehudith received for all of her belongings.

Nevertheless, I called on another neighbor and asked for a bundle of rugs that my mother left with her. She at least did not deny that she had received them, but she said that since no one else was returning anything, she wasn't about to be the first and only one to do so. "Why should I?" she asked. "The rich got everything from the Jews. Now why shouldn't I get something, too?"

I had nothing to say to her. She wanted to know why I needed the rugs. I said that maybe I would be able to sell them so I could buy some food and clothes. She looked over at a few loaves of freshly baked corn bread. She cut off half a loaf and handed it to me. I walked away thinking that she probably expected me to thank her.

She had taken a bundle of rugs mother had handwoven expressly for my trousseau. Now I had a half a loaf of warm bread instead. I also had a pot of jam from the plums in our garden. There was nothing else left for me in Berezov.

Everything that happened there depressed me. Marika noticed how morose I was and how I had deteriorated.

She could not read or write, but she realized what was happening to me. I looked as if I had awakened from a bad dream. I was forlorn, and hardly ever smiled. I commuted between Chust and Berezov, settling in neither, belonging nowhere. I was mistakenly depending on the generosity of my enemies to give me a bowl of cornmeal tokan.

Marika wanted to help. Not knowing what to do, she asked, "What ever happened to that nice young man who used to come to your house? Your mama said that he was a very good man." I thought, Oh God, mother must have mentioned him to her; she must have liked him.

Everything that happened to me since I met Avi in Celle now flashed in front of my eyes, my running around to the military to free him. My God.

Marika kept looking at me. "Well," she said, "Is he back?"

"Yes," I said, "He is back."

"Well then...", "Why don't you get married?" She waited. I just shrugged. There was nothing more to say on that subject. It was closed. She understood. I was angry at everybody and everything, at Avi, the Germans, at the whole world that did nothing to save us from destruction. I was even angry at my mother. Why did she have to die and leave me all alone, as if she had a choice.

Marika had a parting gift for me, another of my mother's Sabbath dresses. A black silk one with light gray collar and cuffs, embroidered with small black squares. She found it somewhere and recognized it.

The Ruthenians could not use this one, they couldn't go into the fields to cut grass for the animals, or watch the cows in the pasture, in a black silk dress. My mother wore it on special occasions and when she went to shul. Now it was being passed around. Marika handed it to me, but I was too bitter. I did not want it. Where would I keep it? I didn't even have a place for my weary self, let alone a painful reminder of my mother. I keep seeing those two dresses in my mind's eye. One on the Ruthenian shiksa, and the other with no owner, the original owner was dead, converted into soap and ashes.

On my last day in Berezov I took the quilt that I had been using to cover myself, to Marika for safekeeping. She was the only one upon whom I could rely. I did this, in the event I had to come back to Berezov, but I prayed that I would never have to see that town or Carpathia again. When I carried the quilt to Marika, Mihalie, the peasant who lived in our house, met me. He saw me carrying the quilt and became very upset because I had not given it to him. Everybody was eager to enrich themselves on Jewish property. He had lived in our house rent-free. Now he was accusing me of taking his milk, and here I was feeling guilty. I was quite embarrassed when he mentioned the milk. I had hoped that he would not notice the loss of the small amount I had taken.

I did exactly what I used to do in Bergen-Belsen. I stole what he called milk from his barrel. It was actually homemade cottage cheese from fermented milk. The peasant kept the barrel in the room from which the Russian soldiers had removed half the floor covering. By that time I was experiencing hunger pains but just couldn't digest any more plums. So I dipped my cupped hand into the wooden barrel and ate from my

325

hand. It was delicious. I did this several times in the hope that he wouldn't notice that small amounts were missing. Now, after he saw me carrying the quilt to Marika, he was irate. He wouldn't allow me to sleep in his room any longer. It was evident I had to leave and never return. I collected my small pot of lekvar and the half loaf of corn bread, and, for the last time, I walked across the Rika on the wooden bridge to wait for transportation to Chust.

During the three months that I spent in the region that once was my home, I made this trip countless times. Now I hoped I would make it for the last time. It was now the end of September or the beginning of October. I didn't want to come back to Berezov. I never wanted to see my neighbors again, because soon I would start hating the Ruthenians for their treacherous treatment just as much as I abhorred the Germans for what they did to us. True, the Germans had fanned the fires of hate in them; although we lived among the Ruthenians for many generations, the spark of anti-semitism was always there, and it was expressed in many ways. We were always aware of it. But we learned to live with it. We didn't know any better. Why do you detest us so much? Where are your humane feelings? Not one of you showed any empathy when we were dragged along the main road to the station. Not one tear was shed. Not even a goodbye nod. I saw happy, contented faces staring at us, and, may God help you, there were smiles too. Because it was we who were slaughtered, not you. You are the lucky ones, the Aryans. This gives you more rights and privileges in the Universe than we have. And you cannot share it with us; that, I suppose is too much to ask of you.

As I reached the bus stop, a few people were waiting

326

for the bus which arrived twice daily from Toron, a town near the Carpathian-Polish border. The bus served passengers along the road to Chust. It arrived once in the morning and a second time in the afternoon and it was usually filled before it reached Berezov. There was little chance that it would even stop here. We waited for a long time.

At the bus stop I noticed a young Ruthenian girl who was very pregnant. She was wearing a Russian army uniform. The young women in the army were encouraged to bear children for the motherland, in order to replace those who had died in the war. Now that she was ready to give birth, she was on her way to the nearest hospital. Afterward she would go home alone. The baby would be raised by the state "for the glory of the motherland."

The bus wasn't coming. It was quite late. I was feeling anxious that even if it came it wouldn't take on any additional passengers except for the pregnant girl, who had papers certifying that she was privileged, a Russian soldier pregnant with a child for the state. A horse and wagon driven by a Russian soldier came along. It was loaded with wooden ties. First, the Hungarians had almost denuded the Carpathian woods, now it was the Russians. The soldier was middle-aged and did not look too formidable. He stopped for a minute. I thought about what I ought to do. If the bus didn't take me to Chust I would have to return to Mihalie, and I was afraid to do that. He might have killed me for stealing his milk or just in anger for not having shared the Jewish booty. Besides, killing Jews was de rigueur. Not only were they slain by the Germans, but many were murdered after liberation by other countries. Mihalie was living in our house rent free. I wondered what would have happened if I had sold the entire property as I was advised to do. It brought to mind the incident of the hand grenade that was tossed into the apartment occupied by the three men. It was condoned as a normal occurrence. Slaughtering Jews was just another fact of life. The Germans were allowed to kill with impunity. Why shouldn't others do the same? I had said goodbye to Berezov forever. I couldn't return, not even for one night. I asked the Russian driver for a ride to Chust. He moved to the left side on the seat and made room for me. He snapped his whip, shouted "dio" and we were off. I was finally leaving Berezov, my birth place. I didn't even turn for one last look. I had enough of the place, and I made a vow never to return.

By the time we reached Horinch, after just five kilometers, the bus caught up with us. True, there was no room for passengers when it had stopped in Berezov, but they boarded anyhow, on the roof. Some waved to me from that position when they saw me on the wagon. All of them would soon be in Chust. As for myself, I still had a long and arduous journey before me.

Soon after we left Berezov, the driver asked me to step down while he moved the wagon to the side of the road. He became insistent and started pulling me down from the wagon to accompany him among the shrubs and trees for sex. He couldn't understand why I refused. Fighting him off was of no use. I thought I had better use other means to save myself from being raped. My reasoning eluded him. I just kept talking and kept telling him what the Germans did to me. I couldn't possibly get off the wagon. If I remained alone on the road as night fell, I could expect the same abuse from other soldiers. Then dark clouds appeared, and it started to rain. First lightly, then it began to teem. Thank God for this weather. When it started to pour, it seemed to dissipate his lecherous desires. By the time we reached the road that led to Lipscha, the driving rain had developed into a menacing storm. The Russian stopped his horse at the side of the road, and jumped off the wagon. He ran to a lone house near the road. I followed him. No one, of course, was outside in this terrible weather. We sat in the house for a long time waiting for the rain to stop. It just let up a bit. But by this time he had lost interest in me, and I could relax a little.

The rain almost stopped, and we climbed back on the wagon, and started back on our journey. Then it started to pour again, but we continued on. I was soaked to the skin, and also cold. The rain and strong winds were merciless. By the time we left Lipscha, it was quite dark.

As we reached the outskirts of Chust, he told me that he had to turn to the left to unload the wooden ties. I got off at about two kilometers from my destination and started to walk. Very shortly my shoes were filled with water. Whenever I took a step the water squirted out of my shoes, as I struggled through the wind, rain and a flooded road.

Finally, I reached the little house in which I had been staying in Chust. My half loaf of corn bread that our "good" neighbor gave me for my rugs was a little girl, was sopping wet. I didn't even know whether it would be edible. Gratefully, I entered the little house and looked among my few possessions for something dry for a change of clothes. The girls from Berezov were all there including my cousin Riva. One of them said that Avi had been looking for me. I raised my head, hopefully. Maybe he had returned having realized that his infatuation with the other girl was just that, an infatuation. But the faces of the girls were grim. Finally, the older of the two sisters began to speak. Ruchel and her younger sister Liechu had surprised me one Saturday afternoon when I was alone in our house in Berezov and feeling lonely. They had heard that I was in Berezov and came over. I didn't know that they had survived. They told me that they had been on a death marches from the eastern countries to Germany, when the German Reich was beginning to crumble. They marched for weeks with no food and little rest. They were removing Jews from places that were about to be liberated. They marched them along the roads. After they reached Germany, the sisters found a propitious moment and stepped out of line to hide somewhere along the road.

After the others moved on, they walked to the nearest village to look for work. They decided to use the story that they were Ukrainians whose home and family had been destroyed in the bombardments during the war. They only spoke Ruthenian among themselves, so as not to betray themselves by speaking German. Since they were not tattooed with a number and did not wear concentration camp uniforms, they were able to get away with it. A German farmer hired them to work on his farm for food, and he allowed them sleep in his barn. He even made each of them a dress from the same material. They mentioned that good food they received on the farm and they both looked well-nourished.

When they heard that the war was over, they returned to Berezov. I was delighted to see them. They had stayed with us in the little run down house on Izo Street. On one occasion the older sister, Ruchel, pretended that she was a gypsy and read Avi's palm. She told him what everyone knew by this time about his change of heart and girlfriends. Now, it was Ruchel again who mustered enough courage to tell me that Avi had come to invite me to a celebration of his engagement to the other girl.

I said nothing. What was there to say? I swallowed hard and there was a lump in my throat. I had just narrowly escaped being raped by a Russian soldier. I was wet to my skin, cold, tired and hungry. What a fine end to a fine day.

That night I lay in the broken bed, but I didn't sleep. In the morning, a hazy sun shone partially dispersed the dense clouds. It was a nice fall day. I learned that there was a train in the evening at eight o'clock leaving for the last stop in Carpathia. It didn't go any further because the borders of the Carpathians had been closed by that time.

The Russians weren't permitting to anyone leave. Those who tried to cross the border was shot at. That, however, didn't stop people from trying. It had just become more difficult and more dangerous. I informed my cousin Riva of my decision to leave. She agreed to come along with me. We were warned that until the train reached Chust, it was so unbelievably crowded that we might not be able to get an board on the first try, that people usually had to attempt it two or three times before they succeeded in squeezing into the packed train.

We left ahead of time. We each wore three dresses, almost everything we possessed. We took nothing along except a small bundle containing the corn bread and the pot of prune jam. When it became dark we walked out silently into the night, hoping that we would not encounter any Russian soldiers asking a lot of questions about our destination. The few pieces of jewelry that Marika returned to me I hid in some dough that I made with flour and other ingredients. I also baked small cookies. I placed each piece of jewelry in a separate cookie and baked them, hiding all traces of their contents. I put a few in my pockets hoping that they would be safe there. We waited in the shadows for the train not wishing to attract attention.

When the train arrived at 8 o'clock, it was terribly crowded; filled to capacity.

People were hanging out of the windows. Some stood with only one foot on the steps, and the other in the air. Others were suspended from the doors and a number even on the roof. I thought that I would never be able to board this train. Then I convinced myself that I definitely must. To board this train seemed impossible. Even to try was foolhardy. But try we did, and we miraculously managed to squeeze into the train. I remembered having one foot on some one else's. As for the other foot, I couldn't find any room for it. So I managed on one, clutching my bundle pressed tightly against my belly. We rode that way the whole night through, packed like sardines. Few people left the train while many more tried to push in. By early morning of the next day we arrived at the town of Chop, which was on the border between Slovakia and Hungary. But how to cross the border? That was the problem that had to be solved. There were other people who also wanted to leave. I went to get more information while Riva guarded the bundles. We did not want to be conspicuous with them. I heard a rumor that there was a gentile who, for a good fee, smuggled people across the border. I tried to find him. I met a young man and his sister walking in the same direction. We found the old man and he agreed to smuggle us out of Carpathia, but only the three of us, not four. I tried to convince him to take Riva also, but to no avail. He would only take three and only with very little luggage.

I didn't give him a definite answer because of Riva. I went back to where she was waiting. It was in the afternoon and there was only one more train to Chust. If we couldn't get across the border, we would have to return to Chust and find some other way. We boarded the train to Chust. As it started to move I told Riva that there was a possibility of crossing the border, but that they didn't want to take her along. She said that she didn't mind going back alone, and that if I could get out, I should go. By now the train was moving quite fast. There was little time to waste. I left my bundle and jumped. I had seen the Russians doing this many times. They rarely waited a stop. So I thought that I could also do it. Well, I could not. As I jumped I fell on my knees and face, seriously injuring my knees.

As I tried to rise a Russian soldier ran towards me. It was too late to run from him or to try to hide even if I could walk. He helped me to my feet, placed his hand around me and led me away. I realized that I was in a great deal of trouble. I regretted having left the safety of the train. I decided that when I was being questioned I would say that I accidentally fell from the train, as I told the soldier who came to my aid. Meanwhile I looked for an opportunity to escape from my captor.

I found none. Instead, he brought me to a first aid

station. He said something to another soldier in a white coat who asked me where I was injured. I pointed to my bleeding and bruised knees. He then washed and cleaned my knees, applied some ointment and bandages. They both noticed that my entire body was covered with sores. They made some comments about what I should do about them that I didn't understand.

When the soldier in the white coat finished, he left me. The other one, who brought me, took me by the arm and walked me out. He told me to be careful while on speeding trains and also of soldiers. "This town is a border station," he said. "There are many military men here who can hurt you." Then he said "Zdrastwute devushka," (farewell) and returned to the first aid station.

I could not believe it. I was free, he didn't arrest me. When he had led me away, I thought: This is it. They will torture the truth out of me, that I was really trying to run away from their paradise. I would be imprisoned, and they would throw away the key. From what I knew about the Russians, these things happened all the time.

I hurried to the house of the smuggler. The sister and brother were waiting for me. They asked where I had been for so long. "It is late," they said. "Where is your luggage?" I told them that I had none. After we paid the fee in advance, we left his house and were told to sit in the wagon. He said that if we were stopped along the way, we were to tell them that we were going to gather produce from the fields. He had equipment in the wagon.

We rode for a long time. When he stopped, he told

us to get off. He left the wagon and said that from there on, we had to proceed on foot. He walked in back of us and told us that if we encountered a border patrol, he would disavow us, claiming that he had never seen us before. We should back him up. He told us that he had something he could tell the border patrol about his business in the area. He would not reveal what it was, and he counted on us to keep him out of trouble.

We started to walk, passing fields with wild vegetation, marshy grounds and a lot of mud and puddles. The march seemed endless until we came to a forest. Our guide stopped there and announced that he was not going any further. "Go through the forest. The border is somewhere in the center. Be careful not to step on anything man-made, because there might be wires attached that will trigger alarms. When you cross the forest you will be in Slovakia. A town will not be too far away. Get there as quickly as you can. In town you will be safe. Look for a friendly person, ask for a certain name and go there." God, why can't I remember the names of those people to whom the smuggler directed us? We did exactly as we were told. When we reached the house about which the smuggler told us, it was nighttime and dark. As we entered the house, I realized that it was Friday night. The eve of the Sabbath. Not that one day or evening was any different for me than the next one. They were all the same. But there I saw something that made me remember that it was Friday night. The table was set for the Sabbath meal with a white table cloth and candles that were lit at one end, and at the other, two loaves of challah bread covered with an embroidered napkin. Just as it used to be in our house when there was a home.

I thought that after the war no one observed traditions anymore, that everything called tradition and religion had died along with the Jews in the gas chamber. In this house, however, it was still a revered ritual. A family of brothers, sisters and cousins were getting ready for the evening meal. We told them that the Ruthenian who smuggled us out of the Carpathians had directed us to their house. They said nothing. They were probably used to getting unexpected guests from across the new frontier. We were invited to sit at the table and partake of the meal. They didn't have to ask twice. I hardly had anything to eat all day. The brothers told us that they were making slivovitz (a Polish brandy) from the abundant crop of plums in the area. They resumed their business when they returned from the concentration camp.

The meal was served on china with the proper silverware. This was new to me; after my internment I had eaten from a china plate only once. While I was in Chust I had accompanied my cousin Sima and some other people to a restaurant of sorts. It was in a private home. The meal was cooked by a young woman who had returned from Auschwitz in January of 1945 after the liberation of Auschwitz by the Russians, and she later started catering to those who could afford to pay for a wholesome meal.

In the "restaurant" were some civilians and a Russian Jewish officer, who preferred to eat home-cooked food instead of rations. The meal we had was delicious. Unfortunately I could not go back there again. I had received some money from the sale of our camer and it was running low. There were two small buildings in our yard in addition to the house. One was a stable for our cow and the hay. The other was the camer which was a small structure divided into two rooms,

one for the chickens, the other for the geese. When I
returned I found that the roof had caved in. Some
one, who wanted to use it for firewood, offered me
some money for it. I wish I had the sense to sell more
of our property, as one of my father's Ruthenian
friends advised me. He suggested that I sell our house
and all the land we owned, everything, accept
American or British money for it and go far away.
Since I sold nothing but the little building, I did not
have much money. Later I learned that the Russians
had destroyed all the Jewish houses in Berezov and in
other towns. They left only one Jewish house in
Berezov.

I could still taste that chicken. And now, for the
second time, I was having another fine meal. The
portions that the women served, however, were very
small. They had to stretch the food for three additional diners. I received a slice of the challah bread, a
little soup and a small helping of the main course. It
wasn't enough to satisfy my great hunger. I was
seated at one end of the table. On my right was a
young man, my traveling companion, who was about
twenty-four years old. His sister, a teenager, was
near the center. Both sister and brother were handsome. The young man wore polished boots. In the
aftermath of the war there was a tendency among some
survivors to clothe themselves in German attire. Some
did it right in the concentration camp. Especially
those who became wardens and capos and all the other
ugly job-holders in the death apparatus. After the
war, those who could afford the fine boots that the
Germans loved, wore them as a symbol of manhood,
charm and especially prosperity.

I had barely finished eating when two Russian officers
entered the room. They were quite drunk. We were

337

scared that they might start asking questions about who we were. Instead, they demanded a huge drink of slivovits. After swallowing their drinks one of them walked out, but the other one sat down near me. He reeked of alcohol. He greeted me, "Zdrastwute, te krasiva (You are pretty). Where are you from?" I realized that I had to answer. If I told him that I came from any place other than Moscow or Leningrad, he wouldn't know where it was anyway. So I mumbled Berezov. "What!" he said, "You are from Breslaw? I fought for that place and I was wounded in the battle." He immediately started to remove his clothes to show me his wound. I said hurriedly that I believed him, but that I was not from Breslaw. I thought bitterly that I didn't even know where Breslaw was. I had never even heard of it. (I learned later that it was a large city in Germany.) But the drunken soldier did not hear me. He became very excited that I came from Breslaw and started to yell that he fought for me and demanded that I have sex with him.

Since I did not move from the table he started to scream, "Ya za tebe voyoval, I battled for you, and now you will have sex with me." He felt sex was his due, and if I didn't submit of my own free will, he would take me anyway. He started to drag me away from the table. He was very drunk. He repeated that he fought for me. The young man who was our host came to my rescue. He began to pull him away, offering him more liquor. He started to shout that it was his legitimate right to have me.

While one of the brothers kept plying him with more alcohol, the other whisked me away to a little room at the side of the building. He told me to lock the door from inside. The small place had nothing in it but a narrow bed and a chair. After I locked the door, I sat

down on the bed and remained there a very long time.
I would have much preferred to share a room with
other people rather than being alone in hiding. I certainly would have felt more secure. I did not undress,
as if my clothes could protect me from the Russian's
fury.

Bless you, you good hearted strangers for all you did
for me. I am sure that I was not the only one on
whom you bestowed such generosity and kindness.
How else would the smuggler have known about you?
Forgive me for not remembering your names.

The besotted soldier raged outside most of the night.
Towards morning, he quieted down. Then I fell asleep briefly. At daybreak I was awakened by the host.
My two companions were waiting outside. We were
given told where to go and how to cross the border
again into Hungary, where we were all headed. We
followed his instructions and arrived safely at the station across the border where we waited for a train to
Budapest. I wanted to pick up my few belongings
there, including the items Avi had taken from the girl
in Prague. They were hidden in my distant relative's
house.

The train for Budapest was not due for another few
hours. The other girl remained with their little suitcase in the station while her brother and I went into
town to look for food. We were not successful. We
were all very hungry. It was Saturday noon and we
hadn't eaten since Friday night. One housewife offered to sell us a little milk. We returned to the station to wait for our train which we boarded when it arrived. We traveled for the remainder of that Saturday. Most passengers were headed for Budapest. In
the afternoon I saw a young boy, probably in his late

teens, board the train, carrying several large sacks made of rough cloth. In the evening he removed from one of these a large home baked loaf of white bread and a big pot of butter which he spread on bread and ate. He mentioned that he was going to Budapest to sell these items. A woman also got on the train at the same station. She, too, had food with her, for the trip. She ate one of her thin sandwiches. I watched the both of them eating, and I fantasized devouring their food.

Later, at nightfall, all the passengers fell asleep, except me. I couldn't. I was too hungry. I had not had any food since Friday night, and even then the meal was too small to appease my great hunger. Now my empty stomach was growling.

I looked around to make sure everyone was sound asleep. I rose and tried to reach the bread in the young woman's bag, but it was impossible to remove. It was at the very bottom of the bag. Reluctantly I gave up. Then I tried the woman's bag which was easier, and I removed the sandwich. It was small, indeed. I finished it in a few bites. It certainly did not assuage my hunger, but it was better than nothing.

I kept sitting in my place when the other passengers started to wake up. Again, the young man ate his bread and butter.

The woman, too, reached for her sandwich, but could not find it. She delved deeper into her bag. She looked puzzled, but finally stopped searching. We all continued our journey until we reached Debrecen, a large city in Hungary. There, we were ordered off the train and informed that it would not continue on to Budapest. We would have to wait for the next one which was scheduled to arrive on the next evening.

Everyone started to scatter, looking for friends or relatives with whom to spend the time. I had no one. My two companions were also alone. At night it wasn't wise to be out in the street or in any public place such as the station with all the Russian soldiers roaming around, looking for watches to steal and girls to rape. Besides, we were illegal entries in Hungary. The Carpathians were now a separate entity. If caught, we could jailed or sent back to the Carpathians.

We decided to go to a hotel. It seemed to be the only place to spend the night in a strange city, but there were no vacancies. We were promised a room in the morning. Meanwhile, we settled in on arm chairs in the lobby. Others were sleeping in them too. In the morning we were given a room with a double bed and one single sofa bed. We decided that the two girls would sleep in the bed, and the man on the sofa. It was a nice clean bed, but the charge was high, and I could hardly afford it. I wouldn't have minded remaining in the lobby until the evening. My money was being depleted. I still had some stashed away in my girdle. My male companion had to pay for the room in advance. In the evening we returned to the station to wait for the train.

My companion asked me for my third of the cost of the hotel room. I had some difficulty reaching inside my girdle. He refused to wait until we reached Budapest, and insisted that I pay him immediately. I stepped outside between two cars and there I lifted my dress in front of other passengers to remove the money from the inside of my girdle.

When we arrived at the Budapest station, we went our separate ways. I headed for my distant relative. When I got there, he was not home. I knocked on another door of his large apartment, where I found a woman. I inquired about my relative. She said he would probably return soon and I could wait for him in her apartment if I wished. I don't know what made her do what she did. As I was sitting near a table, she placed a plate containing very little soup in front of me. I had been traveling for three days to get to Budapest, a trip that should have taken, at most, twelve hours. All I had eaten was the pilfered, thin sandwich. Her few drops of soup did not satisfy me. I hoped that my relative would have some food in the house for me.

When he came home, he did not offer me any supper because he had no food for himself. Budapest had changed from a city of abundance to a place where almost everything was in short supply. Bread was rationed. Other commodities were virtually nonexistent. At least I had a place to sleep in his house. He marveled at how well I looked, and how much I had improved since I was in Budapest last. "The country did you a world of good," he said. I reflected that the plums from our garden were nutritious for me after all. I wished I could have some again, right then and there. On the next day I showed my relative the boils on my body. I was afraid to do this during the previous evening, because I feared that he might not allow me to stay with him lest he contract a contagious disease. I did not want to risk it, and be forced to look for another place in the late evening.

When he saw my skin, he said that he had a Russian friend who was a doctor whom he would consult. After two days the doctor stopped in. I was asked to show him the dark sores on my body. He said it was very serious. Since I wanted to go to Czechoslovakia anyway, the first thing I was told to do, was go to the Jewish hospital in Prague, where they would take care of it. There was no way that it could be treated in Budapest. There were no medical supplies available.

How would I get to Prague? I thought that I would eventually go to the Sudetenland. There one could easily find a job and an apartment, I was told. The Germans who lived there before and during the war, and had given the Czechs a great deal of trouble after Hitler came to power, had been expelled. They were allowed to take but three kilograms of possessions with them. Everything else had remained in their apartments.

The Russian doctor told me that in a few days he would be travelling to Prague. If I waited for him he would take me there. It was dangerous for a girl to travel alone. I was fortunate to have even made it to Budapest. I waited three days for him. I had not eaten anything since the woman had given me the few spoonfuls of watery soup. My relative had nothing in the house. The following day, when I was already faint from hunger, he came home with a brought a bunch of grapes and asked me to join him. He also redeemed his ration of bread. I helped him finish both. He told me that there was a soup kitchen for survivors and that I could go there. However, it was not near Dob Utco, (the Jewish street) where he lived. The kitchen was a long distance away. I thought that I should not risk getting raped by a soldier infected with syphilis or any other contagious sexual disease for a bowl of soup. I had starved before.

I remained in the house, but I was terribly hungry. I

started to look around, as I had done in Auschwitz when I circled the alley and a woman offered me a little soup. Now I looked around the apartment, and found some dried bread in a brown bag on top of a cabinet. I ate some of it and it was delicious. I was concerned whether it was immoral to take someone else's bread as mine was taken, but the woman whose sandwich I took was gentile, and not uprooted in a concentration camp. The Hungarians weren't starving. They had enough food during the war. As for my relative, he had a difficult time when the Germans occupied Hungary, but he was not transported in a cattle car to Auschwitz. He had stayed home with a few thousand other Jews and managed to outlive Hitler's "thousand year" Reich. The Germans had no time to send all of them to Auschwitz. Finally there was some intervention from foreign embassies. The Swedish diplomat Raul Wallenberg also saved a large number of Jews in Budapest.

A year and a half later, I met my relative again in Lansberg, Germany in a displaced persons' camp. He had remarried, and I had an opportunity to repay him for the bread I had taken. They were in need of food, and the kibbutz in which I stayed could spare some. Everyday I brought a loaf of bread to him, and some other provisions as well. I saw his wife wearing the clothes I left with him. I didn't even mention that they were mine, although he reminded me that I had eaten his dry bread.

At the end of three days, the Russian doctor appeared to say goodbye to my relative and to take me to Prague. I was ready and eager to leave. He was surprised that I had no luggage. I had come to Budapest to get my possessions and meant to take the bundle that I left there, but by that time I had changed my mind. Why, I'm not sure. Perhaps I didn't want to be reminded of Avi and his exploits. Maybe I was afraid that I would be forced to return to the Carpathians, as there were rumors that all refugees from that region would be forced by the Russians, to return to their homes. If I was compelled to go back, I could pick up the things I left in Budapest on the way back. I told my relative that I was leaving my belongings with him, and that I would come for them sometime later. I thanked him for his help, and we said goodbye and wished each other the best of luck. The doctor and I then left for the station. When the train arrived it was packed, mostly with wild Russian soldiers. As they saw me, they roared like a pride of lions, "Barishna, barishna," they all cheered. Some rose to be among the first to take their turn with me. The doctor told them firmly, "This is my barishna. All of you stay away." They moved to make room for us. We squeezed in among them and sat down. They were a lively group, singing, clapping their hands and stamping their feet all the way to Prague. One played a harmonica while the others sang along. Each time another soldier entered the car, he headed in my direction. The doctor continued to keep them away.

When we arrived in Prague, I bid goodbye to the doctor and thanked him for his help. I then went straight to the Jewish hospital. I was examined by the head doctor and was admitted right away. I was told I would have to stay for a week at least, to cure my skin disorder. They had very few medical supplies and food; they even lacked soap. At the end of the week I was instructed to take a warm bath to wash off the black ointment they had applied to my body twice a day. The water from the faucet was tepid, not hot as it was supposed to be. The piece of soap I was given was so small that it didn't lather. I could hardly wash the black ointment from my body. I did the best I could. The attending physician told me that I could stay and work in the hospital and live with the nurses and the other personnel. They would train me as a nurse's aide. Later I could apply for a test to become license. I thought I would be better off in the Sudetenland, so I declined their offer.

When I arrived there, I visited to a city named Ustinat-Labem, where I was told I would find former inhabitants of Berezov. I located some of the Adler family from the Kuzy, two sisters and a brother. They had an apartment, and they allowed me to stay with them.

At the job placement office, I was hired as a salesgirl in a bakery. When I reached the place I was told that what they really needed was an office worker, not a sales person, but I could still stay and they would train me. I worked from six in the morning until ten at night. Lunch was served for all of the workers. I was employed there for about three weeks when the German girl who previously worked there returned from the hospital. I was then dismissed away after being told that I was a dirty Jew for taking a job for which I was not qualified. I was required to do the bookkeeping, and the owner discovered an error in my figures. I had been working seven days a week, and was too tired in the evening to think about correcting.

After I was fired, I packed my few possessions and travelled another city, Chomutov, also in the Sudetenland and not too far from Usti. I had heard that my cousin Sima was living there. I found her living with a large family of brothers and sisters who were her friends. I joined the group and started to look for a job. I was sent by the employment agency to an address and arrived there at about the same time as a gentile girl, who was also sent to apply for the same job. At that point I wanted to return to the placement office to look for something else. I knew that I could not compete as an office worker since I was only a beginner. But the owner asked me to stay, handed a piece of paper to both of us, and started to dictate. I had never done this before, except in elementary school, and that was, it seemed, in a different lifetime. The other girl grabbed the only good, sharpened pencil from the desk. The one I had to take was only an inch long. The man began dictating a letter to a government agency. The names he mentioned were strange to me, and I could not keep up with his rapid delivery, so I stopped in the middle of the test. The other girl continued to take the letter.

He finally stopped dictating, looked at both papers, and then began insulting me because I was Jewish. My face turned red and, even though it was cold, I felt very hot. By this time I was glad to step out into the cold air. I still had to find work, not only to support myself and to obtain the meager rations of bread and other items that were available only to those who worked, but also because those who were unemployed, especially Jews, were frequently accused of being smugglers, or as the Russians called us, "Ivrey speculant."

I went back to the placement agency and asked for any job that was available. I was sent to a watch factory. They accepted my application, and I started to work on the following day. The job was not too difficult, but it was boring and monotonous. Work started at 6 AM, six days a week, eight hours a day. After about three months, the original tenants in the apartment, the three sisters and two brothers, left. I really didn't know where they went, but I suspected they were on their way to Palestine illegally. An older brother, who left Chust, their hometown, for Palestine before the war, had returned to Czechoslovakia to visit those of his family who survived the Holocaust. He was a "Shaliach," a person on a mission from the Holy Land to recruit people to settle there. He wore a British uniform, since he had served in the British army as a member of the "Jewish Brigade."

The most shocking characteristic about him was that he wore a yellow Star of David on the left sleeve of his green army jacket. I could yet understand why Jews would wear the yellow star by choice and with pride. We had been so humiliated by the same emblem. He told me that the Jewish brigade were composed of volunteers eager to help the British fight the Germans and that they had asked to be identified by precisely the same emblem that the Germans chose to degrade the Jews, that infamous yellow Star of David.

When his brothers and sisters left, only the two of us, my cousin Sima and I, remained in the apartment. It consisted of two bedrooms, one of which was very small, and a large kitchen. The small bedroom had a separate entrance and it was occupied by a single young man. My cousin and I occupied the larger bedroom and the kitchen. After a while my cousin also left. I was now alone in the apartment.

However, there was a problem: the apartment didn't have a bathroom. It was difficult to wash without one, a bathtub or even a shower, particularly since the winter was very cold. Coal was rationed, so I didn't wash too often. I had to heat water to wash. It was a lengthy and difficult process. Then the same boils that I contracted in Berezov, and from which I was cured in Prague, recurred. I went to a doctor in Chomutov, and he prescribed the same ointment that I had been given in Prague. He told me that hospitalization was not necessary, but that I would have to take bathe in hot water to remove the ointment after applying it for a full week.

I made new friends with a Czech family who owned and operated the grocery where I redeemed my ration coupons. They would occasionally give me more bread than my ration cards called for, and they always talked with me and asked how I was faring. They knew that I had been in a concentration camp and they were quite empathetic. On New Year's they invited me to their home for a party, but I declined. Not only did I have nothing anything to wear, but I had never attended such a celebration before, and felt that I didn't belong there.

They insisted, and said that it didn't matter what I wore. I took out my meager ration of meat, a hundred grams for the entire month, purchased a bottle of liquor on the black market, and took it to them on the night before the party. A number of people were present who were strangers to me, and there was a great deal of drinking. After a few drinks, some of the guests started to say nasty things about the Jews. One older man from Prague, who was an uncle of the hostess, declared, "They speak German." (Yiddish sounds like German and Germany was the enemy). When Hitler invaded Czechoslovakia, the Czech republic crumbled). He also said, "They sell cigarettes." These, of course, were contraband. The Czech government monopolized on the sale of cigarettes. After the war, none were available, not even on rations, except in the black market which was flourishing. The Jews were accused of dealing in all sorts of contraband items. His comments were intended to insult and degrade.

He kept on debasing my Jewishness throughout the entire evening. The hostess correctly surmised that I wasn't enjoying myself and insisted that I have a drink, hoping that it would make me feel better. But I had never drank any liquor before, and I began to feel sick. I wanted to go home as soon as they started the anti-Semitic diatribe, but the hostess wouldn't let me leave. She made some coffee for me (from the black market), and escorted me to a bedroom and urged me to lie down. She also apologized for her uncle. At midnight I was asked to return to the party. As the lights were extinguished, there was a lot of kissing taking place. In the midst of all the gaiety, I was unaffected. When the lights were turned on, the hostess insisted that her only son, who was a student at a nearby college, kiss me. She turned off the light again so he could do this. She had previously tried to get us together, but I had resisted. Maybe she really liked me, but that was certainly not the case with her son, who was virulently anti-Semitic. He would always make anti-Semitic remarks. When I was ready to leave, she sent him to accompany me on the short distance. We hardly spoke along the way. It was bitter cold and I shivered in my thin coat, which must have been made mostly of a paper mixture. In fact, I had been advised by the vendor not to wear it in the rain. That party took place on New Year's, 1946, and was my first attendance at such a celebration since I was free. What celebration? What freedom? During my internment I had imagined that liberation would be vastly different from this. It seemed hardly worth surviving. Here, I was all alone; no one from my family was alive.

Soon afterwards, another Czech friend suggested that I apply for a job in a bakery that he knew needed a salesgirl. I thought it might be more interesting to serve people than to pack watches, which I was doing in a factory. So I left the job in the factory, even though I was told that I compiled a very good record there. Actually, my attendance was excellent. I was never late, and usually arrived early every morning. That was because my cousin Sima was also employed in the same place. She reported for work an hour earlier than everyone else to talk to the man who serviced the machines during the night. Not wishing to walk alone in the still dark morning, I went along with her at the earlier time.

I was hired at the job at the bakery and liked it much better than the job I left. The proprietor was a Russian who decided to remain in Czechoslovakia to operate a bakery business. I sold bread and rolls because no cake was available at that time. My job was to collect the ration coupons and then paste them on a sheet provided by the government. There were a hundred spaces for coupons on each page, which made it easy to count. Customers told me that the proprietor had a German mistress, who, along with her baby sister, lived with him and worked in the store. They had a lovers' quarrel, and she left him. I unknowingly was know doing the work of the mistress in the store.

After three weeks, she returned with her sister. He then fired me rather abruptly without paying me for the three weeks I worked for him. As his excuse, he accused me of having taken money from the register. Well, I was Jewish. What could I expect? So now I was unemployed again, and it would be more difficult to get a new job.

An official from the rent and housing department called on me in my apartment. He brought a gentile family with him and tried to move them in. The official wanted to know who had given me the apartment, and that it was not registered in my name. I explained that I had lived there with the people who had just left. He insulted me and made many anti-Semitic remarks, then ordered me to leave the apartment within the next twenty-four hours or I would be evicted. I packed my meager possessions and went to Teplice, where my cousin Riva lived. I had not been in touch with her since I jumped from the train at the Carpathian border. I learned that she was now working as a salesgirl in a grocery store. She had her own apartment, since her brother, who shared the place with her, was arrested for serving meat to an undercover agent without a ration coupon. He was sentenced to a long prison term, and his license to operate a restaurant had been revoked. I could not find a job and became quite depressed. I was told by a friend of Avi's that he was in the Sudetenland, and I hoped that I would run into him, but that proved to be just another rumor concocted to tease me. I heard nothing about him until a year later. I started to think about leaving Czechoslovakia. I no longer felt at home there, and evidently I did not belong there.

I heard that some youths were allowed to migrate to England. I made inquiries, but was told that I was too old because they only accepted young people no older than up to eighteen. I lied about my age and registered as two years younger than I really was, but it didn't help. Others were leaving for Palestine, but no one told me how I could do that.

In April, there were national elections, to decide the fate of Czechoslovakia. The Communists, using a great deal of propaganda, won the elections in a landslide. They went wild over their triumph. On the following day I bought a cardboard suitcase (the only kind available), and packed my few belongings. What I could not stuff into the case I left for Riva, who always managed to get things. In the afternoon, I purchased a ticket for a train to Ash, the last stop in Bohemia by the German border. I met many young men and women who were travelling in the same direction. When asked for my destination, I was told to say Karlove Vary, a city located before the border stop. It would not attract attention if I did so. Jewish emigration was illegal, but everyone knew it existed, including the government. When I didn't get off the train where I had previously indicated, I was asked whether I might be going to Ash. I nodded. Most of the others were going there too. We arrived in that city without incident.

After alighting, we were led by a Jewish person from Palestine to a camp-style building which contained bunk beds with dark, army blankets. The people there were all young Jews who, like me, were disillusioned with life in Europe after the war. We were trying to leave the continent whose grounds were saturated with Jewish blood. The only way to do it was to return to Germany to await emigration to Palestine. We remained there for three days. On the third one, after being thoroughly searched by the Czech police we were allowed to leave the country. Our luggage was opened and examined very meticulously. Everything was taken away. Only a few personal items were left with each person. A young couple with a baby pleaded with the police to return one flannel sheet which they needed for diapers. They refused. All towels, sheets and other linens were confiscated. They took my bank book for an account in a

Usti-nab-Labem bank.

The two young policemen smiled and flirted with me
while they took away my bank book and were searched
through my meager possessions. However, they tied a
sheet to my paper valise and made straps, so I would
be able to carry it on my back. They said that I would
never make it across the border on foot carrying it in
my hands. They were right. They seized people's
jewelry. They allowed only one watch and a wedding
band for a person. Since I didn't have a time piece, a
fellow emigrant asked me to wear one of his watches
and to return it to him after the search, when we left
Czechoslovakia.

That night we moved out of the building and started
on our journey on foot. We were told not to talk, and
not to answer any one's questions. A Palestine Jew
was leading us, but I never saw him. We trudged
through most of the night across marshy land and
through forests. We finally reached a German sentry
post, where we halted. Our guides talked with the
Germans, and then we were taken to a building where
we spent what was left of the night. Later we were
driven in a truck to a train station. Along the way I
met a woman and her teenaged daughter. I stayed
near them all the while, starting at the Czech border.
A young man recognized me from Bergen-Belsen. He
told me that he had seen me digging beets in the field.
He had been observing us, having nothing better to
do. He was now living in a Displaced Person's camp in
Lansberg. He told me that I might be better off in an
old established camp, rather than in the new one to
which we were being taken. I decided to go with him.
The mother and daughter also accompanied us. We
went to his apartment when we reached Lansberg. He
lived there with his brother. They occupied two small

rooms, one of which served as a kitchen.

We were very tired from the long trip. He gave us some canned food, and we immediately went to sleep in the makeshift kitchen.

On the following day, Saturday, he led us to the camp (his flat was located outside in a German family's house). First, we went to the public dining room where displaced person's, and those who had no families, ate. We expected lunch, but did not get any. We were told that the food was reserved for those who were registered to eat on the premises. The provisions for those people came from UNRRA, the United Nations Relief and Rehabilitation Administration. We heard that new arrivals were not being permitted to register and that the camp had already been pronounced officially closed to newcomers. We had to go back to the brothers' flat. I began to feel that it had not been such a good idea to go to an established camp after all.

The only places that would admit us were the so-called kibbutzim (collective dwellings), where people awaited their turn to emigrate to Palestine. The kibbutz in Germany was designed to prepare its members to live in a commune in Israel where work and benefits are shared. There were several of them in Lansberg. One was a moderately religious one, another was affiliated with the political party, Betar, and a third with the working class party. I checked them out. I finally chose the religious community, chiefly because I found the youngest sister of the people with whom I stayed in Chomutov and who left my cousin and myself the flat from which I was later evicted. She told me that her sisters and brothers had lived in the same kibbutz, but had already embarked on an "Alia

Bet", which meant an illegal emigration to Palestine. She was too young to join that transport and was presently waiting for a different way to get to Palestine to join her sisters and brothers. After the heads of the kibbutz accepted me, I moved in with my suitcase. There was no available bed for me in the women's room. Since the little girl and I knew each other, we were told that we could share her bed.

The boys and girls of the kibbutz were mostly Hungarians, while some were from the territories which were annexed by Hungary at the outbreak of the war. There were also a few from Poland. The two leaders of the kibbutz were Polish. Everybody was required to work, in order a sort of rehearsal of what would later be expected of them in an Israeli kibbutz. All the young men went to vocational school to learn a trade. A German engineer came to the kibbutz to lecture to the boys. The girls were not allowed to attend. They undertook such chores as cleaning, sewing, mending the young men's clothes, and laundering.

Those were very difficult jobs. It took a full day to wash and dry the clothes. We resented the fact that we were supposed to work hard on projects which were not beneficial for us. The boys, on the other hand, were exempt from labor. All that was required of them was training for a lucrative trade. We wanted the same treatment. At a later date, the kibbutz made arrangements with a German woman to pick up and deliver the clothes. It was quite a relief.

The young ladies also served the meals and washed the dishes. The cook, however, was a man because of the heavy pots that the so-called weaker sex were unable to move. They were, however, assigned to help in the preparation of the meals.

One bright summer day when I returned from town, all the women from the kibbutz came out to meet me. They had something to tell me, it was obvious, but I could not understand a word. They were all shouting and talking at the same time. It was hard to learn what it was that they were talking about.

I realized that something special had happened, because they were all smiling and looked happy. Finally, when the din died abated, one of the girls told me that a telegram was received stating that a brother or sister of mine was alive. They didn't know which. That meant that a member of my family had survived. I eventually looked skyward and said " Thank-you, God".

I had never given up hope that some one, somewhere was alive. It had been in the back of my mind ever since a Gypsy woman read my palm a year and a half earlier in Chust. We used to commute between Berezov and Chust on small freight wagons that carried stones from a quarry at the foot of the mountains. It was inexpensive, a fraction of the bus fare, but it was a long walk to and from the train. We travelled in groups only, never alone. Once, when we were coming from the outskirts of Chust towards the city, we encountered a number of gypsies who urgently wished to read our palms. I decided: Heck, why not? For one pengo, let's hear it. She predicted that I desperately wanted to believe.

It often happened during the aftermath of the war that siblings or other relatives who were believed to be dead or lost were found alive. I therefore believed that one of my two brothers, Chaim Hersh or Shmul Moshe might be still be among the living. I was rather skeptical of a sister's survival, since both of them had small children and, therefore, would have gone straight to the gas chamber upon their arrival at Auschwitz. I knew that Alta, my older sister, could still be living had she given her child to someone as she was advised to do by a veteran prisoner, who told her that they were killing the children together with their mothers. But she failed to do thus and died in the gas chamber with her child. She therefore could not possibly be alive. Neither could Rivka. She was in the cattle car with my parents and me. She and her child were gassed. My brother, Azick was dead, shot in a ditch and buried along with his family in Kamenits Podolskiy. He was the first of the family to die at the bloody hands of the Germans. We heard from a Ruthenian, who was at the Russian front, that my brother Baruch Bendit, who lived in Ungwar, the capital of Carpathia, was dead. The Germans poured gasoline on his barrack and he was burned alive. Another man from Berezov had also expired in that inferno. But miracles did occasionally occur. Almost everyone who survived owed his or her life to some kind of miraculous intervention.

But who got the telegram? What did it say? I was very anxious. The girls knew very little. I hoped that the two men who were in charge of the kibbutz would have more information. They did not. They only knew the fellow who received it from a friend the town of Windsheim, also in Germany. Somebody living there sent the wire to someone in Lansberg, who, in turn transmitted the information to the kibbutz. This man in Windsheim was supposed to know which member of my family was alive. I pleaded with the head of the kibbutz to ask the fellow in Lansberg to send a telegram asking him to wire back who it was and the address of my family survivor. He did send a telegram and got a reply from his friend with the address in

Windsheim of my brother or sister. We were also asked to please send a suit along. It was a vague message, with only an address but no name, so I decided to go to Windsheim and find out for myself. I was asked to take along a suit.

The kibbutz did not want me to travel alone. They sent a young boy along as an escort. The kibbutz, Bnei Akiba, also had an affiliated one in Windsheim. We were instructed to go there, and stay for the Sabbath and return Sunday if it was just a hoax. It also occurred to me that it might be a mistake. The war had ended almost two years earlier. By now, the record of survivors was complete. Someone might be playing a stupid and very cruel game with me. But I was adamant about checking it out. We were also given a few cans of food for the kibbutz in Windsheim , so as not to impose too great a burden on them. We set out to the train on a Friday, in the early morning. We changed trains twice. I was told by the kibbutz elders to postpone my trip until Sunday, but I couldn't wait. I was too anxious to know whether anyone from my family was alive.

At the first junction, as we got off, we asked somebody about the train to Nuremberg, where we were supposed to change trains for a second time. The person pointed across the tracks. We did not see any passage to the other side of the track, and very anxious to get to the train on time, we walked across the railroad tracks, since it was such a short distance. As we did this, the transit police rushed us from all sides, and grabbed our arms and took us to the guard house. I pleaded with them to release me so that I would not miss the train. The boy who escorted me offered to remain in custody if they would let me go. Tearfully I told them in tears that I was going to meet a brother whom I hadn't seen since the beginning of the war. What did I expect from the Germans? They had seen plenty of Jewish tears and were not moved. Our pleas were of no avail. We were both detained and we realized that we would miss our connection at Nuremberg for Windsheim. Finally, after much talk, and a payment of a fine of ten marks, we were freed.

After our release by the transit police, we entered the station. We had a few hours to wait for the next train for Nuremberg. There was a sudden commotion in the back of the station. A black baby was found in a garbage can. The bustle did not last. A nun who happened to be in the station took the baby away. No one was greatly surprised; this was not an unusual occurrence. Many black babies were abandoned this way. The girls of the "super race" were not overly particular. They willingly engaged in sex with anyone for a piece of chocolate or a pack of cigarettes.

The next train on that day did not leave until three o'clock in the afternoon. We decided to wait for it and not to return to Lansberg. We arrived at Nuremberg and were told that there was no train to Windsheim that day. The last one had left a number of hours ago. I was at the end of the line once again to ask the same clerk if he hadn't made a mistake. He recognized me and remembered that I had previously asked him about a train to Windsheim. He became very angry and started to shout at me that there were no more trains to Windsheim that day, did I understand? I remained in the station. We had plenty of time to get to the city to find for a hotel.

I noticed people boarding a train and the train seemed almost ready to depart. I asked the passengers if the train might be going to be going to Windsheim. They all said yes. I couldn't believe it. I was told repeatedly by the clerk that there was no train to Windsheim, and here there was one. We jumped on the last car just as the train started to move.

As I sat down I noticed someone in a British uniform. Upon a closer look I recognized him as Yitzchok, the "Shaliach" from Eretz Yisrael who had come to Chomutov, Czechoslovakia to see his sisters and brothers at the place where I was living earlier. I had also seen him one other time, briefly, when he visited the kibbutz in Lansberg. He also recognized me. He told me that he was on his way to the kibbutz in Windsheim for the Sabbath. I explained why I was going to Windsheim and that I didn't know how it would turn out. I asked him whether it would be alright if we remained for the Sabbath in the kibbutz. He assured me that we would be welcome. I felt better, more relaxed, and the time passed very quickly.

Since we rode in the last car, we were the last to leave the station. The "Shaliach" excused himself and headed straight for the kibbutz, informing me that he had to prepare for the Sabbath. My companion and I headed toward town. We wanted to check on the address we received. As we emerged from the station, I noticed a group of people in the distance, mostly men, standing in a circle and conversing. I started for that group. They looked Jewish, and I hoped that somebody would direct us to the address I had. As I approached their circle I asked in German, "Would somebody know where the certain 'Strasse Nummer Drei' ist?" "Malka!" I heard someone shout. "Baruch Bendit!" I cried, "Is that you?" We were in each others' arms, weeping and laughing. We held each other for a long time, unable to speak. When we finally regained our composure, we looked around us. The men with us were standing like statues watching the scene that had just taken place. Some had tears in their eyes. Later they told and repeated the touching story of how a sister and brother met after a separation of many years, each believing that the other was dead. They said it was so heart rendering that they wished they hadn't been present. However, those who just heard the story said they wished they had seen it.

The following day as we were walking, people pointed at us. "You see, there are the brother and sister who met after a long time." We held hands. Baruch Bendit wasn't at the train station by chance. He came there to wait for me. He just knew I would be on board. When the first train from Nuremberg arrived and he found that I was not on it, he came to the arrival of the next one. We talked that Friday night until very early in the morning. However, we didn't have enough time to apprise each other of everything that happened to us.

Baruch Bendit had been conscripted by the Hungarians for hard labor in a work battalion. He toiled for a few months in a bakery in Sighet. He did not fare too badly there. Everyday after he finished work, he was allowed to go in to town. He was free from six to nine in the evening. After he became well acquainted with the guards, he would return after nine. The other conscripts had the same experiences. The guards looked the other way. They became quite friendly, especially when they were received little gifts which were bought in town.

While in Sighet, Baruch Bendit saw the sealed cattle cars that transported the Jews to Kamenits Podolskiy. Some heroic people from Sighet delivered food and drink to the unfortunates, in spite of the vigilant guard. After the Germans were defeated, Baruch Bendit passed by Kamenits Podolskiy, the graveyard for so many Jews.

On Yom Kippur, the Day of Atonement, wanting to observe the holiday, he feigned illness. He was examined by a doctor, who said that he was fine. He was put in a carcer, a small dark cell in which he could not move or even sit. He was there for a few hours. Many other Jews from his battalion were attempting to sneak out of the camp to attend services in a nearby Shul. It created a quite a stir. A high ranking officer arrived. When he learned that it was a Jewish High Holiday, and not a mutiny, as other officers characterized it, he ordered a guard to escort all the Jews to a synagogue. But they were still required to finish their work before they were allowed to leave.

Baruch Bendit was released from the carcer. He went to the main synagogue in Sighet. The rabbi was a young man. He was standing at the pulpit close to the holy Ark. He beat his head against it, crying bitterly and lamenting the tragedy that had befallen the Jews. Word was just received from Kamenits Podolskiy that all those who were transported had been brutally murdered. As the rabbi related the ghastly details of the execution, the entire congregation wept loudly. Hysterical cries arose from the women's section in the balcony. Between sobs the rabbi shouted: "God, why? How can You let this happen? If it was decreed by You, Almighty One, that the Jews should perish, at least let them not die at the hands of their most virulent enemies, the Germans."

Baruch Bendit noticed a familiar looking man entering

the synagogue. His face and chin were covered by a scarf. He went straight to the rabbi. Baruch then realized that this man was the head of a little yeshiva in Drahive where he and Azick had studied. He was also the rabbi and ritual slaughterer of the town. He was difficult to recognize, because he no longer had his long beard. He had just returned from Kamenits Podolskiy, where he lost his entire family. A Ukrainian man had saved him, and promised that he would smuggle him out of Poland, but he would have to shave his beard to appear less Jewish. He arrived in Sighet after walking for many days, and confirmed the bitter details of the massacre of Jews in Kamenits Podolskiy.

Later, he was sent to the Russian front to dig ditches, clear mine fields, build protective walls for the Germans and the Hungarians, and of course to serve as targets for the Russian cannons. On his long trip to Russia he had seen many Jews in striped pajamas, working at different sites. They looked like walking skeletons. Baruch had a large loaf of bread in his rucksack. He tossed chunks of the bread to the men in the striped pajamas. The starved workers threw themselves on the bread. The Hungarian guards demanded to know who had thrown the food. No one answered. By that time the bread was gone.

At another stop he saw two very pretty girls. They spoke German fluently and Baruch thought they were German. But there was sadness in their eyes. They asked the men in the train where they were going. They did not know where they were being taken. Later the girls acknowledged that they were Jews from Slovakia. They said, bitterly, that they were brought to the front by the Germans to serve as "mattresses" for the German officers.

After the train ride, they marched for many more days in the bitter Russian cold. The Hungarians rode in wagons which were loaded with equipment. The Jews were forced to walk alongside the wagons. When the horses could no longer bear the frigid weather, they simply stopped and wouldn't budge. The Hungarian bastards let the horses go, and ordered the Jews to get into the harness and pull the heavily loaded wagons. The Hungarian soldiers themselves stayed in the wagons, along with the equipment. They were not going to walk in the snow. They were too refined. The Jews had to pull the heavy load trudging through the deep and frozen snow in fifty degrees below zero. The Hungarians brutally beat them when they couldn't walk fast enough. Baruch said that most of the time, the Hungarians were worse than the Germans. (I doubted that this was possible.)

The Hungarians beat the Jews to amuse themselves as soon as they left the Hungarian territory and entered occupied Poland, the Ukraine and Russia. As soon as they crossed the Hungarian border they became maniacal.

At one point, the prisoners were forced to relinquish all of their money and jewelry. Whatever they had: watches, rings and even pens. They were ordered to undress in the freezing weather and run. They were beaten on while in the nude. As a result, Baruch suffered a head injury. Blood spurted from his eyes and he was unable to see where he was walking. He was with one of our cousins who had the same name, and this man led him by putting his arm around him. He served as his eyes, and so saved his life. Had my brother lagged he would certainly have been shot.

Many men from Ungwar had been conscripted at the

same time. Among those was a medical doctor. They raised some money among themselves and gave it to the doctor for buy medical supplies to use at the front. The Hungarians did not offer any medical treatment for the Jews. This Jewish physician examined Baruch and gave him some medication.

When the Germans were forced to retreat, they ignited gasoline that was poured over the barrack the Jews occupied, including the two Baruchs. In a matter of seconds it was engulfed in flames. My brother grabbed his shoes and his clothes, and because he was near the door, managed to escape. The other Baruch also escaped, but when he got outside he realized that he had left with only one of his shoes. Without these he would be dead in minutes in the Russian winter. He rushed back into the burning barrack for his second shoe, and never came out again.

As the Germans and Hungarians retreated, they continued to chase the Jews like mad dogs. One night Baruch found himself outside in the bitter cold. There was a pile of straw in the yard close to a house that the German and Hungarian soldiers were using for sleeping quarters. The Jews were not allowed into the house. Some of the Jews burrowed into the straw for the night, but there was not enough room for all of them in that straw. So Baruch leaned against the pile, and being very tired from walking and running, he fell asleep. When he woke his feet were itching. After a few days, a very bad odor emanated from them. He realized that when he dozed off against the straw, his feet froze and now they were very painful and beginning to deteriorate. To make matters worse, the Jewish doctor had no medication for him to help relieve the pain. He had to march along with the retreating armies on his frost-bitten and painful feet.

As they trudged on, they halted occasionally to dig ditches in an effort to stop the rapidly advancing Russian army. When Baruch was ordered to retreat again, he could no longer walk. Along with him, about ten people decided that they would attempt to stay behind and let the chips fall where they may. They were all sick and couldn't march any more. At the time when everyone was ordered to leave the area, the sick group tried to hide by digging deeper into the straw. Just prior to the Germans departure from the area, a number of soldiers were ordered to search the straw for deserters. They plunged their bayonets into the straw to check for Jews who might also be hiding. It was sheer luck that the bayonets did not penetrate any of them. When the soldiers had finished, they announced that no one was hiding in the straw and left.

The Jews remained in the barn for many days, waiting for the Russians to liberate them. The front was quiet, they had no food, and no idea about what had happened on the battlefields since they heard no shooting.

Baruch developed a high fever, during which he had rather vivid dreams. In one of them he saw his father dressed in his Sabbath caftan, shtramel and the tallis. Father informed him that very soon something extraordinary would happen. Baruch woke and after a while he envisioned the same scene repeatedly and with the same message. He saw father so clearly that when he moved towards the door, Baruch cried out, "Father, don't go." All the others woke and asked what had happened. Baruch told me that it was not a dream. He was not asleep the second time, he was sure of it. He was wide awake and he saw his father there. He related his story to the rest of the people.

The religious among them said that it would be appropriate to recite a few chapters of Psalms, which they did. One rabbi among them pulled out a small prayer book from a secret pocket and they all joined in intoning.

Suddenly, they heard loud shouts outside. They were sure that it was finally the long awaited Russian army. Instead, a high-ranking German SS officer appeared. His jeep stopped right in front of the barn where they were all staying. Baruch was sure that the Germans were told about their whereabouts in the village near by. How else would they have known to come directly to the barn? They all knew their death was imminent. This was the last SS group that retreated from the Russian front. It was their job to shoot those who tried to surrender to the Russians. The officer asked who they were. They answered that they were sick workers. They could not, however, hide their true identity from him. They still wore the yellow bands that identified them as Jews. He walked out, and they heard him shout orders.

They all began to recite the prayer that Jews say before death, since they were sure that soon soldiers would enter and shoot them. Instead, food was brought in; three loaves of bread, one can of meat, American candies and cigarettes. Baruch's frost-bitten reeked so badly that the odor permeated the entire barn. The officer asked what it was. Baruch showed him his feet. The officer left and returned with some bandages. The men were dumbfounded. They could not believe their eyes. But they were still afraid that they would be forced to go with the retreating Germans. They, of course, wanted to wait for the Russians.

The officer, to their great relief, informed them that in about three hours they would be liberated. I couldn't believe that a German would actually behave so humanely towards a Jew. I could only think that he must have been a reincarnation of the ancient Prophet Elijah, since I never met one German who was in the least bit friendly. I asked Baruch whether this German officer was aware of the fact that they were Jews. He assured me that he could not possibly have mistaken them for any other people. But I still think that if this man was indeed a German, he must have, by some stroke of luck, failed to recognize who they were. The officer wished them good luck with their imminent freedom and said that the Russians were only eighteen kilometers away. He advised them to hide in some safer place since there would probably be some shooting before the Russian army arrived. They heeded his advice and moved to the place he suggested. At exactly the time he predicted, they were liberated by the Russians, who knew exactly where to look for them. The Jewish prisoners ecstatically thought that their long nightmare was over, but they were mistaken.

The Russian liberators treated them as they did any other prisoners of war. They were placed in a camp with German and Italian prisoners and were given no food, but only a few sacks of "suchares," dried out bread, once a week. People died from hunger, disease, unsanitary conditions and were then thrown into a church. When it was filled with bodies, they were tossed on the barren ground nearby. Someone announced that the Red Cross was coming to inspect the camp. The Russians made a hasty attempt to dispose of the corpses. They brought wagons pulled by cows and Baruch was ordered to help remove the corpses, but he was too weak for the job, so they beat him. A friend from Beregsas, Carpathia, wearing a Russian hat and pretending to be an overseer, freed Baruch from that labor.

After the Red Cross commission left, the Russians announced that all those who could walk were to go a quarter of a mile to pass an inspection. Those who were unable to do so would remain in camp without food. Baruch couldn't walk. He was too sick. He wanted to be left to die in the camp. He no longer cared anymore. His friend from Beregsas, Shiyovits, would not leave him. He held on to him and helped him walk the quarter of a mile. He never would have made that distance on his own. Baruch passed the inspection but fainted immediately after.

He awakened in a hospital lying on a mattress and was told that he had typhus. He did not know how he got there, but later he learned that Shiyovits had carried him on his shoulders all the way to the hospital. In addition to the high fever he suffered from severe diarrhea which the Russians had a difficult time curing. They had very few medical supplies; they just had those which were brought over from the United States. A German doctor suggested that they treat him with activated charcoal, and fed with baked potatoes (which he enjoyed) that generally used to stop diarrhea. When his fever finally broke, he was told that he would recover. Shortly afterwards, he contracted malaria, and suffered very severe attacks every second day. At one point he was so cold and involuntarily shivered so violently, no matter how many blankets used to cover him. Then suddenly, he would get hot. All the blankets would be removed to no avail. No medicines seemed to relieve him. They tried quinine, with no success. They finally gave him some American-made tablets which were effective. He remained in the hospital for an entire year.

Each time they discharged him, his high fever soared and he had to be readmitted to the hospital. Once, he was already at the train station when he was seized by an attack, and had to be hospitalized. The Russians began to accuse him of feigning these spasms in order to avoid work. The doctors, however, informed the authorities that this illness could not be simulated. Actually, the doctors found Baruch to be useful to them in the hospital since he spoke both German and Russian, and could serve as an interpreter for the German patients and the Russian doctors. He would even join the doctors when they made their rounds.

The sick Germans were usually brought from the camps on stretchers. They were undressed before they were put in beds. They usually wore two or three pairs of pants and shirts. When they were discharged and returned to their camps they received one pair of each. The rest of their clothing was traded for extra food. Most of the Germans also owned gold jewelry which they exchanged for more urgent necessities such as food and special medications. In the hands of the Russians they were not as haughty as they were in the concentration camps.

Baruch had acquired a gold cross and some other trinkets for acting as an intermediary between them and the Russians. The Russian authorities knew about these barters, but pretended not to know about them. One day, rather unexpectedly, on a tip from a Russian nurse, they conducted a search. She was not satisfied with the amount of jewelry she had already taken from Baruch and wanted more. As a result the authorities confiscated Baruch's collection of small treasures. However, they did not search the Russian workers.

371

After they took everything from him, he was determined that the next time they would find nothing on him. When he later acquired some money and jewels he hid in a hole in the wall which he made by removing a loose brick. But once again he lost his valuables when a fire burned down the ward. After spending a year in the hospital, they discharged Baruch for the last time.

The Russians did not treat the Jews as allies who waited to be liberated by them from the Germans and the Hungarians. Instead they treated the Jews as enemies. Baruch was sent to a labor camp, where, as in the previous camp, hunger, and disease prevailed.

Every morning, corpses were found with parts of their thighs cut out. The inmates were punished severely for cannibalism if caught, but this did not stop them from continuing the practice. Their hunger drove them to madness. Baruch and another man sneaked out of the camp through a sewer, and went looking for food. They knew that they would die if they didn't do something soon. They thought that since they knew Russian, they would get by. Walking around the countryside they came upon a peasant's hut. A woman was at home, and they asked her for food. She gave them a piece of bread and, because they were very hungry, they started eating immediately. She was angry, and regretted having given them anything, calling them "bes boszne," (godless people). They understood so they stopped eating and crossed themselves. Now she seemed pleased. They finished the bread and left.

Two Russian soldiers seized them, holding guns to their heads. They were ordered to raise their hands. The soldiers wanted to shoot them, then had a second thought. They would turn them over to higher authorities to receive a large reward for having caught "two spies." At one place the two young soldiers who appeared to be all of sixteen years of age forced them to walk through a stream of very cold water, in which pieces of melting ice were floating. A Russian soldier had previously appropriated Baruch's shoes. During the Russian winter a good pair of shoes was a lifeline, and Baruch knew it. When he was conscripted he bought the best pair he could get. He had managed to safeguard them through his experiences with the Hungarians and the Germans, but not the Russians. The first Russian soldier who spotted them had taken away his feet-preserving shoes. He couldn't wear them on his frozen feet, so he carried them over his shoulder. The two soldiers who escorted them at gunpoint noticed that his feet were wrapped in rags, but, nevertheless, they forced him to walk in the icy water.

The stream flowed between two mountains. The soldiers walked along the banks, but forced their prisoners to walk in the water for no reason except to indulge their own sadistic pleasure. Although Baruch and his friend tried talking with the soldiers to placate them, it did not help. When they were not able to walk fast enough in the melting slush, the soldiers would beat them. They brought them to a high ranking officer, expecting a large reward or at least a medal for catching the two spies. This officer recognized them and told them in Yiddish, so that the soldiers would not understand, that they were very lucky that they were not shot on the spot by the two soldiers while they were roaming through the countryside. The Russian soldiers had instructions to shoot first and ask questions later. The soldiers were dismissed, and were clearly not happy with the outcome of their escapade.

They were not yet out of the door and the officer could still hear them curse him "yep twoyu mats", for the Russian Jew. Baruch and his friend were glad that they had found someone who might be willing to help them. They explained to this officer why they sneaked away from the camp, and why they could not return as the officer had advised them. That camp was certain death, they told him. The officer then suggested another one. "Walking around without papers is inviting death, too," he said. He told them that not only did the camps have no food, the population at large had none either. They asked if he could help with a document, which he gave them. Then they walked through the area, asking people for directions to the new camp.

When night came they walked into any house and asked to be permitted to sleep on the floor. One house in which they stayed was occupied by a woman alone. Russian soldiers arrived searching for food. They found a few small potatoes under her bed. The woman wrung her hands in anguish and pleaded with them not to take her potatoes, for that was all she possessed. But the soldiers turned deaf ears to her plea, and took them. In another house Baruch and his friend were invited to sleep in the family bed. They told their hosts that they had lice and wouldn't want to jeopardize to them. The hosts replied that it didn't matter, they too were infested.

At long last, after much suffering, they reached the new camp at Gorkiy. The there conditions were somewhat better than those in the previous camp, and they had a better chance of surviving there. Soon food became more available even in the camps when the United States started to ship supplies to the Russians.

At this camp Baruch was assigned to work a detail first at the camp lazaret and later on another job. By then almost all of the Russian men had been sent to the front. They had only a token number of soldiers assigned to supervise the camps. In Gorkiy one Russian soldier escorted a few hundred German prisoners to the various work places. They decided to use prisoners for supervisory jobs. They selected Baruch and other Czechoslovaks, Poles, and Jews. They gave them arm bands bearing the letters VK on them. They helped the Russian soldiers lead the other prisoners to work. Baruch wore a German army coat. These coats were warmer than any of the other ones. They were quite effective in keeping them from freezing. Once an upper echelon Russian civilian employee in the camp mistook him for a German. He came to Baruch to chat since he had heard him speak almost perfect Russian. He told him that the Russians were fighting the wrong enemy, and said, "we have nothing against the Germans. The real enemies are at home, the Jews and Stalin who is practically Jewish. He had surrounded himself with Jews like Molotov, who was married to a Jew." Baruch never told him that he spoke with the real enemy.

Later, fifteen hundred Hungarian prisoners were brought into camp. They were assigned to five barracks. Baruch was appointed the head of one of the barracks. The camp commandant was a major. He carried on a vendetta against the Hungarians. He hated them even more than he did the Germans. He had been seriously wounded when a Hungarian threw a grenade in his direction. He was been buried in a pile of rubble for hours. The major told the leaders of all

375

the barracks to seek revenge against the Hungarians.
One of the prisoners in Baruch's barrack, a man from
Munkach, Carpathia, pointed out all the Nazis in the
group. He also told Baruch exactly ho each Nazi
treated the Jews. He in turn mistreated the Nazis. He
singled them out for stern retaliation.

One of the camp's doctors was a Russian Jewish
woman. She ordered Baruch to treat the Nazis in the
same way he did the rest of the prisoners. He tried to
explain what they had done, but it didn't make any
difference to her. "In camp," she said, "they must be
dealt with fairly." She was a doctor, not a politician.
She did not care about what they had done. She told
Baruch that if he did not obey her, she would have
him placed in a carcer. The Russian one was a narrow, underground hole. Later she reported him to the
major, and he was ordered to his office. The doctor
was there. The major started to lecture him about
how in Russia every one was equal. Russians, Germans, and Hungarians "wso rovno" (all are the same).
When he finished, he walked out. Baruch then suggested that the doctor listen to two Jewish girls who
were brought to Gorkiy from Auschwitz. They were
telling anyone who wanted to know, what was happening in Auschwitz. The doctor insisted that she did not
want to hear about it. When Baruch walked out of
the office, the major was waiting for him. He patted
him on the back and urged him to keep up the good
work. Baruch was more careful after that.

At long last, a year after the war was over, some of
the people from Russia were released and were allowed
to return to their previous homes. Every one who
wanted to leave Russia was required to register.
Baruch did so and attested that he was a Carpathian,
and wanted to go home. They rejected his applica-

tion, and was not permitted to go home to Carpathia. The Russians had annexed that territory. He was told that he could remain where he was, since there was no difference. All the territory was the motherland. However, he did not want to stay in Russia so registered again. This time he gave his home address as a town in Slovakia, the name and other details of the place he had learned from another man. Each person registering was cross-examined to confirm that they were telling the truth.

At long last, he was aboard the train, breathing a sigh of relief at finally leaving the "motherland". The two girls from Auschwitz were also passengers. All the others were released male prisoners. After a few days of travel, Baruch arrived at Chop, a main train junction in the Carpathians. Chop was just a few kilometers from Ungwar, where he and his wife Lenke had lived, and where he had worked in a bakery for many years. He left his rucksack with a friend and told him that he would be back before the train moved on. He then took another train to Ungwar and stopped in the bakery in which he used to work. All of his gentile friends and some Jews who had returned were there. They all were very glad to see him. They told him that his wife had survived too.

He wanted to go home immediately, but they advised him not to go to his previous apartment. Instead, they urged him to stay in the bakery, where he could have his job back. He could not understand why they were all acting so nervous and confused, and why they all stuttered. When he insisted that he was going to go to his previous home, one man offered to go with him, but Baruch refused.

When he entered his apartment, he saw a fellow

baker, half-dressed and lying on the sofa bed while his wife Lenke was kneading dough. He understood at once why every one at the bakery was so apprehensive and nervous. She had married his friend and fellow worker. When Lenke saw Baruch, she became very pale and could hardly speak. Finally, she mumbled that she was glad he was alive. Baruch wanted to leave immediately. She asked him to accompany her into the other room. She told him that she would divorce her new husband, and asked him to stay. Everything would be as before. He to started hesitate. She wanted to further placate him with talk. She then told him that I was alive and that I had gone to Czechoslovakia. Immediately after hearing that, Baruch informed her that she could stay married to the other man.

He hurried to catch the train to Chop. He arrived at the station just before the train started to move out. There were many people there, and some tried to buy his papers and his seat on the train. A great deal of money was offered for places. No one traded for tickets. They all eagerly wanted to leave Russia, and had waited too long. Now he was happier. Although his wife had left him, he, at least, found a sister.

The train began to move, and it soon crossed the border to into Slovakia. There, Russian guards appeared at every door of each car. Only those with proper identification were allowed to leave the train. Each one leaving was accompanied by a guard who accompanied him or her to the town hall to be certified as coming from that town. Baruch became very nervous and worried. He was not Slovakian. What would happen to him when the guard brought him to the town hall to check his home address in the birth register? He started to think about bribing the guard.

He was afraid to approach him. Besides, he had nothing of value to offer him. He started to watch the guard at the door of his car. At the right moment, when he looked away, he left the train without his rucksack, with only the shirt on his back, and lost himself among the pedestrians. Soon after, he arrived in the Sudetenland, he was told that I had gone to Germany. He took the same route to get there as I did, and as soon as he arrived he started to look for me.

In Germany he asked every person he met about my whereabouts. He also prevailed on his friends make inquires. Each person travelling to a different location in Germany was asked to help locate me. One of his friends called on the central committee on refugees in Munich. He asked about me and gave them my full name. He was told that they were sorry but they had no information about me. A woman who happened to be in the office overheard the conversation. She said that she was residing in the Lansberg Displaced Persons camp. She was working in the food distribution center. She thought that she had seen that name on the list of members of the religious kibbutz. As soon as Baruch heard about this he sent a telegram to a person who lived in the camp to check on the authenticity of the story. That was how Baruch and I found each other in a D.P. camp in Winshiem.

My travel companion remained for the Sabbath in the Winsheim kibbutz and returned to Lansberg on the following day. I stayed for a few more days. Another man from Berezov was living in Winsheim at the same address as Baruch. He was David, the son of Esther Mirl, the widow. He was married in the Carpathians after the war. (David was a cousin of Avi's.) His wife Mindle told me that she met Avi in Chust. He asked

379

for her advice as to whom he should marry since he had two choices. He loved one of the girls while he had sexual intercourse with the other. Apparently he had made love to her in Prague, right after he left me in the train to wait for his return. Not knowing either one, she advised him to wed the one with whom he had sexual relations. Had she known me, she admitted, her choice would have been different.

Thanks, but no thanks!

Baruch and I decided that we would go to Israel together on "Aliyah B," an illegal emigration.

After I returned to Lansberg, members of the kibbutz went on a little vacation. When the first group returned, I, too, was allowed to leave with a few other members of the kibbutz. My lower back and feet, which started to hurt so painfully in Bergen-Belsen while digging beets, had never improved. I did nothing about it except suffer. I never had had the opportunity of consulting a doctor. The resort we visited was situated in a very nice area. The food, however, was not kosher, so we ate only breakfast and prepared sandwiches for lunch. There was a lake nearby. We went there every day, rented two boats and rowed on the lake. While I was basking in the sun, I suffered severe back pains which prevented me from rising. I was brought back to the hotel, and was confined to bed for the rest of my vacation.

After returning to the kibbutz, I visited to the Lansberg medical facility which provided free treatment. They did not take my complaints too seriously, but they promised that I would be free of the pain in a short time and I believed them. My physical therapy consisted of a bow with many electric bulbs which was placed on my back, generating tremendous heat. I was sure that this would eliminate my back pains, but it didn't really help. Then they tried pills and needles, but also to no avail. I was then admitted to the hospital in Lansberg for a regimen of complete rest. I later was transferred to the Jewish hospital in Munich on the Muhle Strasse. I stayed there for more than three months, while I under went countless tests. They even punctured my spine and took specimens of my bone marrow for examination, and prescribed all sorts of medicines, but alas nothing helped. I returned to the kibbutz with more acute pain than I ever had previously. Baruch visited me in the hospital several times. Once he brought me a huge Star of David that he baked made of white bread dough. He told me that he had difficult time removing it from the oven. I loved it, although I didn't eat that much of it.

When I arrived back in the kibbutz I met two new members. The first was a rather obese man from Poland. Soon after he arrived, rumors spread that he had been sterilized or castrated by the Germans. As a result, no one befriended him. He became an outcast from the kibbuta community and subjected to a great deal of sarcasm and clowning. After a while he was forced to leave the kibbutz.

The other new arrival was a girl from the Carpathians. Soon after she was admitted, every one knew her secret. She had been raped by a Russian soldier in Budapest, and contracted syphilis from her attacker. She had served as an interpreter for the Russians and the Hungarians. I thought that she was handsomely rewarded for her services.

While she was being treated for the syphilis, the members of the kibbutz looked upon her as if she were a maimed person. People who suffered the most from the Germans or by the war, were shunned by the other survivors who were fortunate enough not to have been hurt too badly. At least, they thought, they were in good health. However, many diseases, physical and mental, became evident much later. When I returned from the hospital, I too was regarded as being damaged. Some members of the kibbutz refused to have anything to do with me, as if my back pain was a contagious disease. The only girl who befriended me was Lilly, who had a heart condition. The two of us felt isolated. Lilly and I became very close friends. We thought that we would never be separated and that we would go to Israel together. However, it did not happen. One of the young men from the kibbutz started to spend some time with me. He taught me mathematics, which I liked very much, as well as other subjects that he was studying.

A Yiddish show was presented in Lansberg, and the kibbutz members were going to see the show. It was the Yiddish version of Fiddler On The Roof. It was billed by its Yiddish title "Tovia der Milichiker." There weren't enough tickets available, so Lilly and I were told that we could attend the next showing. The young man preferred to stay home, too, because I was not going. His brother was the assistant to the head of the kibbutz, and when he realized his sibling's interest in me, he intervened and aborted the friendship before it developed into something more serious.

The young ladies of the kibbutz were rewarded for their devoted service to the members of a congress which took place in the building just below the kibbutz. Their awards were certificates to Israel. These documents entitled the bearers to legal entry into

Palestine while it was still under British rule. I was one of the recipients of that privilege. The kibbutz assistant wanted me separated from his brother. I was even given some pocket money for the trip. The rest of the members of the kibbutz would have to emigrate illegally. In the early spring of 1947 I was notified that I could leave for Palestine. All those with a permit were transferred from the American held territory in Germany to the British section.

Lilly, however, was not as "lucky" as I was. She left Germany a short time after I did, and on July 7 (three days after my arrival in Palestine), she, along with all the other kibbutz members, boarded an illegal ship in France named "Yetziath Europa" (Exodus from Europe). The British navy intercepted them as soon as they left the small harbor near Marseille. Six warships escorted them until they almost reached Haifa harbor. The British wanted to send all of the 4,500 passengers to Cyprus where they usually sent illegal refugees trying to enter Palestine. In Cyprus illegals were interned in camps. The passengers of the Exodus refused to be taken to Cyprus. Near the port of Haifa, the British attacked the Exodus and a fierce battle ensued. There were many casualties. Thirteen British soldiers died and many were wounded on board the Exodus. The ship was forced back to France, but the passengers refused to disembark when they arrived there. The ship remained in French territorial waters for six weeks. The British decided to take the vessel to Hamburg, where they forcibly removed each passenger. They had spent a total of two months aboard the Exodus. I later learned that Lilly was very sick and was taken off the boat on a stretcher when they reached Hamburg. All of the refugees were placed in two concentration camps near Hamburg where British armed guards and dogs kept them under surveillance from watch towers. They were interned there for six months. They were finally freed when the state of Israel was established. Lilly later married the kibbutz cook, Mordche, and they settled in South America where he had relatives.

After a number of days I arrived (for the second time) at Bergen, just a few short miles from Bergen-Belsen, where the site of the once infamous concentration camp. A few days after my arrival, a number of other people and I hired a vehicle for the short trip to the concentration camp location. At this time the place looked vastly different from the way it looked when I saw it for the first time in early January of 1945, when the Third Reich was crumbling. For one thing, now it was spring and the sun was shining. At the entrance to the camp were two wooden barracks alongside each other. Families with children lived in the barracks. A monument was also erected in April of 1946 honoring the martyred Jews of Bergen-Belsen. The inscription on the monument reads: "Israel and the world shall remember the 30,000 Jews exterminated in the concentration camp of Bergen-Belsen at the hands of the murderous Nazis. Earth, conceal not blood shed on thee." There is another monument with inscriptions in thirteen languages, including Yiddish and Hebrew. When I entered the camp, where once the inmates' barracks were situated, all traces of them were gone. Everything was destroyed.

Trees were planted where the barracks once stood. Saplings were growing erect.

Where the kitchen was located, only the cement floor remained. The shoes that were once piled high at the gate to the crematorium had also disappeared, along with the crematorium. Nothing was left, only charred ground remained in and around the pits where the corpses were once burned. The air was no longer fouled by the sickening odor of burning flesh. Even the birds returned to Bergen-Belsen after a long hiatus of at least three years when Bergen-Belsen housed the unfortunate innocents. The birds couldn't bear the putrid emanation from the piles of nude, emaciated bodies lying in front of every barrack. And yes, I no longer envision the procession of wagons loaded with dead bodies on their way to their final destination, cremation. Now only the trees would be mute reminders of what transpired on that soil.

There are a number of cemeteries in the Bergen-Belsen region. The unfortunates who died just after they had seen some light at the end of the dark tunnel of internment were buried there. They were liberated, but unable to enjoy their new freedom. They were gone, never to return. I visited those cemeteries, and read a number of inscriptions on the simple wooden boards which served as grave markers. What was I looking for? A familiar name? A brother? A friend? Udel and Frida who died in the Bergen hospital and were buried somewhere in the vicinity of Bergen without even a simple marker for graves? There were also a number of mass graves, which were identified as such. At one of these the marker indicated that a few thousand had been buried there.

On one Saturday afternoon while I took a walk, as everyone else seemed to be doing that day, someone out of the large crowd hugged me so unexpectedly and aggressively that I almost lost my balance. "Monci, you are alive. You are alive." she shouted. I looked into the face of Emma, the capo from the peeling kitchen of Bergen-Belsen. She embraced and kissed me and kept repeating, "You are alive. You are alive. I can't believe it." She looked about the same as she did when we were in Bergen-Belsen. We talked a little, and asked me what I was doing in Bergen. She was in the company of a young man.

We remained in Bergen for a few weeks, and were then moved to a different place in Germany, also under British control. It was just a camp and it was awful. Our food consisted of a soup which was as bad as the concoction we received when we arrived in Auschwitz. It was unpalatable. Those with money were able to buy additional food. We lived on the one piece of bread daily. Someone told me about a cherry tree not too far away. I would go there every day, and pick a few cherries from the lower branches to supplement the bread.

Our sleeping quarters were quite poor. The berths were similar to those we had in the concentration camps, except that there were only two layers, instead of three. Loose straw was strewn in the berths, without a cover for the straw, or a blanket. I was issued a "stateless" passport in that camp.

Later, we traveled to Marseille. We stayed there for about two weeks on the top floor of a rather hotel high but without an elevator. I had a few francs which received when I converted my German marks. I went into the city to see what I could buy. I stopped at the window of a lingerie shop with many nice nightgowns on display, but they were so expensive that all of my francs were not enough to purchase even one of them.

But I thought it would be nice to own a pretty nightgown. I had never had one before. I went into the store to inquire whether they had anything for less money. A man and a woman were in the store. I asked about the gowns in German, but they did not understand me. The woman motioned for me to wait, and disappeared through a side door. She soon emerged with another, older woman, who asked in Yiddish what I wanted. I told her about the gowns, and she translated my request for the younger one, who just shook her head, indicating through the translator that she was sorry, but she had nothing cheaper.

The older woman began to question me about where I was from and what I was doing in France. I said her that I was on my way to Palestine. She wanted to know how I survived the war and asked what had happened to my family. She accompanied me out of the store to indicate the direction to take to return to my hotel. But instead of just telling me how to get there, she walked with me all the way. Then she asked if she could visit with me on the next day and take me out, so that we could continue our talk. I agreed, and we made an appointment for two o'clock on the next afternoon. She arrived promptly and took me to an ice cream parlor. We sat in a quiet corner and talked.

After telling her about my experiences in the war, she began to talk about her own. During the Nazi occupation of France she hid in a gentile family's house, where she successfully avoided persecution. She complained that she did not derive much pleasure from her only daughter, whom I had met in the store. She married out of the faith, even though her mother had objected and the marriage wasn't a happy one. The woman was also saddened to learn that her daughter could not bear children. Before she walked back to my hotel with me, she invited me to her home for lunch on the following day, and told me to come early so that we could have more time together.

On the following day, her daughter was present. The woman informed me that her daughter wanted me to know that she was sorry that she was unable to converse with me because of the language barrier. She had prepared a kosher lunch so I would have no qualms about eating. The meal was not only kosher, but delicious as well. It was fried flounder with potatoes, with a wedge of lemon for the fish. I was told to try some of the green olives on the table. I never had tasted olives before. I started to cough. I had not expected them to taste the way they did. She told me I would be eating lots of them in Eretz-Yisrael. "They are quite popular in the Middle East,"

I stayed for a long time after lunch. She told me that she lived alone in that large apartment, and that she was divorced before her ex-husband died. "People make terrible mistakes," she said. She was happily wed to a lawyer, and lacked for nothing. One day she had to see the doctor. Along the way she realized that she forgot something, and returned home. When she entered, she found her husband and the maid in bed. She left immediately without taking anything, and insisted on a divorce. Her pride was devastated. She received her divorce but lived a lonely life ever since.

She suggested that I stay with her in Marseille, and said that it would be very difficult for me all alone in a new country. How right you were, Esther. It was more difficult than I imagined. She was not very wealthy, she said, but she would send me to school, so I could learn French and other skills that I could later use to earn my own livelihood, if necessary. When I did not agree, she thought that I might be afraid that there were no young men with similar backgrounds to mine in France. She assured me that, in fact, there were some, even in Marseille. My certificate for a legal entry to Palestine would not be wasted. They would give it to someone else. At a later date, if I wanted to go there I would be able to do so. But I could not forfeit the privilege of legal entry while others were trying desperately to get there even illegally. I had already decided to leave Europe. I could not stay among the people who were responsible for the Holocaust. I wanted to be as far away as I could from Europe and Germany. I had made up my mind, but as it turned out, I made a big mistake.

When the mother and daughter realized that I adamant about going, they urging me to stay. As for Palestine, the mother said, she couldn't help me. She had no one there except a distant relative in Tel Aviv, whose address she gave me. If I decided to go to America, she had a sister there who could offer some help. She had another sister in Paris, whom she said we could visit and explore the city. She was sure I would enjoy it. The mother then presented me with a little gold charm of the Ten Commandments. It was her mother's, she said. She could not pass it on to her daughter for whom it was of no use. She asked me to remember her name, Esther, in the event we ever lost contact, and she hoped that if I had a child, I would name the offspring for her. Of course, she said, after you name the first one for your mother. Sorry, Esther, I had two miscarriages but did not give birth to a daughter to name her for you or my mother. Then they gave me some clothes, and a piece of beautiful cotton material, from which I later made a dress which I wore for a long time. They even packed some sweets and fruit for the boat ride. The packages were wrapped in paper from the daughter's store, with the name and address of the family printed on it. They wanted to be sure that I had their correct address. I promised that I would save one of the papers, and told them not to worry. They took me to the ship in a taxi, and asked me to write as soon as I reached Palestine. If I changed my mind about emigrating I could always come back. I would be welcome in their home.

I became very sick on the ship. I had never been at sea before. The papers I wanted to save with their address were lost. When I realized what had happened I was very upset. But I still had the address of Esther's sister in Paris. She had entered the address herself in my memo book. After I arrived in Palestine, I asked someone to write a nice letter in French, explaining to Esther's sister what had happened, and asking her to answer and to send her sister's address in Marseille, or at least to forward my letter to her. I never received an answer from Paris. I bought a chain for the little charm she gave me, and wore it on my neck for a few years. I still have it. I don't wear it anymore, but I look at it often and remember Esther and her daughter. I am truly sorry that we lost contact.

I had another misfortune aboard the ship because I was seasick. When we arrived at Haifa harbor and docked, a rumor spread that the British were confiscating immigrant's jewelry. I was shocked. Now the British, too? First it was the Hungarians, then the Germans, and now even the British were robbing us. Would there ever be an end to Jewish persecution? I remembered that when I left home and went into hiding I sewed my money into the lining of my coat, passed an inspection by the Hungarians in Chust, and brought the money safely to Auschwitz. There, of course, the Germans relieved me of my coat, along with the money it contained, in the bath house. So now, to prevent the British from taking my earrings, I removed them from my ears and safely hid them in my clothing, or so I thought. Instead, when I wasn't too careful, they fell to the deck of the Kedma, our ship. This was her maiden voyage from France to Palestine. A man found them, and went around the deck asking who had lost a pair of diamond earrings. At the time I was suffering from a severe aching, felt nauseous and feverish. My seasickness blunted my appetite and I ate nothing during the entire five day journey.

In my misery I did not realize that the earrings were mine. The man circled the deck a number of times trying to find the owner of the earrings. Since no one claimed them he kept my treasured possession. In fact, the British did not examine the incoming refugees for earrings or any other jewelry. They just looked for electrical appliances in order to collect customs duty. Ironically, I could have worn them openly without any problem. When my headache abated and I realized what had happened, the man was gone.

Then, my mother's engagement ring was stolen from me while I was watching Israel's second Independence Day parade in Haifa in 1949, almost three years after my arrival in Palestine. I had kept the ring along with another charm in a shoulder bag. When I wasn't paying attention, three sailors who were standing behind me, stole my ring and the charm. When I discovered my loss I became ill and was hospitalized. Nobody answered my advertisement in the paper offering a reward for the return of the ring. It was gone forever.

When the war ended, the D.P. camps in Germany were over-crowded with survivors of the Holocaust, people, like me, who were disillusioned with life in the countries of their origin. Just as I did, they crossed many borders, and came to the American and

British zones in Germany from all over Europe, in the hope that from there they would be able to emigrate to more friendly countries.

All but a few left, mostly to Israel and the United States. The majority of those who arrived in the United States were given material help including finding apartments, jobs and helping with the rent for the first few months. But not many received psychological assistance. At that time few even realized that we might need such rehabilitation as urgently as we did the material aid. No one knew the depths of our psychological scars, not only from the selections and the other cruel German abuses, but also from the loss of our families, possessions, and our homes and communities.

After the war, when the Germans were once again flourishing economically, they offered compensations to survivors. Many of us objected to receiving what was characterized by the Germans as "wiedergutmachung," (making reparations). We who objected, called it "blood money." We said that no amount of money could even assuage us for the terrible wrongs the Germans had inflicted on us and our families.

However, others, who where desperately in need of financial help, did press their claims for reparations. I was among those who did not want their self-serving bribe. However, after I realized that many survivors had applied for the wiedergutmachung, and that the state of Israel was receiving goods from Germany as compensation for those who had perished, along with the fact that I desperately needed the money, I finally decided to apply. This entailed my standing on long lines, convincing witnesses to testify that I was, indeed, in a concentration camp, and being asked to swear on the Bible, which I refused to do. Then I was required to sign a statement attesting I was telling the truth. I was one of a host of victims waiting for "blood money" from our tormentors.

The Germans took their own sweet time. After a number of years, when the money finally arrived, the five hundred Israeli pounds that I received did not even make an appreciable difference one way or the other. All I could buy for that sum was two pairs of shoes. Did they, at last, pay me for the shoes they seized from me in Auschwitz? Did the five hundred pounds even begin to compensate me for the cruel winter I suffered in Auschwitz and later in Bergen-Belsen without shoes? It was all a huge ironic joke. When I was in the United States in about 1964, my doctor at Mount Sinai Hospital where I was being treated, convinced me to claim damages for the poor state of my health. He also wrote a letter attesting to the severity of my injury addressed to the German authorities in charge of the wiedergutmachung. My claim was rejected explaining that they had asked me in a letter, after I had received the five hundred pounds, whether I had any further claims. They said that since I had not answered, at the time, I lost my chance to receive reparations for damages to my health. It seems that I had offended their delicate sensibilities. I had wounded their German pride. Of course, I never received such a letter, though they might have sent it. I explained through my lawyers that I might have been in transit between Israel and the United States. It did not help.

My attorneys later requested a one time allotment to help me in my dire need. Their answer was always the same. Because I had not answered their letter, their obligation to deal with me ceased. So my dear Ger-

393

mans, now I owe you a reply to your letter, even though it may be a bit late. But as the saying goes: Better later than never. Here is your answer:

You bloody German bastards. You killed my father and my mother. You murdered my two sisters and three brothers. You crippled me physically and mentally, and you have the tenacity to ask me whether I have any claims against you? You bet I have. But you will never be able to repay me. Not even in six million years. Your infamous name will go down in history for the degradation you committed and for the most detestable crimes ever recorded in the history of mankind. You created the hells of Auschwitz and Bergen-Belsen so evil that they beggars description. Pat yourselves on your collective backs. You out-deviled the devil. You Germans can never be absolved or pardoned for your dastardly crimes. Even the soil saturated with innocent blood you shed can never be cleaned. Wherever any one of you walks the streets of the world, children of all nations will point an accusing finger and say: These are the conscienceless butchers who killed blameless people, including babies, in cold blood. You enjoyed the carnage. You had an orchestra playing beautiful music while you herded men, women and children into the gas chamber. You rewarded your devoted lackeys with extra food and liquor for participating in the slaughter. You performed your depraved atrocities with zeal. You even mercilessly killed us one half hour before the allies entered the camps. We were treated as animals, without food and water, in filth and under conditions that bred sickness everywhere. You seized us from the four corners of Europe and brought us to slave in your factories of death. You employed high technology to destroy us at a faster pace because you were in a great hurry to get rid of us. To breathe the same air that we did for a little while longer would have been unforgivable for you. You needed desperately to breathe "pure" air, uncontaminated by Jews. You fostered and fostered a Josef Mengele on us, who with a flick of his gloved hand sent two and a half million of us to our death.

Dr. Mengele, after you sent them to the gas chamber to die, you often watched them through the peep hole after the Zyklon-B poison gas was dropped on them. You, with obvious glee, watched them writhe in pain and agony while the gas was asphyxiating them. You looked quite content, very pleased and proud of your deeds when you casually pointed your finger to the right and to the left, one of which always meant death. I can't help but feel unbridled hatred for you. May you taste the curses of Auschwitz on your skin as you made us live through it.

Tell me Dr. Mengele, how do you sleep? Do you have nightmares like the ones I suffered through all those years? Do you see your victims in your dreams writhing in pain? You cold blooded murderer. I wish that you could live for a thousand years, and that every night of your life your victims haunt you until you scream in pain just as they did, while you and your fellow criminals enjoyed macabre jokes.

And if you are dead, Dr. Mengele, may you burn in hell for all eternity. Amen.

Epilogue

A popular saying among the Germans in Auschwitz was that no one leaves Auschwitz except through the chimney. At the war's end I thought that gave the to the adage. Those who had survived that camp had really left it. However, as time passed I came to realize that the Germans were partially correct. Only our bodies had Auschwitz, but our minds and souls remain there even after fifty years.

I am still in Auschwitz. I will live there for the rest of my life. In my daily routine, every time I eat and drink, the camp seems to come alive. When I see food being thrown out, I think of how it would have tasted in Auschwitz, if only I were fortunate enough to have had it. Every piece of bread I eat reminds me of Auschwitz; of how precious a single slice was. Auschwitz comes vividly to mind when I stroll along Thirteenth Avenue in Brooklyn, N.Y. where mothers and children walk on a sunny day. The children often drop whatever they happen to be eating. When I see a piece of bagel or pretzel, or a piece of fruit on the sidewalk, I immediately think about Auschwitz where I would have eagerly picked up all these discarded foods and eaten them gratefully. I have heard about similar reactions from other survivors, who, like myself, to this day hoard food and clothing in their houses as a contingency for another holocaust. I always carry food in my purse in the event of an emergency. Starvation might be just around the corner. I am sensitive to words that don't normally bother others. For example, the uttering of the word "gas" instantly makes me shudder. How can anyone mention it so casually? Don't they know that it conjures up scenes of writhing death of innocent people by Zyklon B? The same is true of "smoke." When I see a cloud of smoke rising from a factory chimney, I recall the tall ones in Auschwitz. A knock on my door at an odd hour also makes me shudder. Highly polished boots, uniforms, all bring back terrible memories that I try desperately to forget. A simple fence brings to mind the tall electrified barbed wire ones in Auschwitz. While riding in a subway train, the closing of the doors brings back the claustrophobic fear of being trapped in the gas chamber with its resulting deaths.

When I lie down on a bed, I think about how much different it is from the bare, dirty floors on which I slept. I start to cry whenever I am reminded of the camps, or whenever there is talk about a family member who perished there.

All those things that happened so many years ago have been suppressed during the fifty year interval. But as I grown older they have been surfacing periodically into my awareness. I had so thoroughly suppressed the memory of being beaten over the head with the butt of a rifle by an SS guard in Bergen-Belsen, that when my doctor at Mount Sinai Hospital where I was treated for severe headaches asked me whether I had ever been beaten over the head in the concentration camp, I replied "No." I did not even remember the episode. Now that I am nearing the age of my mother when she was put to death in the gas chamber, I think how terrible it must have been for her when Dr. Mengele separated us, and she was left alone, without knowing where she was. How sad and lonely she must have felt. She ran off, alone, to her untimely end in a place in Poland she never heard of, robbed of her children, to face her horrible death alone.

This scene is quite vivid in my mind, and won't fade; it becomes more graphic as time passes. It is constantly in my mind's eye. An older woman all alone in a lion's den. The "cultured" killers lying in wait for her, ready end her life, without pity or remorse. I feel terribly guilty that I separated myself from her, and allowed her go off alone. I am sure that Dr. Mengele would not have objected if I had chosen to go with her. One more Jew in the crematorium would have made little difference to him. We were all destined for that fate, sooner or later, and I would have eased the loneliness of my mother's last moments in this world. She would have had her last daughter at her side when she died. Why didn't I run after her behind Dr. Mengele? I still might have found her. I would have made her very happy I come. She wanted me with her. I keep thinking: If I had a daughter, and she abandoned me in my adversity, how would I have felt?

When some of the horrors of the concentration camps are depicted on television, I can't ignore it. I must watch, and then it upsets me greatly. When Gerald Green's story, "Holocaust" was aired on television, I was sickened by it, but I watched it to the end. I feel the same when I visit Holocaust shrines or memorials to the dead, such as the Memorials to the six million Jews who perished conducted in Madison Square Garden in New York. Many synagogues throughout the city organize these memorials every year. When there are lectures and meetings on this subject, I must attend, even though I know how depressed it will make me feel, how upset I become.

It is generally acknowledged that the Germans lost the war. They really did not lose it. What was lost? The world they wanted to conquer? They were never deported from their homeland. They were forcibly separated from their families and homes. They were not interned in concentration camps and jammed into gas chambers and later converted into soap, lampshades, and ashes. I lost the war. The six million of our innocent people who were exterminated along with those who survived, lost the war.

Yes, indeed, the whole Jewish people were the losers, not the Germans. We were not only vanquished but we lost everything, our families, relatives, friends, homes and all our worldly possessions. We even lost our God. Most Germans lived happily ever after, in tranquility and in abundance with their families, in peace and prosperity enriched by our labors and possessions, while we, their surviving victims, whom they did not have enough time to kill, were left with our bitter memories and our unending pain, our nightmares and our illnesses. We wandered all over Europe and elsewhere searching for relatives, a home, a place to rest our weary bodies. Instead of finding a loved one, we mostly learned how and where this or

399

that member of our family died. I only heard that my brother Shmual Moshe was seen in Auschwitz, and then nothing more about him. How many vanished in Auschwitz without a trace?

When the war was almost over, the Germans expected reprisals for their criminal behavior. They knew that their guilt was palpable. As one of their high-ranking Nazi officials said just before Germany collapsed: "If they do to us what we did to them, then God help us." There were no reprisals. They were not made to pay for their crimes against humanity. Maybe it was cowardice on our part that we did not seek revenge for what they did to us. We were too sick, too weak, exhausted mentally and physically from our terrible ordeals. We could hardly stand on our feet, let alone seek retribution. We were looking to rehabilitate our shattered lives. We left the avenging to the Allies. They had done nothing to save us from the Germans. The least they could do was to deal harshly with the culprits. Well, they did not. They treated the Germans rather gently. When the Soviets blockaded the western sector of Berlin in 1948, the United States Air Force airlifted food and medicine to West Berlin. Thirty-one young American lives were lost in order to feed the Germans. The Nuremberg trials were a mere slap on the wrists. Many criminals were freed for good behavior after a short internment. Others are still free, escaping justice.

After the war, the Germans had the effrontery to claim that they did not know what was happening in the camps. They must have lost their vision, their hearing and their sense of smell for twelve years, because all one really needed in Germany in those years was a sense of smell. The bodies that were cremated in the camps emitted an awful stench that permeated the air for miles, and the people in the surrounding areas could correctly have guessed what was happening in those death camps. They saw transports of barely living skeletons locked in cattle trains like animals and watched by armed guards. And these fine and gentle creatures never saw any of us. Of course they didn't. We were not human beings to them. Just dirty, contaminated Jews. Why even glance at us? Their superior Aryan hubris didn't permit it. They have much to atone for, though they claim they knew nothing about the existence of the death camps.

Their husbands, sons, and brothers not only cremated the corpses in Auschwitz whom they first gassed, but they also threw living children who were snatched from the mothers' arms into burning ditches. How could you? Damn you. How could you? What punishment is adequate for your consummate evil deeds? I can't think of any just deserts that would adequately satisfy the enormity of your crimes.

The rest of the Germans went along with the Nazis for the profit that accrued to them. During those fateful years, and when the Third Reich began to crumble, they saw Jews being driven like mad dogs by the Nazis as they moved them from one concentration camp to another, so as not to allow them to be liberated by the Allies. They marched the hungry wretches, sometimes for hundreds of miles from the Eastern countries to places in Germany they still controlled. My cousin Sima, for instance, was forced to march in the dead of winter from the Riga concentration camp in Latvia to Germany. As a result of that long harrowing trek, she suffered from severely injured feet, losing large parts of her toes. Not only were they forced to trudge in the bitter cold without adequate clothing, but they were also starved. After marching for days without food or water, they finally stopped at a farm. The SS guard ordered the farmer to cook potatoes for the prisoners, who were so grateful to the SS for the potatoes that they were waiting to eat, that they almost forgot the hardships along the way. When the potatoes were cooked, the German ordered the farmer to grind the potatoes into the straw just as he did for his cattle. The farmer obeyed. When the potatoes were thoroughly mixed with the straw, he gave it to the women who could not eat it, no matter how hungry they were. The straw cut their tongues and gums. The vast majority of Germans had to know what was happening to the Jews of Europe whose possessions they seized. They took clothing and other goods bearing labels from all over Europe. They certainly knew where these clothes came from. They consciously chose not to think about it. Yet all those so-called cultured and refined Germans said they never saw a Jew mistreated or wronged during the war.

No German admits that was on the staff at Auschwitz, Bergen-Belsen or any other of the numerous camps all over Germany and Poland. Instead, they swear that never in all their lives did they harm a Jew. No, they even had Jewish friends. So what happened to the Jews of Europe? Where are all those large communities of Jews from Poland, Hungary, Czechoslovakia and all the other countries of Europe? Did they just vanish? Was it an act of God that caused their disappearance? Ask the Germans. They know the answer. They deliberately planned and carried out the final solution to the Jewish question. And what was that? The total annihilation of European Jews.

When somebody mentions to the Germans the hardships of the war which they started, they complain that they also suffered during the war years. Of course they did, poor dears. They had no real coffee, not enough cigarettes and liquor. But we drank muddy water from puddles and ate scraps of food unfit for even a pig.

Not only did the world stand idly by when we were suffering in hell, but when the few survivors, crippled physically and psychologically, emerged from the death camps, we were chided for allowing ourselves be murdered and humiliated. Children were ashamed of their parents for having been in a concentration camp. No one wanted to read the meager literature on the subject that existed. What transpired in those camps was too brutal for anybody to read or hear about, and besides, every one wanted to forget.

Bystanders could disremember, but how does one ever forget when one has lost his or her entire family? How could I lose sight of the fact that the Germans made soap from the fat of my sisters and their babies. When men tortured other men so mercilessly no words could adequately describe what really happened. Men became beasts, first to exploit the weaker, and then to systematically obliterate them all in the name of a monstrous ideology. Even for those who survived the conditions the Germans created in those camps left virtually no possibility for the oppressed to even lead normal lives in the aftermath.

First, there was the knowledge that one's parents, brothers and sisters along with their young children were put to death in the gas chambers. The sudden separation, and loss of one's family created a sense of loneliness and alienation. Even in cases where there were two or more young sisters with no children and capable of working, they were often hopelessly separated from each other. Secondly, we literally

lived on top of each other; the overcrowding was unbearable. The systematic starving, constant beatings,
and the hard labor seven days a week wreaked our
bodies and souls very quickly. And lastly, the terrible
ordeal of the selections; the knowledge that at any moment the whistle could blow, and every one would
have to line up before the infamous Dr. Mengele who
would be selecting bodies to fuel his fires. Watching
the thick, black smoke of the crematorium rising to
the sky day and night was extremely frightening: not
even the sun could break through those black clouds
and smoke that stank of burning flesh; all that was left
of your father, mother, sisters, brothers, relatives
and friends. You woke and went to bed with sickening odor of cremated bodies assailing your nostrils.
That is, if you made it through the day. Otherwise
you were the fodder. That one had to wash with soap
that was made from the bodies of relatives and friends,
was devastating. All this did improve the low morale
of the inmates. No wonder the nerves of the survivors
were shattered.

When the war ended, and we were liberated from the
concentration camps, we wanted to talk to someone,
to share our great grief and our sense of loss, but no
one waited to listen to us. The world that was indifferent during the holocaust did not display any sympathy or provide the psychiatric care that we needed to
rehabilitate ourselves. As a result, the survivors,
having a need to talk about their experiences, talked
to one another. In my experience, whenever two or
more of us survivors met, we talked about hardly anything else than the episodes that had occurred during
our internment. This went on for a long time, and
then, suddenly, the survivors themselves did not want
to hear about what had happened in Auschwitz or elsewhere. If one of the survivors brought up the

holocaust, others would belittle him behind his back, saying that all he could talk about was the concentration camps.

We finally got the message that nobody respected us for having survived. If we thought of ourselves at the war's end as being heroes for having survived, we now found out otherwise. Now we were being blamed by the rest of the world for having let ourselves be taken to the slaughterhouse like sheep, without fighting back. It seemed as if people were accusing us Jews, rather than the Germans, for the slaughter, when in fact there was very little we could have done. We were surrounded by a hostile population that had been instigated by anti-Semitic propaganda. The non-Jewish population also was tempted to get the possessions of the deported and murdered Jews. The Jews were not organized. The main power in the Jewish community was in the hands of the rabbis, and the rabbis of that time were anything but capable of conducting a revolt against the mighty German army, which had conquered almost all of Europe in a blitzkrieg.

In places where there were youth organizations, there had been some revolts and a few Germans even got killed too. That was the entire victory. These few revolts were highly praised especially, in Israel. They praised the few who stood up against the mighty Germans. They built monuments to the Warsaw ghetto uprising. They built settlements, and named them for the fighters of the ghettoes. Everyone, the old and very young who were surrounded by a hostile population whose minds the Germans had contaminated with anti-Jewish propaganda, could neither fight nor hide from the murderers. To those who had not even known or believed what their destiny would be, since it had no predecessor in the history of mankind, they went like sheep to the slaughter. To those who perished, Israel built a memorial called "Yad Va Shem."

However, those who miraculously survived the holocaust and emerged with scars from the terrible ordeal were looked upon like inferior creatures, weaklings who could not fight for their survival or their dignity. Nevertheless, they were used by the Jewish agency as a way to achieve an independent state so that the survivors would have a home, a place to go. However, as soon as they were brought to the shores of Israel, they were dumped in "mabarot" (transit camps) or wherever, and their plight was largely forgotten. No one received any material or psychological help of any kind in Israel.

The Israelis had a very negative attitude about the holocaust in the post-war period. They were ashamed of what had happened to us, the Chosen People. Chosen for what? To be persecuted? They looked at all the survivors as if a stigma was attached to us because we had let the nations of Europe step on us and humiliate us. Maybe the sons and daughters of the holocaust survivors are such terrific fighters for their freedom and their dignity to compensate for what their parents lacked during the war. The Israelis did not want to hear or read of what had happened to their brethren at the hands of the Germans. They chose to ignore the fact that Rommel, the brilliant German field marshal (nicknamed "the Desert Fox") who commanded the Afrika Corps until the British forces stopped him in Egypt in 1942, stood almost at the gates of Palestine. What would have happened had the Germans marched into their haven, as they marched into Hungary, Poland, France and Czechoslovakia? The Arabs would have gladly and gleefully joined the Germans in robbing and exterminating the Jews, just as the nations of Europe did to us. But thanks to their good fortune, the Germans were driven back, and they were spared our fate.

It was no secret that most of the Palestinian Arab leaders supported the Nazi program for the extermination of the Jews. The Grand Mufty of Jerusalem, Haj al Heusseini, spent the war years in Berlin and Rome taking part in the Nazi effort to induce the Arabs to collaborate with the Germans.

Many who happened to be listening to me talking about the holocaust in Israel did so out of patient endurance, and in silent indifference. Many, even in Israel, were blase about what had happened to us. For example, I was once traveling on a bus from Tel-Aviv, and a lady next to me engaged me in conversation. She asked me to describe my experiences in the concentration camps. I replied that no matter what she heard about it, the truth was worse than any words could express. Then I told her about how I lost my whole family, save for one brother. She then volunteered that for her the war years were very good, indeed, even profitable. For her, the war should have lasted for at least another year. She would have then made even more money. I bitterly thought that if the British hadn't come when they did, the many typhus-stricken, starved, dehumanized skeletal figures of Bergen-Belsen would have been dead, including me. But all she had been concerned about was her money.

The Germans killed six million, and so many of those who survived are spiritual cripples. The past hounds us. It cannot be forgotten, and it is relived day and night. The nights usually bring back the nightmares.

All those terrible experiences; trying to hide from the Germans in places which offer very little shelter, trying to make myself invisible, while the SS was searching everywhere. I have dreams of being nude in a public place and being terribly embarrassed, and a dream that a big black bull chases me in the street. I try to run away from it as fast as I can, but I cannot run fast enough. The bull almost catches up with me. Other people are in the street as well, but the bull ignores the others and runs after me. It aims for me. I wake up in terror. I don't care to go back to sleep. In other recurrent dreams I always lose something, such as my pocketbook or any of my things. I have many other indescribable horror dreams.

The mental and physical ailments that concentration camp inmates contracted last a lifetime. Most are not curable; if anything, the symptoms get worse with time. The pain in my back and legs, which I contracted in Bergen-Belsen digging out the beets from the frozen ground in the open field, without adequate clothing, never left me. The back injuries never healed, no matter how many doctors I went to, or what treatment they gave me. The pain never ceases. While the Germans, our tormentors and our executioners live happily, we are left with our nightmares, our pains and our pills for every ailment, and we are left with our terrifying memories. We are even afraid to love, because to love someone means to lose him. We cannot suffer any more losses.

When I was tattooed it was not terribly painful, but the pain grew as time went on. After thirty years the emotional pain associated with my tatoo became so severe that I couldn't stand it any longer. I decided to have it surgically removed in Mount Sinai Hospital in New York. It was suggested that I talk to a psychiatrist before the surgery. The psychiatrist was very encouraging. He said he thought it was a good idea for me to go ahead with it. As it turned out, the physical pain associated with having it removed was excruciating. For over a year the wound wouldn't heal. The wound was constantly burning, itching, reopening and bleeding. They tried to relieve the pain, but nothing helped. In addition the emotional torment associated with the wound has been even worse than the torment that had been associated with the tattoo itself. I now feel even more guilty that I didn't stay with my mother and the wound reminds me that I even tried to run away from the guilt. The wound constantly calls out to me: Why did it all have to happen? Why did the world let it happen? Why did God let it happen? We cried to God the minute the Germans entered Hungary, "God, where are you?" The last words of most of those who went to the gas chamber was most probably a cry to God. I did not have to hear it to know that my mother and father called, "Shema Yisrael Adoni Eloheinu Adoni Echad."

But God was in the German ranks. He answered their prayers to help them annihilate the Jews of Europe. The only God I saw in Auschwitz was wearing an immaculate German uniform and shiny boots. God's insignia was a dead skull with crossbones. No, God wore an insignia of six million dead skulls on his uniform: Six million Jewish, innocent skulls, including those of my father and mother who were pious and prayed to him. My parents dedicated their lives to serve him, and He let the Germans stuff them into a gas chamber to suffocate and be converted to ashes.

I am aware that anger and hatred are not the nicest of emotions. Love and forgiveness are much more attractive. These are precisely the emotions, namely

409

bottomless hatred, anger, and prejudice, that led to the wholesale slaughter of the Jews. Wouldn't it be nicer if I could say that I have forgiven and forgotten? But the truth is that I haven't. As hard as I've tried, I can't forget and I never will. And as to forgiving and loving, how do you love your mother's murderers? I'm not yet convinced that the Germans regret what they did and that they would not do it again if the opportunity presented itself. They were mighty proud of themselves when they killed innocent men, women and children in cold blood.

They can't claim that they did it in a minute of insanity. It would be easier, maybe even possible, to forgive if one could make oneself believe that they were insane. But they were not insane. These were not the deeds of a few perverts. They were not perverts, just ordinary people from ordinary walks of life: the tailor, the teacher, the baker, and the doctor. Don't forget the doctors who took the Socratic oath and who performed medical and psychological experiments on human guinea pigs. They knew perfectly well what they were doing. To dispose of over six million bodies took more than just a few insane individuals. It took and entire nation working cooperatively.

One criminal, Adolf Eichmann, was brought to trial. Other criminals live as free men everywhere. Nations who did not give asylum to the doomed Jews accepted the Nazi murderers with open arms. I feel that every German alive from that generation ought to be put on trial. They were all accomplices to the murders, whether actively or passively, by not voicing their objections to the wholesale slaughter of the Jews.

I am grateful that it was I who had the chance to write

but one line of this sad history of our people and to describe, however poorly, how we suffered and how we died. Had our executioners been victorious, they had intended to write a glorious page of world history, which meant the erasure of the Jewish people from the face of the earth.

I also wanted in this narrative to describe German inhumanity and beastly brutality. If I did not do this I failed in my task.

But foremost, I wanted to tell the story to those who say the Holocaust never happened. Some people claim the Germans never did the things that we, the survivors, are accusing them of. They say the Jews made this tale up to get sympathy. They are already trying to rewrite history to make it suit their purposes, while some of us survivors are still alive. We say very loud and clearly, "they did."

The Germans most certainly did all that is in this book and much much more. If those six million who perished could speak, my story of survival would be no comparison. They would tell you first-hand how they were tortured, starved, beaten, shot and drowned and how they suffocated in the gas chambers that German ingenuity erected.

I was the lucky one. I survived. They didn't. The least we can do for them is to keep their memory alive. We have to remember their tragic story. They don't want to be forgotten. Bad enough nobody remembered them when they died. This is also their story and in their name I offer this little prayer: God Almighty, don't ever forgive or forget what the Germans have done to us in Auschwitz, Bergen Belsen, Dachau, Maydanek, Treblinka.......

411

A Postscript

When this narrative was about to go to print, my beloved brother, Baruch Bendit, left this world. I am heart-broken at his passing more than I can say. I can hardly contain my pain and sorrow. I grieve for him even more than I grieved for the rest of my family when they were all torn away so cruelly from this world. Then I did not have even that bit of comfort to be able to mourn for them.

Many years ago when at the Russian front, my beloved brother, Baruch Bendit, almost died from a fall when he hit his head against a stone. Although he was revived by his friends, he had wanted to die. He had begged them to leave him there. He did not want to go on living any more. Life was not only too dif- ficult, but hardly possible. As he himself had said: "If I had died then, I would have died like a dog and been thrown into a ditch somewhere. "Nobody would have ever known where and when he died and where he was buried.

Fate, however, wanted it that he die in the street, falling down to the pavement, hitting his head on the cement. He was all dressed up and on his way to the synagogue for prayers on the first day of Rosh-Hashana, the Jewish New Year. He died like a saint, clutching his prayer shawl in his hands as he fell down. The blood from the wounds he sustained spattered on his white shirt as well as on his prayer shawl.

Baruch Bendit, you were the humblest of men. You were so content with what you had. You never asked for more. Every piece of bread was to you a heavenly gift. Baruch Bendit, why did you have to die? Why didn't I die instead of you? You finally had everything to live for: a home, a nice family, and many, many friends who all loved you dearly. I now have nothing to live for. I am now the lone survivor of that once large family.

Baruch Bendit, I want to say again what I said when I saw the casket you lay in for the last time, before you were put on a plane, on your last journey to your final resting place. The place you had chosen yourself only a weeks before you passed away so suddenly, on the beautiful Har Hamenuchot overlooking the city of Jerusalem:

Baruch Bendit, I beg slicha and mechila (forgiveness) had I unintentionally ever sinned against you. Be a Melitz yosher (advocate of peace) for all of us. Dearest brother, go to heaven and tell Avrahan the Patriarch that he wanted to give one son, only one family member to the Almighty as a sacrifice. I have given my whole family to Him. His was only a trial. My loss is for real. God has taken away my whole family from me. Go to the heavenly throne and tell the Almighty: "...that her appointed time is accomplished, that her iniquity is pardoned, for she has received of the Lord's hand double for all her sins." (Isaiah 40:2) May your saintly soul rest in peace with all the righteous in the Garden of Eden, Amen.